DO NOT REMOVE
CARDS FROM POCKET

SUCCESSFUL BUSINESS OPERATIONS

TO IRIS

Successful Business Operations

*How to Develop and Exploit
Competitive Advantage*

◇

LEN HARDY

Basil Blackwell

First published 1990

Basil Blackwell Ltd
108 Cowley Road, Oxford, OX4 1JF, UK

Basil Blackwell, Inc.
3 Cambridge Center
Cambridge, Massachusetts 02142, USA

British Library Cataloguing in Publication Data

A CIP catalogue record for this book is available from
the British Library

Library of Congress Cataloging in Publication Data

Hardy, Len.
Successful business operations: how to develop
and exploit competitive advantage/Len Hardy.
p.   cm
ISBN 0-631-17626-8
1. Success in business   I. Title
HF5386.H253   1990
650.1—dc20   90-210   CIP

Typeset in 11 on 13pt Galliard
by Enset (Photosetting), Midsomer Norton, Bath, Avon
Printed in Great Britain by
T. J. Press Ltd, Padstow, Cornwall

Contents

◇

Preface

◆

For real success a business needs a winning strategy backed by effective and efficient operations. Strategy and operations are complementary. It follows that this book is complementary to my earlier work *Successful Business Strategy*.

It is based primarily on my personal experiences and observations. I was fortunate in that my earlier business appointments were in medium-sized companies where I was able to play a part in strategy formulation and then to be actively involved in getting results in the market-place through operations.

My study under a Leverhulme Research Fellowship, carried out many years ago, was a valuable experience for me. I was able to discuss business with many skilled and successful operators. I still value the time they gave me.

However, my major experience centres on my lengthy period with Lever Bros in the highly competitive soaps and detergent industry. I was fortunate to be a member of the Lever board for more than twenty years, with six years as marketing director, and over ten years as chairman.

Business operations in Lever were always serious, challenging, and very enjoyable. I greatly appreciated the skilled and positive approach of my colleagues. I also appreciated their most willing help.

The views and opinions expressed in this book are, of course, mine and they do not necessarily represent the views of the Lever company or of the people in it.

This book outlines a practical approach to successful business operations. It sets out to help practising business executives. It is also intended to help students of business, particularly those who have yet to experience the great satisfaction of 'making it work' in the market-place.

Len Hardy

◇

Introduction

◆

Real success in business demands successful business operations. If a business is to survive and prosper it must have a winning strategy backed by successful operations. Without effective and efficient operations there can be no real success.

There is no shortage of companies that have developed brilliant strategies and yet have failed. They have failed because they lacked the ability to turn the strategic plans into effective action in the market place, the real world of business. Quite simply they have failed because they were ineffective business operators.

■ *This book is about winning in business. It is about the development of competitive advantages and their exploitation in successful business operations.*

THE CHALLENGE OF COMPETITIVE BUSINESS

My business experience has shown me that it can be both challenging and exciting to formulate a winning strategy. It has also shown me that it can be even more satisfying to 'make it happen' in the market through successful operations.

My book *Successful Business Strategy* considers the formulation of a winning business strategy for an operating company. Strategy and operations are complementary, and so this book is complementary to my earlier one.

Both books are based primarily on my personal experience and observations over many years in business. This includes the experience

1

I gained with a Leverhulme Fellowship research study which covered many consumer markets. It also includes my periods in the printing, electronics and food industries, and in particular my lengthy period operating in the highly competitive soaps and detergent industry and in the markets within it. The views expressed have been tried, tested, and proven in a hard and demanding school.

Lever Bros is one of the UK's leading companies in the manufacture and marketing of consumer products. My first senior appointment in the business was as company operations manager. It was an excellent experience and served me well when I later became sales director, then for six years marketing director, and for over ten years chairman of the company.

As marketing director I was very closely concerned with strategy and operations, and as chairman I took ultimate responsibility for both. It was a most active time for the business as it progressed to become leader in no less than six of the seven major markets in which it competed actively. During this time the company developed a number of its established brands, such as Persil, Domestos, and Lux toilet soap, to dominant market positions, and also introduced to the market-place a series of highly successful new brands (including Persil Automatic, Comfort, Frish, Shield toilet soap, and Jif). Many of these moved forward to become outstanding market leaders and among the biggest brands in the UK grocery markets.

Creating a new brand and launching it successfully into a big market, developing it, defending it against competitive attack, bringing it through to market leadership and a satisfactory level of profit contribution can be a stimulating experience. The stronger the competition in the market, the better the feeling that accompanies success.

Equally, guiding a brand to a wider coverage of store distribution, developing a higher level of plant productivity, or finding a 'better way' to process the product can also be rewarding.

These are all examples of business operations in action. For success they require effective creativity, a high level of skill, a willing effort, and a positive approach.

Business operations can be challenging, exciting and at times frustrating. They can also be most enjoyable.

There is an important additional satisfaction which comes with successful operating. The record shows very clearly that out of the cut and thrust of competitive operations the consumer certainly benefits.

To be successful the operator must earn the consumer's money; his brands must pass the consumer's 'best-value' test, and they must do this on a continuing basis.*

■ *Of course, if the operator is to be truly successful into the longer term his brands must both pass the 'best-value' test and make a satisfactory level of profit. This is the real challenge of competitive business.*

STRATEGY AND OPERATIONS

There is a general view that strategy takes care of the long term and operations the short term. This view tends to over-simplify the relationship between strategy and operations.

The strategic plan provides for the use of the total resources available to the business in a manner and form calculated to achieve the objectives of the business in a given time period. Normally it is concerned with the longer term.

Operations are concerned with actually putting the strategic plan into action. Operations make the strategy work. The strategy may plan for the growth of a new market and provide for a brand to enter and dominate it. Operations have to create and develop the brand, and then launch it successfully.

It is true that operations are normally concerned with shorter-term activity. But it should always be appreciated that the longer term is made up of a series of shorter terms. In effect, a successful strategic outcome will be the result of a series of successful operations.

The dividing line between strategy and operations can, on occasions, be very unclear. The two are completely complementary. They need each other, and only when they are both of the highest quality, and correctly aligned, can real success be achieved.

There is one important respect in which strategy and operations differ; it is in the number of people likely to be involved in their planning, formulation, and actual implementation. With strategy the probability is that only a limited number of people will be concerned. Often the business strategy will be formed by the chief executive and a very small group of senior assistants.

---

* Throughout this book, the masculine pronouns are used for simplicity and clarity. These should not be regarded as gender-specific.

With operations every employee must be involved. There is no escape; everyone in the business has a part to play. Ensuring the necessary clarity of purpose and concentration of effort within this larger group of people is an essential requirement for successful operations.

■ *Management leadership has an important part to play in strategy development. In operations this leadership contribution is of even greater significance, and its effect is likely to be recognized more easily.*

PEOPLE, MANAGEMENT, AND LEADERSHIP

It is an often-quoted fact that the two most valuable assets a business has are its brands and its people, and neither appear on its conventional balance sheet.

The value and importance to a business of its brands is of basic significance and is accepted and emphasized in this book. In essence, their strength is in the strength of the company.

■ *This book also recognizes the vital importance of people in a business. If it is accepted that brands are of major significance, and that brands are created, developed, and exploited by people, then the importance of people must be of the very highest order.*

It is acknowledged here that the people of the business should be its most valuable asset. Within the total number of people a specific group, the management, are of paramount significance.

■ *If a business is to be fully successful its people will need a high level of skill, and a willingness to give a full effort. However, of even greater significance is their attitude. The* right *attitude, and the enthusiasm that emanates from it is the* key *to the extra contribution from the people of the business which makes the difference between a good performance and one that is better than all others. Management has a responsibility to provide the people of the business with a leadership which encourages and ultimately ensures the development of a positive attitude right through the whole business. Enthusiasm, sometimes considered a naïve and unsophisticated quality, is invariably present in large quantities in any operation that consistently produces superior results. Management should encourage and actively develop an enthusiastic approach.*

All members of management have a part to play in helping to develop the right *attitude and enthusiasm in the business, but the major responsibility rests with the top management and, in particular, with the chief executive.*

The chief executive, in his approach, his attitude, his behaviour, and by his example will set the style, the tone, the atmosphere, and the pace of the business. If his leadership is right *for his particular business it could certainly represent a competitive advantage, probably a significant one.*

THE BUSINESS PURPOSE: MARKETING

The purpose of a business is the creation and satisfaction of customers. Without customers there is no business.

When a customer makes a purchase he always buys the brand or product which in his view, at the time of purchase, provides the *best value.*

■ *You create customers by providing them with what they believe to be* best-value *and you retain customers by ensuring that, after trial, your product or brand continues to pass their* best-value test.

The business objective, whether it be profit, market share, or sales volume, can only be achieved through the fulfilment of the business purpose. It's impossible to realize a profit, or improve market share, until you have made a sale.

Within the business everyone should be conscious of the importance of customers; everyone should be anxious to play their full part in customer creation and satisfaction.

However, the prime responsibility within the business for customer creation should rest with marketing. Customers are created through brands or products. Marketing has responsibility for the health and progress of the brands or products of the business.

Marketing should be at one with the purpose of the organization. It should be at the heart of the business and should permeate every part of it. Marketing starts and ends with the customer. By the use of research studies it attempts to discover the product the customer wants. It works with basic research, development, and production with a view to ensuring that the product manufactured conforms with the customer requirements. It endeavours, by the use of salesmen and other means, to maintain adequate stocks of the product with the traders through whose hands it must pass on its way to the customer. By the use of advertising and promotions it attempts to create and build customer demand for the product.

THE BUSINESS OBJECTIVE: PROFIT

It is quite possible in the shorter term that a business may have as its main objective an increase of sales volume, or the improvement of market share. But if it wants to survive and to prosper into the longer term its main objective will have to be profit. Stated a little more fully, the objective will need to be at least a satisfactory profit return on the resources invested in the company.

Of course, the business man who merely achieves a satisfactory level of profit is unlikely to be considered an outstanding success. Real success in business demands superior results – results which are ahead of those of competitors, and ahead of all those other companies that may be competing for additional resources.

In theory the owners of the business should set its objectives. In some cases theory and practice are at one and the owners actually do set the objectives. The sole owner who plays a dominant role in managing the business is a good example of this.

However, in many cases, and particularly in big businesses, the owners do not set the objectives. They delegate this task to the board of directors. In particular, the task is delegated to the chief executive, the person the owners appoint to manage the business successfully and in their interests.

While the chief executive will be fully aware of his responsibilities to the owners, in setting his shorter-term objectives he is also likely to be influenced by certain other pressures.

If his business is a public company with a share quotation on the Stock Exchange then the very short-term profit returns may be of significance. If his results are reported on a quarterly basis then his objectives will need to allow for this. The stock market may forgive him one bad quarter, especially if he has warned of it, but if it is followed by bad second and third quarters the effect on his share price could be disastrous. From an unduly depressed share price many other problems are likely to confront him.

Liquidity is always important. The old saying 'You go broke through lack of cash, not lack of profit', is basically correct, although the shortage of profit may be the key reason you are short of cash. Ensuring an adequate supply of cash must feature among the business objectives.

If the business is to have a future, if it is to develop and to grow as it needs to do if it is to meet the expectations of its owners and its employees then it must make progress in the market. It will need to develop its established products and brands, and introduce successful new ones. The development of sales volume, and in turn market share, must at some time feature as a *key* business objective.

The chief executive may like to have high profit, plentiful cash, big dividends, and major market share growth across his markets, all included as *key* objectives for the short term. But if he believes in setting realistic objectives there is a very high probability that he will need to compromise. He may, for instance, go for growth in market share in some of his markets; in others he may need to sacrifice share for profit and cash.

■ *Setting the shorter-term objectives for his business is one of the chief executive's key tasks. He should always be sure that, despite the compromises he may be forced to make, he is moving the business forward through the shorter term towards his longer-term strategic aims.*

COMPETITIVE ADVANTAGE

A competitive advantage is quite simply an advantage your competitors do not have.

All competitive advantages are of value. Those of the greatest value have the ability, if they are exploited fully, to improve a brand's market share. Competitive advantages of this strength and ability are described here as significant.

When a manufacturer is considering a business opportunity, one of the key questions he should ask in his assessment and selection procedure is: 'Can I develop a significant competitive advantage for use in the exploitation of this opportunity?'

If the answer to this question is a firm 'yes', then the particular opportunity should certainly be moved forward for further consideration. There may remain some specific reason why it is not *right* for the business, but at least it will have jumped one of the most important of the entry hurdles.

If the answer to the question is 'no', then the opportunity should be rejected unless there is some special overriding reason for its acceptance.

BUSINESS OPPORTUNITIES

Successful businesses make and take opportunities. Expressed in slightly greater detail, successful businesses search for business opportunities which, when they have found them, they assess and evaluate. They then select for action those opportunities which they believe they can exploit more effectively than their competitors. Once they have made their selection, they marshal their resources and concentrate them on the development and exploitation of the chosen opportunities.

■ *There are always opportunities available to a business. They have to be searched for, but they are always there. Recognition of the fact that 'there is always a better way' is acceptance that there are always opportunities available.*

The enterprising and successful business never stops looking for new opportunities. In some considerable part its success is directly related to its skill in selecting the *right* opportunities to move forward for development and exploitation.

When a business stops looking for opportunities it has started to decline. Cost reduction projects, value analysis and similar moves can have a material effect on shorter-term results. They are necessary and valuable exercises. But if the business is to make real progress over the longer term it must make and take business opportunities.

BRANDS

This book is concerned with the manufacture and marketing of brands and products. All companies market either brands or products. Some brands are well-known household names and are sold to consumers, via the retail trade, with the support of extensive advertising and promotion. Other brands are of a different nature, they may be for instance, machine tools, life assurance policies, or a plumbing service. But they are all brands, and they have a number of significant factors in common.

A brand is a name. If the manufacturer has done a good branding job the name will come to represent in the consumer's mind the fulfilment of a purpose, a standard of performance in meeting the purpose, a price-level, and a personality. Over time brands, like people, develop personalities. It is important that the personality should be the *right* one for once it is formed it is very difficult to change.

■ *Brands exploit marketing opportunities. Brands provide the company's revenue and without revenue profit is impossible. Through its brands the company makes the direct contact with its ultimate customer, the consumer. The company is judged by its brands. They are all vitally important to a company and should be developed with great care and attention – strong brands should mean a strong company.*

PRINCIPLES AND TECHNIQUES

A view held widely within business management circles is that the 1980s witnessed far-reaching changes in the reasoning and approach of the more progressive business managers. The view goes on to reason that this development has outdated many of the approaches followed by successful businesses through the 1950s, '60s, and '70s.

In considering this issue it is important to differentiate between principles and techniques. Principles are considerations of basic significance. They go to the root of the matter; they serve as a foundation from which other views and approaches are developed. Invariably principles are formed and tested through time. Once established they continue to apply into the longer term.

A technique is a mode of execution. It is a way of achieving a particular objective. Techniques can come and go rapidly. Unlike principles they are often influenced by the fashion of the day.

Of course, good techniques can be of considerable value. Leadership in the development and application of a worthwhile technique can bring a competitive advantage. Failure to appreciate the value of a particular technique can bring about a major disadvantage.

The established and tested business folklores are principles. The lore for brand success in a new market is a simple one: 'Get leadership early and then be sure you grow at least as fast as the market.' Through time a number of techniques have been developed which can provide assistance in actually gaining the leadership. Of course, the techniques which were helpful in the 1950s may not have been suitable for the 1970s or '80s. But the principle was applicable through the whole period and will continue through the 1990s and beyond.

Principles are invariably based on good sound business economics. Techniques are more likely to be concerned with the short and medium term and with the achievement of a particular objective at a given level of cost.

Through the 1980s the widespread introduction of the computer, particularly the form of computer that is available to senior executives on a personal basis, has encouraged the development of many new techniques. The 1980s also saw, throughout the world, the rapid growth of business schools and other management training facilities which acted to stimulate technique growth. The atmosphere created by these various technique developments may have given the impression that there has been a major change in principles.

■ *The view taken in this book is that there has not been a major change in principles through the 1980s. Time and experience may have added certain refinements, but the tested and proven principles have continued, and will continue into the future.*

Are the business principles *always* right, and should they *always* be followed? In by far the majority of instances the principles are correct and clearly they should be followed. On rare occasions it may be right to 'buck' the principle. Deciding just when and how to do this successfully requires a particular quality of fine judgement, and probably a degree of good fortune.

The principles of strategy are often quoted, but the principles of operation rarely get the same level of publicity. This is understandable as business operations have not received the same high level of academic and research study as business strategy.

In this book we are primarily concerned with the principles in business operations: certain of the more widely employed techniques also receive consideration.

THE OPERATIONS PLAN

The company's strategic plan sets out the longer-term aims of the business and goes on to state how, where, and when these aims are to be achieved. Through his business strategy the chief executive directs the company's efforts and resources in a manner calculated to 'win the war'.

■ *The operations plan is for a shorter period, normally covering a year. Through the operations plan the chief executive directs the shorter-term activities of the business. The plan sets priorities, and concentrates the use of resources. In effect, the operations plan sets out to turn the strategy into action. The operations plan is concerned with winning battles rather than the war.*

A war is made up of a series of battles. While a general may lose a battle, if he is to win the war he must win the *key* encounters. The business man is in exactly the same position as the general. If he is to achieve his strategic aims he must be successful in his *key* operating activities.

BUSINESS OPERATIONS: A PRACTICAL APPROACH

The practising business manager or student of business anxious to improve his knowledge of business operations will soon come to recognize that helpful literature available on the subject is strictly limited.

Studies on specific subjects such as advertising, sales promotion, and production techniques, all of which go to make up operations, are more plentiful. But there are very few studies which cover the complete field of business operations.

The actual formulation of the company operations plan is a subject which has received even less attention. This is very difficult to understand for it is a subject that is vitally important to any company aiming to achieve real success in business.

■ *One of the main aims of this book is to suggest a practical approach to the formulation and application of a successful company operations plan. This book is primarily concerned with businesses engaged in the manufacture and marketing of consumer goods. However, it is suggested that the basic approach which the book outlines is applicable on a wider basis to businesses in both the industrial and service sectors of industry.*

There is a need for an operations plan in all businesses. There is a need to direct and concentrate resources on the exploitation of the major opportunities. A requirement to develop and exploit competitive advantages, and a need to ensure that the brand (be it soap powder, industrial equipment, a life assurance policy, or a plumbing service) represents *best value* to a satisfactory number of the potential customers to whom it is directed.

The *marketing tools* are present in all companies, although of course the manner and the form in which they are used will differ widely from company to company.

The responsibility of management to provide the business with leadership of the highest order is most certainly applicable to all sectors of business, as is the need for a positive commercial management.

■ *Finally, and most important of all, the need for business management to appreciate the importance of getting the company operations plan right, and then to pursue it with skill, effort, and enthusiasm very clearly applies to all businesses.*

THE ORDER OF THIS BOOK

This book is divided into eight parts. In this introduction a number of the basics with which we are concerned have been discussed. The discussion has been brief, but it is hoped that it is sufficient to set the scene for the more detailed considerations which follow.

Part I is concerned with the company operations plan, its purpose, its formulation, the time period it covers, and how it is controlled. The formulation of the plan is central to the development of successful operations.

Four fundamentals are discussed in Part II. Two of these – best value and competitive advantage – are conceptual; the reasoning behind them is basic to successful operating. The third and fourth fundamentals – the market and competitors – are of a more factual nature.

A progressive business maintains a continuous search for business opportunities which it believes it can exploit more effectively than its competitors. The three chapters in Part III review business opportunities in detail. In particular, one of the chapters considers the development of competitive advantages to exploit marketing opportunities.

Brands are the pillars on which the strength of the business is founded. The marketing man works to build and strengthen his brands through the company operations plan. He has a series of *tools* to work with in his brand development task. These *tools* include the product, advertising, promotions, pricing and the sales force. The marketing *tools*, their purpose and their use in operations, are examined in detail in the six chapters contained in Part IV.

Leadership is a most difficult topic to cover adequately, and is the subject of many contrasting views and opinions. However, in a book that is primarily concerned with successful operating it cannot be ignored. The *right* leadership of a business can in itself represent a significant competitive advantage. The chapter in Part V considers business leadership and also contains views on the important issues of people, morale, and company culture.

Part VI of the book considers the significance of good commercial management. Often thought of purely in terms of 'control', good commercial management can make a contribution to operational planning which extends far beyond control.

The final chapter in Part VII is concerned with the actual formulation of the company operations plan. The stage-by-stage approach outlined is intended as a guide. It is concerned more with principle and reasoning than it is with detail.

The approach is essentially a practical one. It aims for simplicity and for the concentration of resources and effort on the development and exploitation of the limited number of major operations which will be of vital importance to the progress and success of the business.

It is accepted that there may be other approaches to the formulation of the operations plan which will be better suited to the needs of particular companies. In the final analysis the key requirement is not that any one specific method of formulation should be used, but that the plan which is prepared should play its full part in ensuring successful business operations.

PART I

1

◇

The Company Operations Plan

◆

The business strategy sets out the plan of action for the company over the longer term. It defines the markets in which the business proposes to compete, how it intends to compete, and where it expects its brands to be positioned. It plans for the development of the business in terms of such factors as new brands, capital supply, liquidity, and major new plant construction.

A winning strategy is essential if the business is to achieve real success. However, even the most outstanding strategy will fail if it is not backed by an effective and efficient operation. The longer term is made up of a series of shorter terms. Failure to meet shorter-term objectives must ultimately mean failure to reach the longer-term strategic aims.

■ *The shorter-term business activity is referred to here as 'operations'. It is suggested these shorter-term activities should be planned and put into action through the company operations plan.*

Skill in the formulation of this plan can in itself lead to a competitive advantage in operations. It is a plan in which timing can be vitally important; the concentration of resource and effort at the right time, in the right place can bring about a superior performance in the market and the establishment of a leading position for the longer term.

Reasonable flexibility within the plan can also be a factor of great importance. A well-timed and judged change in direction can bring

17

a valuable advantage – a skilfully formulated operations plan will have the appropriate flexibility built into it, but it will take care not to sacrifice concentration and performance.

THE COMPANY OPERATIONS PLAN

In many ways the operations plan is a short-term strategic plan; however, there is a major difference between the two plans in their scope for development. While the strategic planners are able to search for their business opportunities on a wide front, and are not necessarily restricted, for instance, to their existing markets, the operational planners are restricted and their plans should always be within the strategic plan.

There is a strong case for arguing that the strategic plan should rate as the company's primary action plan, followed closely by the operations plan.

The objectives of the operations plan will be of the shorter-term variety. However, if they are met through each period they should ultimately deliver the longer-term objectives of the strategic plan. Of course, in real life it is most unlikely that the operating periods will produce exactly the results forseen by the strategy. There may be periods when results are in advance, and there will almost certainly be periods when they are behind.

As the operational periods run their course there may be a need to strengthen certain activities to reach target, or to invest more heavily to take advantage of a particular opportunity that has been created. The operations plan will need review from time to time, and a willingness to make rapid change whenever appropriate. There must also be a refer back from operations to strategy. Operating experience may show that a change in strategy is necessary.

Operations cover every area of the business. Each section has a contribution to make, each has a part to play in moving the business forward. However, no one section is likely to be able to work and to succeed alone; it will need the assistance of other sections if real progress is to be achieved. In effect, there is a need for a co-ordinated effort, a need for a plan which incorporates the contributions of all the various sections of the business. In this book it is reasoned that the *tool* which should bring about this very necessary co-ordination is the company operations plan.

PURPOSE

The purpose of the operations plan is to ensure that the business achieves its shorter-term objectives. The plan directs and co-ordinates the shorter-term activities of all operating sections of the business. It acts to ensure that the company's efforts and resources are concentrated on those *key* activities which will enable it to achieve its objectives. The plan allocates priorities for action. It is the *tool* by which the chief executive directs the shorter-term activities of the business.

Leading from the main plan there will be many project and sectional plans, each one programmed to feed into the main plan at a specified time with a specific level of input (see figure 1.1).

■ *When clearly presented, the company operations plan should act to concentrate, co-ordinate, and inform. It co-ordinates activities and concentrates the use of resources. It informs the various sections of the business just how they fit into the total operations. It is the* key *plan covering the whole shorter-term activity of the business.*

The operations plan is an action plan in that it sets out specific dates and times when actions should take place, and beyond this makes clear who is responsible for the actions.

The plan concentrates on the *special* activities of the business. It is very much concerned with the new brands and products which are to be launched, established brands which are to be re-launched, and special promotional activity. The normal *routine* business must be included as it is part, and sometimes a very large part, of the business activities. However, it is included on a lower level and would not normally receive special effort (see figure 1.2).

This means that the operations plan is primarily concerned with those activities which require extra (i.e. above normal) resource backing. Inclusion within the plan at this upper level provides for special treatment, and a priority in the use of resources.

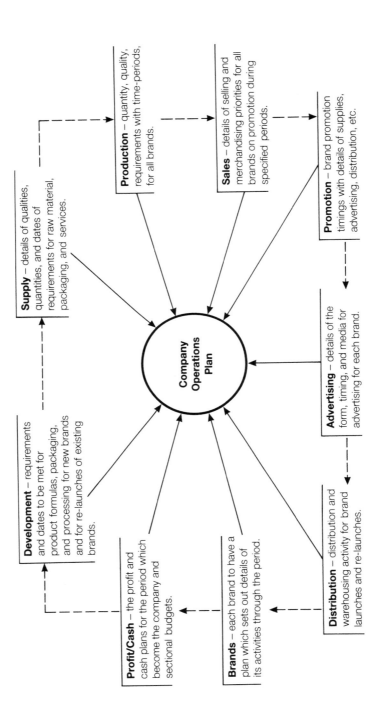

Figure 1.1 Sectional operating plans

The sectional plans are linked directly to the company operations plan. Each section is responsible for maintaining quality, quantity and timing in accordance with the requirements of the main company plan.

Supply – details of qualities, quantities, and dates of requirements for raw material, packaging, and services.

Production – quantity, quality, requirements with time-periods, for all brands.

Sales – details of selling and merchandising priorities for all brands on promotion during specified periods.

Promotion – brand promotion timings with details of supplies, advertising, distribution, etc.

Advertising – details of the form, timing, and media for advertising for each brand.

Distribution – distribution and warehousing activity for brand launches and re-launches.

Brands – each brand to have a plan which sets out details of its activities through the period.

Profit/Cash – the profit and cash plans for the period which become the company and sectional budgets.

Development – requirements and dates to be met for product formulas, packaging, and processing for new brands and for re-launches of existing brands.

Company Operations Plan

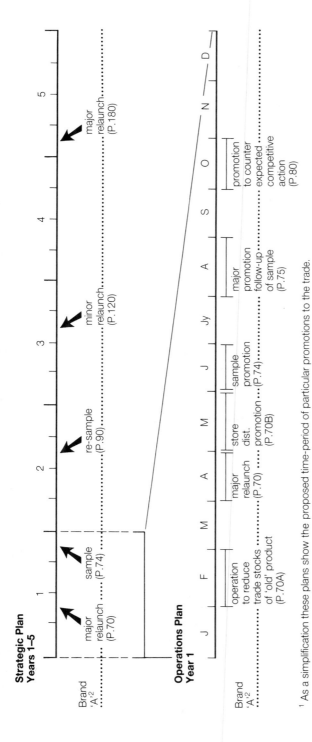

Figure 1.2 The strategic/operations plan

Strategic Plan Years 1–5

Brand 'A'[2]

major relaunch (P.70)

sample (P.74)

re-sample (P.90)

minor relaunch (P.120)

major relaunch (P.180)

Operations Plan Year 1

J F M A M J Jy A S O N D

Brand 'A'[2]

operation to reduce trade stocks of 'old' product (P.70A)

major relaunch (P.70)

store dist. promotion (P.70B)

sample promotion (P.74)

major promotion follow-up of sample (P.75)

promotion to counter expected competitive action (P.80)

[1] As a simplification these plans show the proposed time-period of particular promotions to the trade.

[2] Project (P) numbers refer to individual plans for each project, which should give details of dates for formula finalization, production schedules, distribution etc.

OBJECTIVES

The plan will normally have three main objectives:

- sales volume
- market share
- profitability

To these may be added a number of additional objectives such as the level of inventory (finished stock and raw materials, etc.), and the level of liquidity.

Within the plan, and in addition to the three main objectives each brand should have its own set of objectives, including specific items such as brand distribution, and brand household penetration.

Within the plan objectives should be set for individual periods – these can be weekly, four-weekly, monthly, or quarterly, as appropriate for the particular business.

Performance against these specific short-term targets can be of significance. There is considerable difference between the progress of two brands, both of which may achieve the same total sales volume for the year, if one starts at a high level in January and declines each month for the rest of year, while the other starts at a lower level but increases steadily for each month through the year.

Each brand should have its own objectives for each period of the plan. These will be of special consequence for the periods when the brand is receiving priority treatment.

A series of subsidiary plans, covering every part of the business, should flow from the company operations plan. These would include plans covering production, distribution, stocks, sales performances for regions, areas, by particular accounts, and so on. All of them should link with the company plan and all should have suitable objectives.

There is a need for the objectives within all the plans to be specific. To speak in terms of 'increasing market share' or of 'improving household sampling' is not good enough. Specific objectives are necessary so that resource and effort may be targeted accurately and a specific measure of performance shown clearly when the actual results are considered. Beyond this many of the brand proposals included within the plan will have been passed for action to achieve a specific objective.

FORMULATION

The purpose of the business is to create and satisfy customers. It does this through its brands and products. Strong brands, which can hold a leading position in their market (preferably the dominant No. 1 position) and return at least a satisfactory level of profit, should mean a strong company.

The formulation of the company operations plan is primarily concerned with the brands of the business and the opportunities that are available to them in the market to create and satisfy customers.

At the centre of the formulation process should be a series of brand proposals in the form of:

- A statement for each *major* brand setting out the *key* activities the brand should engage in if it is to:

  1 make satisfactory progress towards meeting its strategic objectives;
  2 exploit to the full the opportunities available to it through the period of the plan.

The statement should also include details of forecast sales volumes and revenues, proposed advertising and promotional expenditures, product costs, and profit contributions.

- A similar set of statements for each proposed *new* brand.
- A similar set of statements for each *minor* brand.

In effect, each statement will be a proposal for the investment of the company's effort and resources in the brand through the period of the plan.

Each one of these statements will require detailed and careful attention. All of the various considerations, such as the market, the opportunities, and the *tools* of marketing (as discussed in the chapters of this book) will have a part to play in the build-up of the brand statements.

The questions that will need to be asked could include:

- Has a satisfactory allowance been made for market growth?
- Have the opportunities been estimated with reasonable accuracy?
- Is the support expenditure (advertising and promotions) adequate for a full exploitation or is it excessive?

- Are the product costs included at a realistic level?
- What allowances have been included for price movements?

It is important to appreciate that while the opportunities for growth brands may be in developing consumer penetration and in turn sales volume and revenue, the opportunities for brands in mature markets may be concerned with a straightforward development of short-term profit contribution.

There is an elementary but nevertheless very important need to ensure that the estimates contained in the various statements are realistic.

They will be of major consequence to the decision as to whether or not the brand proposal should be accepted or rejected. Beyond this they will be of consequence in the allocation of priorities within the operations plan. This means they will have an important contribution to make in deciding which brands are to have priority in the use of the resources of the business. This is one of the *key* decisions in operational planning, and it can be the factor which decides whether or not the business has a successful operating period.

■ *The excess costs and the problems caused by an over-ambitious set of estimates is easily appreciated. Not so easily appreciated, but nevertheless frequently of great significance, are the opportunities missed, or underexploited, by unduly conservative estimates.*

The basic requirement is that the brand opportunities should be examined with great care, and a decision taken as to which ones are of real consequence and for which the business has developed, or can expect to develop, a competitive advantage. These are the opportunities which should receive the highest priority.

Out of the detailed review of the brand proposals should come a plan which is the most advantageous one possible for the business in the market-place. It will be the most attractive plan in terms of servicing and developing the customers of the business: it is from the customers that sales volume is derived and ultimately, given a satisfactory control of costs, will come profit.

There should be a rigorous examination and discussion of the brand proposals. The review session which considers them is one of the most important occasions within business operations. It is really the session when the company's priorities in terms of its brands and the use of its resources are formed for the operating period.

Once the *ideal* brand or product operations plan (i.e. ideal in terms of market-place performance) is in existence a whole series of feasibility studies needs to be carried out. These would cover such factors as:

- research and development
- production
- advertising
- promotions
- sales
- stock holding

- distribution (physical)
- capital developments
- administration
- profitability
- finance

In effect, every section of the business will be involved, every section needs to review its ability to meet the draft operations plan.

The action required of each section goes beyond merely checking an ability to meet the plan. The discussions should consider factors such as the costs involved and how they might be reduced. For instance, if the plan requires a major increase in inventory, there may be ways in which this can be avoided, and these should be examined. Is the sales force unduly loaded at one particular period, and running light at another? Would a simple adjustment of timing avoid this, and is the adjustment free of problems in production and distribution?

There should be a period of extensive liaison between the manager responsible for the formulation of the operations plan and the various sections of the business as they work towards a final plan which provides for the business to take the opportunities available in the market-place and achieve its shorter-term profit objectives.

The approved operations plan, when converted into financial terms, becomes the shorter-term profit and financial plan for the business.

Clearly one of the most important considerations will centre on the ability of the *ideal* operations plan to deliver a satisfactory level of profit.

In the case of a public company which is subject to the discipline of either half-yearly and/or quarterly financial reporting, there will be a need to consider both the periodic and annual profit forecasts.

■ *It is unlikely that the first draft of the operations plan will prove satisfactory. Individual brand plans will need to be considered in detail, and the application of all the various marketing tools reviewed closely. The aim should be to ensure that the plan ultimately accepted for action maximizes the level of profit to be earned while at the same time ensuring that adequate resources are provided for the attainment of the market-place objectives.*

On the financial front there will be a need to ensure that an acceptable liquid position is maintained through the period. This will require that adequate levels of cash are generated by the operations or that cash is provided from other sources. The plans for the payment of such items as capital investments and dividends will need to be covered.

When a company operations plan is finally approved by the chief executive it becomes the central action plan for the shorter-term activities of the whole business. In turn each section of the business should have its own operations plan which is co-ordinated with the company plan and with other sectional plans.

TIMING

It is possible, although extremely rare, for the business strategic plan to cover a time period of just five days. In this circumstance the operating plan would probably cover a period of one day. It is equally possible for a strategic plan to cover say ten years and for the operating plans within it to be of a two-year time period.

These examples tend to be at or near the extremes in time periods. Clearly the ideal time period for the plan will vary from business to business; for most, the strategic plan is likely to cover a period of from three to five years. Within this the operations plan will probably cover one year. Of course, there may well be a number of revisions to the operations plan within the year.

For planning and control reasons it will be necessary to divide the plan into a series of time periods. Normally they will be of equal length, but this is not always appropriate and it may be advisable to have periods of varying length.

It is not necessary for the time periods of the operations plan to be exactly the same as those of the periodic financial accounts although clearly there are administrative advantages to be gained if they can coincide.

WHOSE RESPONSIBILITY?

There should be two *key* plans for action within the business. They may have a variety of names and uses, and in some instances they may exist only in a non-formal manner, but in essence their purpose and ultimate aims are the same. The first is the company strategic plan, and the second is the company operations plan.

The strategic plan is clearly the responsibility of the chief executive. He may receive advice and guidance on its formulation, but the *key* decisions within the strategic plan should be his responsibility.

■ *Equally the* key *decisions within the company operations plan should be the responsibility of the chief executive. Within the formulation and fulfilment of the plan a number of judgement decisions will be necessary. Certain of these may be of such significance that getting them* right *will be all-important if the business is to achieve its strategic objectives. The responsibility for* key *decisions of this kind should not be delegated; they are for the chief executive and he should take them.*

Of course the amount of time the chief executive should give to the more detailed formulation tasks will tend to vary with the size, and form of operation, of the business.

In a small business the chief executive may do most of the formulation work himself. He will probably also direct the operations in some detail. In such a business, if there is a marketing department it is likely to be a small one, with the chief executive possibly acting as marketing director. He may use an assistant from the department to help him with the detailed work and the administration of the plan.

In a large business, where the marketing approach is accepted and an executive marketing department is functioning, the chief executive is likely to delegate the main task of operations plan formulation to the marketing director. He in turn may delegate much of the basic work to a marketing manager or a special operations manager. In a large multi-brand business that is particularly active in the market-place there may be a good case for a full-time manager to be engaged in the formulation, review, administration, and general control of the operations plan.

■ *However, the final responsibility for the company operations plan should rest with the chief executive. The plan ultimately issued to the company for action should carry his stamp of approval.*

REVIEW

The discussion in this book has been in terms of an operations plan covering a period of one year and subdivided into a number of time periods. How often should the plan be reviewed and, as appropriate, revised? The first point to establish is that the plan must be a 'rolling plan', i.e. it should always cover a year ahead and not just the current financial year.

Frequently the planning, for major operations will cross financial years, and may cover time periods of three or more financial years.

If we use a yearly operations plan for the purpose of illustration, then a formal review on a half-yearly basis with an extension of the plan for six months coming out of the review, would in most cases be satisfactory.

The reference here is to a *formal* review of the plan. There will, of course, be a need to ensure that particular operations are reviewed as necessary and adjustments made to them as required.

The need to keep the plan always moving a year in advance is paramount. This may clash with financial planning, where there could be an argument for holding investment plans for Year 2 as late as possible and until reasonably firm results are available for Year 1. The danger in this is that if the operating plans are delayed the 'lead' time for a major operation will be passed and the company forced to use either a weaker promotion or heavier investment in an attempt to save time.

■ *A formal review of the operations plan can involve a substantial amount of operating management time. When it is carried out it is important that it should be done properly. Market trends, consumer behaviour, competitive activities, cost factors, these and other considerations should be included and examined in detail. The need is for a balance. The review should be carried out often enough to ensure that opportunities are not missed and that any developing trends are highlighted, and yet it should not be carried out so frequently that undue time is spent forecasting and planning as against actually operating.*

Reference in the previous paragraph is to a *formal* review. The term 'operations', as used here, covers the shorter-term activities of the business. Tactical moves are important if the 'operational' battles are to be won – and they must be won if the business is to move forward to its longer-term strategic objectives.

Shorter-term actions, not covered in the formal half-yearly operations plan review, will be necessary from time to time. For instance, a very worthwhile market opportunity, which if missed may never appear again, becomes available to a brand at short notice – a review of the appropriate part of the operations plan will be essential. A competitor launches a major attack in a market where the company's brand is leader – vigorous defensive action is required, and an immediate review of the appropriate section of the operations plan will be necessary.

During the course of the business year, particularly in the more active growth markets, there will doubtless be a need to consider many proposals for shorter-term adjustments to the operations plan.

FLEXIBILITY

Clearly, if during the course of the operating year there are to be many adjustments to the operations plan, a reasonable degree of flexibility will be essential. The important question is: 'How much flexibility?' Flexibility normally has to be paid for. It can be provided in many forms; spare capacity is one obvious approach, and additional stock holdings is another.

The level of flexibility appropriate for a particular time-period will be difficult to calculate. Experience of previous periods should be a useful first indicator, but the extent and potential of the various operations planned for the period are likely to be the main factors concerned within any calculation.

For instance, if a new brand is to have a major sampling drive there should be test results available which will provide guidance as to the timing and change in sales volume that the operation is likely to generate in the market-place. But the test will provide only guidance, and in the real world penetration may be raised to say 15 per cent and not 12 per cent as foreseen from the test data. Although the difference is only 3 percentage points, it would represent a 25 per cent difference in volume. It could be unreasonable, and far too costly, to allow for the flexibility to cover for 25 per cent extra, but flexibility to cover say 10 per cent may be acceptable.

In some markets, to be caught with a completely rigid operations plan could be disastrous. In others the form and design of production within the industry may mean that a high degree of rigidity is unavoidable.

There is an important requirement that the manufacturer should have an indication as to how much flexibility, at various levels, actually costs him. This is a difficult calculation to arrive at with any confidence of real accuracy, but nevertheless it is one that should be attempted.

CONTROL

The operations plan is a co-ordinated plan covering the shorter-term activities of all sections of the business. For satisfactory operations it is essential that all sections meet the timings, volumes, etc. of their particular part of the co-ordinated plan. For one section to fail could mean the loss of a whole operation.

It follows that the review meetings referred to in the paragraphs above must act to check the progress of the various projects contained within the plan and ensure that action is taken to avoid deviations. This may mean increasing or decreasing production activities, changing selling plans, and so forth.

Within the business it is important that responsibility for this control function should be clearly assigned to one manager and that he should have the authority to make limited changes in the operations as necessary. And where extensive changes are required he should be able to refer back for a decision to the senior executive who takes ultimate responsibility for the operations plan.

Again, the size and nature of the business is likely to dictate just who within the business takes responsibility for this control requirement. In a large business there could well be a company planning section with a chief planner who has the responsibility. Where there is a manager responsible for the operations plan the responsibility would be his. In a small business the task may be performed as a part-time position by a member of the chief executive's personal staff.

It is necessary that an appointed and responsible person within the business should take control of the operations plan and ensure that all sections of the business know of its progress, are fully aware of adjustments to the plan, and of the part they are expected to play in ensuring that the objectives of the plan are achieved.

■ *The requirement is again a sensible balance. There must be a high degree of discipline within the business in both accepting the requirements of the plan and avoiding unnecessary alterations. Alterations bring complexity, meetings, paper, and so on. Yet there must be a willingness to adjust the plan when adjustments are clearly necessary. These can come from within the business in the form of production breakdowns, supply problems, etc. They can also come from the market-place, in the form of competitive activity. Failure to meet these problems and opportunities could prove very, very costly.*

AN ALTERNATIVE APPROACH

These notes have outlined an approach to the formulation of the operations plan which starts with the customer and the opportunities in the market-place and then works backwards into the business.

It is an approach which fully accepts the business objective of profit making, but brings this into the planning after the opportunities in the market have been fully explored.

In effect it is an approach which reasons that the business strength and its profit-making ability, certainly over the longer term, is contained in the strength of its brands in the market. It reasons that if you build strong brands, and you operate efficiently, satisfactory profit levels should follow.

Having highlighted the opportunities, and considered the costs and revenues their exploitation is likely to bring about, the business must decide which opportunities are to be developed and progressed through the period of the particular operations plan. In making this choice the chief executive should be fully aware of his profit objectives.

There are, of course, many other possible approaches to the formulation of the business operations plan. An alternative approach which has received considerable backing is one that decides just how much profit is required over the period and then works back to an operations plan that delivers it.

An international company that many observers would rate as one of the most successful through the 1960s and '70s is ITT (International Telephone and Telegraph). Under the leadership of Harold Geneen its sales revenue, profits, and earnings per share, grew consistently through the period.

Within ITT companies at this time the operations plan would seem to have followed an approach which in effect started with a statement of the level of profit required. In *Managing* (Harold S. Geneen with Alvin Moscow, Granada, 1985), Geneen writes:

You read a book from the beginning to the end. You run a business the opposite way. You start with the end, and then you do everything you have to do to reach that bottom line. (p. 26)

The argument for such an approach tends to go along the lines that without the desired level of profit there will soon be no business, or certainly no independent business, and this should be faced before detailed brand development plans are considered.

Beyond this, the approach is claimed to stimulate a hard drive for profit right through the business. It is claimed that it keeps very clearly before all managers just what the main objective of the business should be.

The profit approach to the operations plan formulation has many followers and among them are some very successful businesses. When first introduced, particularly if the business has been loosely managed, it is claimed the results can be dramatic.

It is argued that the approach brings a necessary discipline and drive to the business. The chief executive who previously concentrated on a longer-term brand-growth approach and accepted a low level of shorter-term profit suddenly finds, if he is prepared to work hard enough at it, that he can have much of his longer-term development *and* make the required higher level of shorter-term profit target. The approach is claimed to have an even greater effect when it is linked to a well planned management reward system that is directly related to profit performance.

The main argument against the profit-formulation approach is that it is possible for a valuable opportunity (or opportunities) to be missed, or under-valued. Valuable opportunities rarely return; when they arise they should be exploited to the full.

■ *There is no reason why the 'opportunity' approach to the business operations plan formulation as set out here should not be linked with a hard drive for profit. There will be a need for the chief executive to be very clear as to how much money he needs to pay for his brand developments, to organize and plan his priority activities, and also to be clear where he proposes to take profits. It is desirable that the chief executive be forced to face these key decisions rather than neglect opportunities because, at first sight, they appear to have an adverse effect on his shorter-term profitability. In fact, the opportunity approach makes the chief executive decide which are the really worthwhile investment opportunities for the business, and then make sure that other brands and sections of the business contribute at levels which ensure his final profit position is at least satisfactory.*

Key points

1 A skilfully formulated company operations plan can play a vitally important part in the development of a successful operating period. The formulation approach should act to clarify priorities, and to provide for the marshalling of resources for a concentrated attack on the *key* opportunities.

2 The operations plan needs to be sensibly flexible. Excessive rigidity could prove very costly, but it should also be remembered that adjustments are invariably expensive. There is a need for the right balance.

3 The operations plan has an important part to play in providing for the development and exploitation of competitive advantages in operations, but *plans do not get results*. The chief executive should never forget, or allow his management to forget, this simple and very significant point. The people of the business get results through their expertise, their energy, and their attitude. The plan is important, but it is not a replacement for effective management leadership, nor for the skill and enthusiasm of the people engaged in actually turning the plans into real-life activities.

PART II

2

◇

The Best-Value Concept

◆

The 'best-value' concept is based on the very simple fact that whenever a customer makes a purchase, he always buys the particular brand or product which, at the time of purchase, represents 'best value' to him.

This applies to the woman buying detergent in the local supermarket, to the man buying a shirt in a local store, and to the industrialist buying a motor vehicle or a machine tool. It applies to all buyers; that is, it applies to all customers.

■ *Any manufacturer who wants to succeed in business needs to recognize the simple and fundamental reasoning of the best-value concept. If his business is to survive and prosper he must make sales. He must create and satisfy customers, and to do this he needs to be sure that his brands or products represent best value to a satisfactory number of the potential customers to whom they are directed.*

Value is, of course, subjective. Each individual will have his own appreciation of the value of a particular brand or product. The needs and requirements of individuals change from time to time, as also do their economic and social circumstances, and so it follows that their value appreciations will also change from time to time.

The best-value concept is a fundamental factor of great consequence in the formulation of both strategy and operations. It is discussed in my book *Successful Business Strategy*. The concept is a simple one, but nevertheless of major significance and so part of the discussion is repeated in this chapter.

WHAT IS 'BEST VALUE'?

Value is, of course, a subjective quality. For a particular brand it will differ from person to person, and for the individual person from time to time. Small variations can be *key* value considerations for some people. Variations such as the colour of the package or the style of the print, which do not affect the performance of the product in any way can make a material difference in value for a minority of people.

However, for the large majority of people more reasoned brand attributes are the *key* factors in value appreciation.

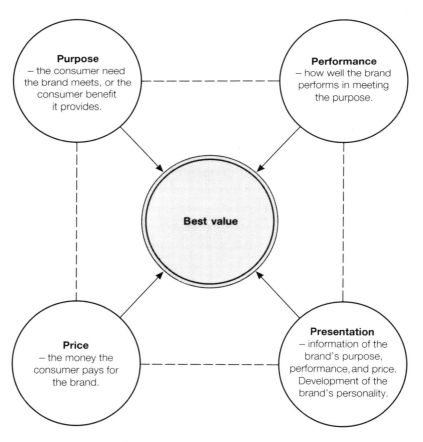

Figure 2.1   The best-value concept

- Are there a series of *key* attributes which the majority of consumers apply in making their *best-value* decisions?
- If so, what are they?
- Can they be applied across all markets?

These are tremendously important questions for any manufacturer. If he wants the customers' money – and he must have it if his business is to survive and prosper – he must provide *best value* to a satisfactory number of customers. Clearly he needs to have a thorough understanding, what might be termed a sound 'feel', as to what represents *best-value* in his markets, and in particular *best-value* to those consumers to whom his brand is primarily directed.

■ *Extensive research, and considerable practical experience, suggests there are certain* key *attributes which apply for a large majority of consumers in a wide range of markets (see figure 2.1). It is suggested that these attributes also apply in the industrial and service markets, but there may be a difference in emphasis in their application.*

The key *attributes in the consumer* best-value *equation are:*

- *purpose*
- *performance*
- *price*
- *presentation*

PURPOSE

Purpose here refers to the consumer need the brand meets, or the consumer benefit it provides.

A brand that fails to meet the basic purpose for which the consumer has purchased it will clearly have only limited value to him.

As a simple example, the woman looking for a dress to wear to a formal social evening is unlikely to find a dress designed and made for beachwear a *best-value* buy on this occasion. Similarly, if a woman is looking for a product to clean her bath, to have any prospect of becoming her *best-value* buy for this need the manufacturer's brand must meet the requirement.

There is, of course, a considerable skill in defining and expressing a brand purpose in the right manner. The potential consumer must both understand and accept it. For instance, it could be wrong to describe a brand that is strong in performance as 'tough', if the consumer interprets 'tough' as harsh and possibly harmful.

There is also a skill in discovering a consumer need that is not adequately met by existing brands. Knowing how to structure and conduct a consumer research study so that the individuals concerned speak freely and precisely about their requirements can provide the base for a valuable marketing opportunity.

Consumer needs change. As people become more prosperous and sophisticated their needs and requirements become wider in nature; the toilet soap needs to clean *and* soften the skin, and the cleaning liquid to 'clean *without* scratching'. This development of consumer needs can provide a marketing opportunity for the manufacturer who anticipates it correctly.

■ *The basic fact is that to have a value to the consumer a brand must meet his need or requirement. It must promise and provide the benefit for which he purchases it.*

PERFORMANCE

A brand's value is markedly influenced by how well it performs in meeting the purpose.

Many brands may have the same or a similar purpose, but they are unlikely to have the same performance. The manufacturer's skill in product formulation, in processing, and in the quality of the ingredients he is prepared to use, can all be significant factors in the way the brand performs.

In a brand's value equation the performance rating that really matters is that given it by consumers, and this will not necessarily be the same as that shown in the manufacturer's laboratory. Specific ingredients which have advanced technological properties, but which do not show through to the consumer in *results*, are unlikely to affect performance appreciation and in turn the consumer view of brand value.

In practice, consumers often have their own approach to performance rating. For instance, users judge their washing powder when they have a particular kind of wash, possibly one where the clothes are heavily soiled. Others make their judgement only when they wash in higher temperature water, and so on. It is an important part of the skill of a manufacturer to know the ways in which consumers judge performance, and to formulate his brands accordingly.

Frequently there will be a need to get from the consumer a comparative rating of performance. In the market-place battle the brand requirement is often to obtain not just a better but a significantly better performance. If the rating of the brand is only marginally better it may not be worth a major exploitation effort. A significant improvement, one that the consumer recognizes readily, could be a very different proposition and warrant substantial backing. The ability to research consumers and to form an accurate view of comparative performance ratings is a valuable skill.

■ *Performance is clearly an important factor in the brand's value equation. The wise manufacturer never underestimates the consumer's ability to make a sound judgement of a brand's performance. There is considerable evidence, from many product categories, to show that over time the consumer can be a very good judge of brand performance.*

PRICE

It is an elementary fact that the money the consumer pays for a brand is its price. Money is a measure and price is very much part of the value equation.

The price in the value equation is always the one which applies on the particular occasion when the buying decision is made. It follows that if a brand is enjoying a special price reduction in a store the probability of it attracting the consumer's custom is enhanced because its value has been improved. At the lower price-level it is more likely to be rated as *best-value*.

As with performance, skill in judging what level of price differential the consumer considers significant, for a particular brand at a specific time, is important.

The manufacturer needs research which will guide him in deciding what is the most favourable price position for his brand compared with those of his competitors. He also needs to have an indication of the degree of movement in consumer demand with various levels of brand price differential. He needs to know the price dynamics of his markets.

The manufacturer also needs to have worthwhile guidance on the relationship between performance and price in his market, or market sector. When once he has clarified and settled on his brand purpose, it is with attributes of performance and price that he will be primarily concerned in any attempts he may wish to make to change his brand value to the consumer.

■ *Of the* key *attributes in the brand value equation, price is the one which can be moved most rapidly. A change in the other* key value *attributes invariably requires considerable time in preparation. This factor can often be of major significance in operations.*

PRESENTATION

In presenting his brand the manufacturer should be concerned to inform his prospective customers of the brand's purpose, its performance and, as appropriate, its price. The presentation will have as one of its main objectives the task of getting the consumer to try the brand and, in the case of regular users, of ensuring retrial.

Obtaining brand trial and retrial, and in this way building sales volume, is the major task of presentation. One of the best ways of convincing consumers that a brand offers best value is to get them to try it. Only in use can they really judge the brand's standard of performance.

Regular users are vitally important to a brand. Before you can become a regular user you must first try the brand. Getting consumer trial is fundamental to ultimate success.

No matter how he sets about the task of presenting his brand, no matter what style, manner, or setting he chooses, the manufacturer is bound to make a brand impression. The package can be designed in loud, gaudy colours, or in soft, gentle colours. The style of the presentation can be noisy and aggressive, or it can be quiet and unassuming. The manufacturer must decide which approach he wishes to use.

The presentation will automatically build a brand personality or, as it is sometimes termed, a brand image. It is clearly better to build a personality which is helpful to the progress of the brand rather than one that is damaging.

This means that the manufacturer should decide on the type, style, and form of personality he wants for his brand. He should decide this well before he enters the market, and he should then ensure that his brand presentations work to develop and maintain that personality.

■ *There is no good reason why a skilled presentation should not fulfil the double requirement. That is, it should do an outstanding selling job, encouraging the consumer to try and re-try the brand, and it should do this in a style which plays its full part in helping to build the desired brand personality.*

There is considerable evidence to show that where a brand has built the right personality this can have a beneficial effect on its value, and it can be a helpful factor in enabling the brand to pass the consumer's *best-value* test.

SYNERGY OF BEST-VALUE ATTRIBUTES

There is undoubtedly a synergy between the best-value attributes in practice. The record shows that for real brand success the requirement is to get the right purpose, the right balance of performance and price, and then to add the right presentation.

The right purpose is directly linked to the consumer need in the market, or market section, at which the brand is directed. With the balance of performance and price, a high-level performance (i.e. high when compared with other brands in the market) can normally command a higher price, whereas a lower level of performance would normally need a lower price.

A low level of performance with a high price is unlikely to succeed. A high level of performance with a low price level clearly has value advantages.

A strong and favourable personality is unlikely to bring a brand success if the purpose is wrong, or if the balance between performance and price is wrong. However, a favourable personality will be helpful, and may cover, to some extent, a slight imbalance between performance and price.

■ *When all the brand's key value attributes are right they will build on each other, and this will act to increase their total value.*

Key points

1 The record shows very clearly that of the successful brands in the household products markets (and the same considerations apply in other consumer goods markets, and beyond this into the industrial and service sectors) a very high number conform to the basic reasoning of the *best-value* approach. They are providing the right benefit, they have the right balance between performance and price, and they have developed a favourable personality.

2 In an established market there may be the exceptional brand which is successful because an outstanding presentation has supported a somewhat inferior product. Such brands are rare and are likely to be found in the more 'emotional' markets.

3 For new brands entering established markets, success for an inferior product attempting to obtain a premium price is indeed rare. When established brands are strongly placed within a market, a new brand will frequently require significantly superior performance with either an equivalent or lower price, if it is to make progress.

4 It is most important that the lessons of the *best-value* concept should be faced in both strategic and operational planning. A brand based on superior presentation alone is unlikely to bring success in the market-place. This approach makes the elementary mistake of underplaying the consumer's ability to make a realistic judgement of performance. Experienced and successful operators never underestimate the ultimate customer.

5 The basic point is that the *best-value* concept, and the reasoning behind it, are backed by considerable market-place experience. It is a concept which is relatively simple in approach, and in many respects can be considered good business common sense. Plans for brand development within either strategy or operations which disregard the *best-value* concept should be questioned very closely. It is possible that for exceptional reasons they may prove to be successful, although the probability is that they will fail. A business strategy or company operations plan which accepts the reasoning of the *best-value* concept, and provides for it in the activites, revenues, and expenditures it proposes, will be more soundly based and much more likely to be successful.

3

◇

Competitive Advantage

◆

Successful businesses search for opportunities. They assess and evaluate the opportunities they find, and then they select for operation those they believe they can exploit more effectively than their competitors. In effect, they select for operation those opportunities where they believe they can develop *a significant competitive advantage*.

■ *The competitive advantage is vitally important, its development and exploitation is at the centre of every brand or product success. Without a competitive advantage there is unlikely to be any real success.*

Within this book a question which is asked continually is: 'How can a competitive advantage be developed in this particular area of operation?' Arriving at a satisfactory answer to this question, and then making it happen, will be all-important for the success of the business.

■ *An acceptance of the approach to business operations which the competitive advantage concept represents can have a major impact on a company and on the attitude and performance of the people within it. The concept is essentially competitive. It is directly linked to the approach which reasons: 'There is always a better way.' In particular, it is concerned with providing a brand or product which meets the specific requirements of those customers to whom it is directed more effectively than do competitive brands.*

45

When the people in a business have been persuaded to accept and practise the competitive advantage approach they will always be working to improve their performance, and in turn to improve the value of their brands to the customer. They will come to accept that they must be better than their competitors in whatever they do – only a superior performance can build a competitive advantage.

COMPETITIVE ADVANTAGE: WHAT IS IT?

A competitive advantage is quite simply an advantage your competitors do not have.

It can be, for instance, a special formula development, a product manufacturing-cost advantage, a particular skill in operating, or the establishment of an exclusive channel of product distribution. The important point is that it is an advantage which is restricted to the operator concerned – his competitors do not have it.

All competitive advantages eventually find their way through to the brand or product *best-value* equation. This is why the competitive advantage is of such major importance – the more significant it is to the customer the more important it is to the manufacturer.

■ *Either directly or indirectly, a competitive advantage enables its owner to give his customer an 'extra', an added value, something his competitors cannot offer. It can be in terms of brand purpose, performance, price, or presentation, or a combination of these factors.*

To be classed as a competitive advantage in the terms of this book, an advantage must have the ability to at least recover its cost. The recovery can be in terms of selling the same volume at a higher unit price, or by increasing total revenue and contribution by selling a higher total volume.

If it is unable to do this it may possibly remain an advantage but it will not be worthy of the title of 'competitive advantage'. Recovery of the cost is, of course, a minimum position: a worthwhile competitive advantage would expect to achieve much more than mere cost recovery.

When a competitive advantage takes the form of a lower unit cost of production and/or distribution the manufacturer can pass it directly to the customer as a price reduction and so increase the value of his brand or product to his customer. Alternatively, he can retain the benefit and increase the brand's contributory profit margin, or use it to support the brand in some other manner, e.g. advertising or promotion.

COMPETITIVE ADVANTAGE AND BUSINESS SUCCESS

All truly successful brands, i.e. brands which are able to achieve and to hold leadership in their particular market sectors and to return a satisfactory level of profit, have a significant competitive advantage.

If the brand competitive advantage is a superior performance then the probability is that it can obtain a higher price, or a better volume. With skilful management both a higher price and a better volume could be possible.

If the competitive advantage provides a lower unit cost then there will be an opportunity to use price more competitively to gain volume, or to take a higher unit contributory margin which in turn can be used to improve brand volume or profit.

Where the business has foreseen the development of a new consumer need and has been able to meet this ahead of competitors it should be able to establish a market position which will provide it with a competitive advantage. Searching out and exploiting the opportunity ahead of competitors should, in itself, provide a competitive advantage.

The success of a business is measured in terms of its performance in creating and satisfying customers, and in meeting its profit objectives. Competitive advantages will be essential for a satisfactory level of business performance.

In many respects the approach to the formulation of business operations should be basically the same as for business strategy. The time period covered may be much shorter, the need for action more urgent; nevertheless, the basic approach should be the same.

The manufacturer will have available to him a number of ways by which he can manage a particular shorter-term position. Each way is, in effect, an opportunity. The important requirement is to select for action that opportunity which will be most effective in meeting the shorter-term objective. The manufacturer's ability to mount an action with which he has a competitive advantage should clearly be a *key* factor in his decision as to which opportunity he selects for operation.

Without a significant competitive advantage an attack on a leading brand is unlikely to succeed; without at least a competitive advantage an attack on either the second or third brand in the market is unlikely to have any success.

Markets where rivals 'slug it out' with brands or products which are almost identical in every respect (i.e. neither brand has a competitive advantage) are unlikely to provide adequate profit levels to the contestants. Such markets invariably drift into becoming price markets, where the only brand differential which applies is that of the periodic 'lower price special'.

■ *Many of the basic rules or folklores of strategy do not apply when one of the competitors has been able to develop a significant competitive advantage.*

The rule that you should never attack a well established leader head-on would normally make very good business sense. However, if you have developed a strong enough competitive advantage, then even the most firmly established leader can be vulnerable to a head-on attack.

It is often argued that a particular business should use a flanking attack. This way the head-on confrontation is avoided and the strong leader is attacked on one or more of his flanks. The statement is often made with the implication that such a move will be relatively simple to apply and will have a greater probability of success. In fact, a flanking attack is unlikely to have any greater probability of success unless the marketing opportunity has been correctly identified and a brand produced with a significant competitive advantage to meet the opportunity.

In strategy planning the important requirement is firstly to identify the opportunity, and then to decide which of the competitors in the market is most likely to produce a competitive advantage to meet it. Sometimes, a manufacturer may be wise to let the most desirable opportunity pass if he feels sure that others

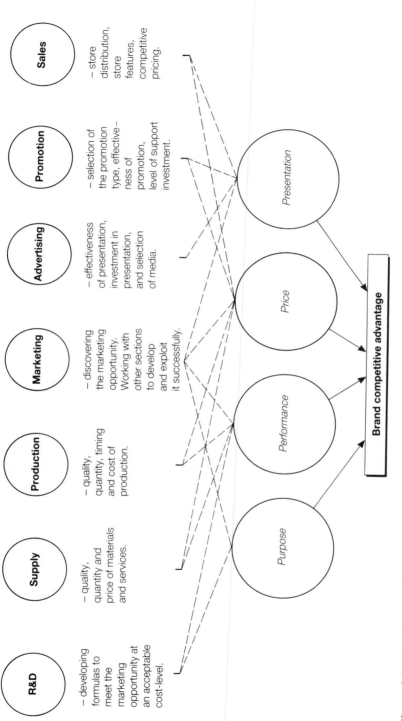

Figure 3.1 Brand competitive advantage
All brand competitive advantages are linked to one or more of the key factors within the brand's best-value equation, i.e. through purpose, performance, price, and presentation. The actual development work is carried out in the various sections of the business – the development links most frequently encountered in practical operations are shown in the figure by broken lines.

are much better equipped to develop and exploit the necessary competitive advantage. It may well be that a slightly less desirable opportunity, but one where he knows he has a real lead in the development of a competitive advantage, will ultimately prove to be the *right* opportunity for him to select for action.

It follows that business managements in strategic and operational planning, should be fully aware of the significance to their brands, and to their business, of developing and exploiting competitive advantages. Beyond this they should take active steps to ensure that everyone else in the business is also aware of this significance (see figure 3.1).

DEVELOPMENT

Significant competitive advantages are vitally important to companies that seek to make real progress; this means they should be important to every business. Yet the facts show that only a limited number of companies have brands or products which hold significant competitive advantages. By far the majority of the brands in the markets have, at best, only a slight advantage. It is probable that if a detailed analysis was carried out it would show that most brands are either 'pets' or 'dogs' – that is, they are brands which do little more than provide a contribution to overhead or possibly a small but unsatisfactory level of profit.

What is necessary for the successful development of a significant competitive advantage? The process starts with the people of the business, and in particular the management. There is a need to have in the business people with a high level of skill, backed by the necessary effort, and resources.

Many businesses have the skill, the energy, and the funds and yet they still fail to produce. The problem usually centres on the attitude of their management. This is a field where a sagacious approach, backed by strong, sensible enthusiasm, and well designed motivation, will be essential if a leadership position is to be achieved.

Competitive advantages can arise purely by chance or good fortune. By accident, a chemist may discover that by mixing a series of ingredients in a particular manner he gets outstanding results. If a company is lucky it may develop a competitive advantage in this way, possibly a significant one, once every ten years. If the company is especially lucky it may get such an advantage more frequently, but it will need to be exceptionally lucky.

■ *Clearly a company that is serious about making progress will not be prepared to rely on exceptional luck. There is a requirement for a systematic approach to the development of competitive advantages. When a company has good people, has generated the right attitude, and employs a 'sensible' systematic approach, it should begin to get results.*

A 'sensible' systematic approach is one that combines the appropriate disciplines with a degree of freedom which encourages the individuals concerned to use their initiatives and, on occasions, to follow their hunches. Achieving the right balance in this approach can be difficult but for good results in this form of activity it is very necessary.

A systematic approach is likely to concentrate on two aims:

1 To meet a marketing opportunity;
2 As the result of planned activity in the business,
   a functional (or departmental) activity;
   b company projects.

Marketing opportunities

The business should be engaged in a continuous search for marketing opportunities. All those markets in which the business competes in earnest, and which are considered to have potential, should be the subject of a series of research studies. These studies should consider the consumers' views of the brands currently in the market, their strengths and their weaknesses. In particular the studies should cover the consumer needs and requirements not currently serviced by the brands already available. The new markets which the business is considering for entry should also be the subject of similar research.

■ *The most valuable competitive advantages, those that can make a significant difference to a brand's competitive position in the market-place, are invariably associated with the* key *brand attributes contained within the* best-value *concept. They are usually associated with brand purpose, performance, price, or presentation. Frequently they will be associated with more than one of the attributes. This is very understandable as these attributes bear directly on the brand's value to the consumer.*

The first manufacturer to discover a new purpose should be well positioned to develop and exploit it in the market-place ahead of his competitors. If he does this effectively he can make the particular purpose the property of his brand.

The advantage of superiority in performance is clear. Of course, it is important that the particular performance advance should be of consequence to the consumer and available at a reasonable price.

Price can always be an important area for gaining a competitive advantage, and a more competitive price has very obvious attractions for consumers.

An outstanding brand presentation can work wonders for brand trial. And if a brand is to become the *best-value* choice of a consumer it is essential that he should try it.

When a marketing opportunity has been highlighted it should be evaluated and assessed. Part of this procedure will be a consideration as to how well positioned the business is to develop a significant competitive advantage to provide for the exploitation of the opportunity.

Following the selection of the opportunity for action, appropriate resources should be concentrated on the development of the required competitive advantage.

It is always possible for the competitive advantage to come first and for the marketing opportunity to follow. For instance, a technologist finds that a new production process provides certain special qualities not available from other brands. Consumer research shows that these qualities are welcomed and valued by the consumer. Here the competitive advantage has given rise to a new marketing opportunity.

The brand development programme should always be looking ahead and should have a number of the marketing opportunities it has discovered lined up for exploitation into the future, possibly covering the next five years. Some of these will be major opportunities, others will be of a minor nature. In each case the aim should be the development of a competitive advantage to aid the exploitation.

Competitive advantages developed to meet a marketing opportunity would normally be sponsored and piloted through the organization by the marketing department. Part of the responsibility of the brand manager should be to ensure that he is fully aware of the opportunities that may be available to his brand with consumers in the market. Beyond this he should maintain a constant liaison with other sections of the business to ensure that the competitive advantages necessary to exploit the selected opportunities are progressed and brought forward for operation.

Planned activities

The development of competitive advantages through planned activity in the business should concern every department, every section, and every person, within the business.

Functional departments and sections

Within each functional department and section there should be a planned and active approach to achieve a continuous improvement in performance. The production departments can improve their productivity levels. The sales department can work at its sales approach, use its people more effectively and advance its overall performance. The administrative section can find a means of producing its invoices and delivery notes more efficiently, and so on.

If these developments take the business ahead of its competitors they are, in fact, competitive advantages.

Sometimes they may be big enough in themselves to rate as significant; more frequently they are likely to be minor advantages but nevertheless certainly worth having. These minor advantages, coming from a whole series of departments, could well represent in total a significant competitive advantage.

■ *Developments under this heading should have a particular value to the chief executive. They provide him with a means of motivating his departmental heads who in turn can lead their staff forward to higher levels of sectional and personal performance. In effect, they provide a means of getting everyone in the business actively concerned in the pursuit of competitive advantage.*

Company projects

Frequently it will be necessary for two or more departments to join together in a particular operation if the optimum gain to the business is to be realized. For instance, joint action between the sales and distribution departments in setting price-list order levels, and thereby influencing distribution vehicle loadings, could bring about savings in distribution costs. The term 'company projects' is used to describe joint operations of this type.

There should be great scope for activities of this kind in every company. Every part of the business should be the subject of a periodic review. There is always a better way, and this applies to every section.

Projects of this kind provide a means of bringing together personnel with varying skills and experiences, and allowing them time to analyse and review, for instance, a section of the business, a brand, or a particular company procedure, with the aim of improving performance

■ *Used skilfully company projects can also have a motivating value to the chief executive. They provide a means of bringing the younger, very bright, people into a direct working relationship with more experienced senior personnel. When a project team with this make-up is led wisely the results can often be outstanding.*

The advantage coming from a project team exercise can, on occasions, be of significance but it is more likely to be at a lower level. However, when the results of a number of project teams are totalled, then a significant advantage could well be possible.

EVALUATION

The young and inexperienced brand manager presents his case for a major brand re-launch. He believes the changes he proposes for the brand are of real significance to the consumer. He looks for a major increase in the brand advertising and promotional support, and requires a substantial effort from the sales force and other sections of the company. He forecasts a large increase in the brand's market share, sales volume, and profit contribution.

In fact, on closer examination, the proposals prove to be a change in pack design and a modification in the advertising presentation for the brand.

Proposals of this kind, and not necessarily from an inexperienced brand manager, have probably appeared at some time in almost every company operating in consumer markets. A similar type of light-weight proposal, possibly in a different form, will no doubt have been presented in industrial and service companies.

If accepted for action they will almost certainly fail in the market-place. Developments such as a new pack design or a new advertising presentation can occasionally represent a competitive advantage but they are unlikely to be of real significance over the medium or longer term. In themselves they are unlikely to be worthy of a substantial company effort. For real longer-term success they will need to be backed by, for instance, a product performance improvement, or a price adjustment.

It is clearly important for management to attempt an evaluation of the competitive advantages it has developed. Just how significant with the consumer is the proposed performance improvement? Can it be noticed in a 'blind product' test? Or is a strong prompt necessary? Is the new purpose development really of substance? Or is it a useful extra, but of minor significance?

Consumer research and other testing techniques are available to the manufacturer to guide him in the evaluation process. In some instances the message will be clear – the consumer thinks the new development is excellent, it is certainly of real significance. In others the test results may be more confused. For some cases a worthwhile test may be difficult to arrange.

However, an evaluation of each claimed competitive advantage is required. And it is accepted that at times this may of necessity be a form of rough estimate. Only when the manufacturer has a clear indication of the value of the advantage in consumer terms can he begin to answer the two key questions:

- What proportion of my company resources, both money and effort, should I place behind the development and exploitation of this competitive advantage?

- Where should this particular competitive advantage feature in my order of priorities?

When a manufacturer places an unduly large part of his resources behind a competitive advantage that lacks real substance the cost can be most damaging to him. There can be a loss in terms of immediate profitability, but the opportunity cost incurred is likely to be of even greater significance. The time wasted in the market-place could be crucial in the competitive battle. There can also be a loss of position with the trade – one failure of this kind may be excusable, but more than one is unlikely to be forgotten and will make later efforts that much more difficult.

A cost which can be even higher in opportunity-cost terms, but not necessarily one that will appear directly in the account books, can be incurred where a manufacturer fails to give a really significant competitive advantage at least an adequate level of exploitation support. The advantage may be copied by competitors, or eventually nullified in some other manner, and the opportunity to make real market progress lost. Such opportunities are very special to a brand – they come on rare occasions and may never be repeated. Clearly they should not be wasted.

EFFICIENCY, EFFECTIVENESS, MORALE, AND CULTURE

It is usual to think of competitive advantage in terms of particular brands or products, or in such forms as production processes, or special methods of operating. This is understandable, this form of advantage is often visible and easily recognized.

However, it is important to appreciate that some of the most valuable competitive advantages are more general in nature and not so readily recognized. Nevertheless they can be of very real competitive significance.

When a company is able to establish a higher level of total effectiveness and efficiency in operation than its rivals it has, in fact, developed a competitive advantage.

The higher level of effectiveness and efficiency will be about an advanced degree of skill, a superior effort, and the right attitude. It is also very probable that a high level of morale and a strong, favourable company culture will have played a valuable part in the development of the effectiveness and efficiency.

■ *Winning and high company morale tend to go together. It will be argued that the winning brings the high morale with it. But there is also movement the other way – a well developed morale can make a worthy contribution toward the winning. A soundly based company culture can also have a favourable effect on operations. A skilled management is always very conscious of this total company performance advantage.*

PROTECTION

Having worked for and developed a competitive advantage, the manufacturer should take appropriate steps to ensure that the advantage remains exclusively his for as long as possible.

Frequently a competitive advantage will require time to reach its full potential. A firm establishment of the advantage will not be achieved over a few weeks, and sometimes a few years will be necessary. The linking of a particular purpose with a brand name, the linking of a given level of performance with a brand name, are good examples of how repetition of the brand advertising, together with a frequent use of the brand, may be necessary before a firm establishment can be expected.

Clearly the protection afforded by patent or copyright is important and where applicable should be used to the full. There is, of course, considerable skill in ensuring that a patent is worded and filed in a manner which provides the maximum protection.

In many cases legal protection for a competitive advantage will not be possible. Then it will be necessary for the manufacturer to provide his own protection.

If the advantage is for a unit cost based primarily on volume production which is in turn dependent on brand market leadership the protection is straightforward – ensure the brand remains market leader and if possible extend the lead.

If the unit cost advantage is based on a particular manufacturing technique the need may be to take determined action to ensure the technique and its operation remains strictly confidential.

Production unit costs are often dependent on the condition and effectiveness of the plant involved. Brand volume may be higher than competitive brands, there may be a very high level of skill present in plant operation, but if the machinery itself is outdated and relatively ineffective, then a competitive advantage based on a superior unit cost is unlikely to survive for long. Protection of the advantage requires the installation of modern, effective plant as rapidly as possible.

The competitive advantage may be the discovery and development of a significant new purpose. When the manufacturer is the first to discover it he is well positioned to make the meeting of this purpose (i.e. the delivery of the particular benefit) his property. If he does this thoroughly, then eventually his brand will become firmly linked with the benefit provision and as others attempt to copy him they could find themselves merely providing his brand with additional publicity. But the manufacturer must take the necessary action to ensure the appropriate link with his brand, and he needs to be aware that the time available to him to complete the task may be limited.

With competitive advantages which are relatively insignificant, yet nevertheless of value to the business, the need frequently is to take action to ensure that they are kept as confidential as possible. The rule 'never talk about a development until it has been surpassed by a further advance' has much to recommend it.

Competitive advantages based on special techniques in presentation, particularly advertising presentation, are likely to have only a limited time-period to be effective. They are often difficult to protect, they can be copied rapidly, and their value quickly undermined. However, when a competitive advantage in product performance is linked to an effective special presentation technique, then the product advantage may be enhanced, and as the product and technique are linked then a degree of exclusivity tends to be afforded to the technique.

The degree of protection a manufacturer is able to provide for his competitive advantage can clearly be a key factor in its value and in his plans for its exploitation.

CONCENTRATION

A significant competitive advantage is clearly of great value to a brand, and in turn to the owning company.

When a marketing opportunity has been identified and selected for operation by the business it is vitally important that the competitive advantage which is to be at the centre of the exploitation in the market-place is specified and action taken to speed its development.

■ *One of the most important operating rules is to appreciate that success will invariably require a concentration of effort and resource. The business is unlikely to have the resources to explore every opportunity open to it. It will need to be selective, and to concentrate its resources on the limited number of openings which are most likely to produce the required results.*

Key points

1 Every successful brand has a competitive advantage, frequently a significant one, which it has developed and exploited.

2 Successful brands go to make a successful business. Every company should be concerned to ensure that it has within it an ability, and a practice to develop and exploit competitive advantages.

3 In simple terms, an outline for brand marketing success would read:

- Find the marketing opportunity. Assess and evaluate it.
- Define the competitive advantage necessary to exploit the opportunity.
- Decide whether or not you are positioned to develop the competitive advantage more effectively, and more rapidly, than your competitors.
- Accept (or reject) the marketing opportunity for action.
- If you accept, concentrate resources on the development of the opportunity and in particular of the competitive advantage.
- Marketing opportunities are exploited by brands. The competitive advantage must be incorporated into a brand, either an established brand or a new one.
- When you have developed the competitive advantage check its value with the ultimate customer. If you have a competitive advantage of significance be sure you exploit it to the full.
- Be sure the *key* factor within the brand competitive advantage is given full protection.

4 This simple outline approach emphasizes the great importance of an ability to develop effectively and rapidly a competitive advantage to exploit the marketing opportunity.

5 Acceptance of the competitive advantage concept can have a major impact on the thinking, behaviour, and performance of the people within the business. It encourages a competitive approach, one that reasons: 'there is always a better way', and then goes on to accept that the better way must be created, developed, and exploited ahead of competitors.

6 All competitive advantages are worth having. The most important are those of real significance. Advantages of this kind can move the market share of a brand. A business that is intent on achieving real success must build an ability to create, develop, and exploit significant competitive advantages.

4

◇

The Market

◆

Clearly the market in which a brand competes, its size, and its rate of growth or decline are vitally important factors in the formulation of brand strategy. The value of obtaining the dominant leadership of a growth market, and then carrying it through to a highly profitable position during maturity and eventual decline, is well accepted. Similarly the opportunity cost incurred by the big operator who concentrates his resources on a particularly small market, or the possible trouble for the little company that tries to establish a major position in a very large market without full preparation, are strategic considerations which are linked directly to the market.

■ *The market and its development are also of great significance in business operations. The longer-term growth of a market is made up of a series of shorter-term steps, some of them small and others large. Failure to foresee the development of these steps, particularly large ones, can mean the loss of brand position, possibly of brand market leadership. Recovering a lost position of this kind can be difficult and expensive.*

Knowing the current size of his market or markets is of major importance to a manufacturer. Beyond this he needs to be sure of the market's state of development. Is it still a growth market? Has it moved into maturity or decline? Other factors of significance concern the market's regional development, and also its spread by social class, consumer age, occupation and so forth.

In the study of the economic prospects and market developments operations and strategy are closely linked. Essentially operations are concerned with the shorter term, normally a period of no more than twelve months ahead. In particular, the need is to specify accurately any possible market 'breaks' – major moves up or down in the market volume. Strategy is normally concerned with the longer term – but the breaks will be important to the strategist as they can be key factors in deciding the pace of development, and eventual size, of the market. To foresee a break in good time, and ahead of competitors, could provide the opportunity to develop a significant competitive advantage; to miss a break could be extremely costly.

This chapter is primarily concerned with the market and its part in operations. The opening section of the chapter considers the economic outlook. In preparing his operations plan the manufacturer needs to take a view of the economic prospects for the time-period covered by the plan. The economics for the period will have an effect on the movement of the market; beyond this they may provide for other opportunities in operations.

ECONOMIC OUTLOOK

In strategy formulation it can be reasonable to deal in broad terms when considering the economic outlook. A forecast that reasons in terms of five years of steady growth with a short period of no growth in the later stages can be acceptable. The strategist can work within these terms.

Such a forecast would not be acceptable to the operator. He is concerned with a much shorter period. He needs to know the pace of growth through his operating period, and he wants to know the actual months where no growth is expected. He is looking for a much higher degree of accuracy over a much shorter time-span.

Economic forecasts covering a whole range of items such as government monetary activity, taxation changes, population movements, consumer spending, housing completions, construction activity, etc. can be purchased from specialist consultants.

In the larger companies there may be a case for retaining a specialist staff to work full-time on these and other forecasts. Smaller and medium-sized companies would probably buy from outside consultants.

The general forecasts which deal with the development of the economy form a background for the more specialized forecasts that are concerned with the movement of those factors which are known to have a material effect on the markets in which the business already competes or expects to compete in the future. It is the more specialized forecasts which tend to be of real significance to the operator.

The good operator will know which of the economic and other outside factors are likely to have a material effect on the movement of his markets, and which are of interest but of limited influence. For instance, to a washing machine manufacturer, a small increase in the general level of incomes may be of interest. However, a big drop in the minimum level of the hire-purchase deposit rate, or its complete removal, could be of real significance and something that might cause the market to explode.

The specialist forecasts will need to go beyond the economic field. It could be important to know how the housing completions are expected to rise in general, how this rise is spread regionally, and also the type of houses involved. Textile production may be an important issue, with details of styles and colours. The number of motor-cars expected to be sold in the period, with the lead from this to the probable demand for tyres and other equipment, may be of significance. The weather could possibly be an item of importance, and the manufacturer who has discovered a fully reliable means of forecasting it would certainly have gained a competitive advantage.

The list of special forecasts will vary from business to business depending on the markets in which they compete. The aim must be to produce a series of forecasts that provide a guide as to when, where, and to what extent these various outside factors are likely to provide opportunities for the brands of the business through the operating year.

In operating battles timing is always important. If conditions in March are likely to stimulate consumer demand for a group of the company's brands then they must be delivered to the shops in February. This probably means they need to be produced in January. If the February sale to the traders is missed, then the business could go to a competitor. And then the manufacturer must face the need to encourage the consumers to re-try his brand, and to switch from a competitive brand.

Judging the extent of any likely opportunity arising from the forecasts is always difficult, and yet it can be important. If the opportunity is a big one then it must not be missed. Preparing for it may be costly, and if it does not materialize, or materializes in part only, then the cost of unused preparation could be extensive. Of course, the cost of missing a major opportunity could be much higher. This emphasizes the need for sound and well timed forecasting.

■ *Good forecasting faces the facts as it sees them developing. This means that it foresees good years – and on occasions it foresees bad years. The opportunities present in years of economic expansion are more easily recognized, but there can also be opportunities during years of economic recession. For a manufacturer who is well resourced a year of recession can provide an opportunity, and possibly a relatively inexpensive opportunity, to buy market share. For the strong man in a market a recession, can be a good time to go on to the attack. Of course, it will be helpful if he can be sure that the competitor (or competitors) he has targeted to receive his offensive is going to be weakened by the recession.*

EXCHANGE RATES

At one time the currency exchange rates of most of the international trading countries were fixed by agreement. That period has passed and now the major international currencies are subject to a free market movement.

This means that within his economic forecasting the manufacturer must provide a forecast covering the movement of the currencies which are likely to affect his business through the period of his operations plan.

If he buys imported raw materials the exchange rates will be of significance to him. If he buys processed materials based on an imported product, then the exchange rates will also be of consequence. There is unlikely to be a trading company of any size that isn't affected directly or indirectly by the movement of exchange rates.

It would be difficult, and probably unduly complex, to attempt to forecast accurately the movement of every currency that is likely to affect the business operation, but it should be possible to cover the limited number that are of real consequence.

The competitive advantages that can come from accurate exchange-rate forecasting are many. Of course, the longer-term movement of selected currency values should be a strategy formulation factor, but there will also be shorter-term movements which provide opportunities in operations.

■ *The movement in the exchange rates of countries supplying raw materials is an obvious area for competitive advantage. The requirement is for a double win – an accurate forecast of the movement of the raw material price and an accurate forecast of the movement of the appropriate currency exchange rate.*

The decision as to which currency is to be used for the billing of export sales can also be an area of opportunity. Frequent changes will cause confusion, but changes are possible and it is important they be made the right way.

For companies that are required to remit dividends to parent companies in overseas countries the exchange rate can be of great significance. If the parent company has requested and expects profits and dividends of given levels in the home currency, then the exchange rate can be *key*. If it is favourable for the subsidiary it will leave cash and resource available to buy market share in the local market or to invest in other projects. If the rate is adverse it will mean belt-tightening in the subsidiary operation. Clearly forecasting the exchange rate correctly will be of importance to the subsidiary – and to its competitors.

It is, of course, possible to take out a form of insurance through the financial markets to provide cover against major swings in the currency exchange rates. This can protect against extensive loss, but it should be appreciated that exchange rate swings are difficult to read accurately and there must always to be a degree of risk, even with insurance.

THE MARKET

The market we are concerned with here is made up of people. Its size and value will be determined by the number of people who can be persuaded to spend their money on the brands and products which are available in the market. The amount of money they spend on each occasion, and their frequency of purchasing, will clearly determine the total size and value.

In considering the market and its development it is suggested the manufacturer should use these headings:

1 current size
2 natural development
3 the special forecasts
4 promotional influences
5 price influences
6 the market potential

Current size

It is important for him to know the current size, and recent trends, of the market or markets in which his brands compete. Knowing where the market is now, and how it got there, can provide valuable guidance on the opportunities it offers and its potential for the future.

The requirement is to have a detailed view of the current market including its total level, its level in its various segments, the consumer or household penetration, quantity consumption per consumer, the regional levels within the national market, and any other outstanding features.

For most of the larger consumer markets information of this kind can be purchased from the professional marketing research companies. In some instances it may be necessary to supplement this purchased data with specially commissioned research.

The analysis of the market's movement over previous years should confirm its position as either a growth, mature, or declining one (see figure 4.1 for a typical market development pattern).

Analysis of the data covering consumer (or household) penetration, and its development, should show the possible opportunity under this heading. Similarly, the consumer consumption levels should indicate possible opportunities, as also should the regional data.

In effect, the manufacturer should be able to build a picture of the market with details of its strengths, weaknesses, and most importantly its opportunities. The requirement is for information under all the appropriate headings for the manufacturer's brands, and also for competitive brands, operating in the market.

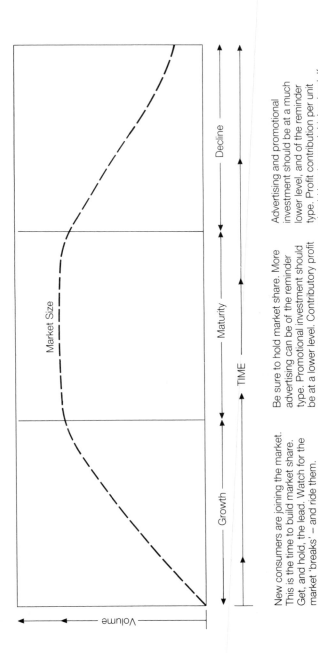

Figure 4.1 Market development

A typical pattern of market development. The rate of growth and decline will vary from market to market as will the time-periods of growth, maturity and decline.

Natural development

The natural development of the market is the development which will take place if there are no exceptional happenings such as a strong promotional battle, a new brand entry, or a particular environmental influence. It is important to calculate this level as it acts as a base from which other levels may be measured. From the manufacturer's viewpoint it is the level that he can expect if he and his competitors decide to keep their investment in their brands to a minimum.

The special forecasts

How are the developments contained within the special forecasts likely to effect the market? If the promised cut in hire-purchase deposits materializes how big a lift will it give the home appliance market? And will the extra number of washing machines in use make a major difference to the consumption of washing powders? Will the expected increase in the birth-rate mean a material increase in the consumption of baby foods this year, or will the increase come next year?

This form of question needs to be asked of the special forecasts. The requirement is to quantify any market movement and to put a time position on it. Will the lift come early in the year, say in February, or will it be later, say in September? Clearly the timing can be of great significance if the operation is to be successful.

The special forecasts can have a material impact on the main market, but frequently they will be of greater significance to specific market segments. On these relatively small sectors they can have a major impact.

The movement in living standards can often mean a move forward for the premium section of a market. It can also augur well for leisure goods and items of a luxury nature. Similarly the movement in considerations such as unemployment levels can mean an uplift in the demand for a particular type of product.

The requirement is to identify those special forecasts that are likely to affect the markets and market segments in which the manufacturer has a brand or intends to have a brand, and then to bring them into effect on the volumes as they are likely to apply through the operations plan period.

Promotional influences

If you invest heavily in a door-to-door sampling scheme, and you have prepared your effort wisely, then the probability is that you will expand the total market. You may introduce new users to the category and expand the use of existing users. Similarly if you engage in an extensive brand advertising investment aimed at gaining new triers, and you have a brand that represents best value to a satisfactory number of consumers, then you are likely to expand the market.

Markets grow under two basic approaches – firstly by an increase in consumer penetration, and secondly by an increase in usage which leads to higher consumption. It follows that any promotional expenditure which works on these factors is likely to increase the size of the market.

■ *Every market passes through a period when there is an outstanding opportunity to develop penetration, and an examination of the current level is clearly a* key *factor in highlighting such an opportunity. If current penetration of households is low, and it is known that there is a wider demand available if only consumers can be induced to* try, *then an investment in brand penetration can be expected to expand the total market. Of course, it is important that the brand concerned has the ability to become* best-value *– this means that if it is an entirely new brand it must represent better value to consumers than the brands that are currently available.*

It is important to differentiate between product or category penetration and brand penetration. An extension of category penetration is likely to expand the market, but this will not necessarily apply for an individual brand. A brand development in penetration may be very worthwhile for the particular brand concerned, but the increase achieved may come from other brands and not from an expanding market.

On occasions a move as simple as the development of the store distribution of the product category can bring about an expansion of the market. Where distribution weaknesses of this kind are shown they can usually be corrected without extensive promotional investments.

■ *Reading the market accurately and appreciating when a penetration opportunity is available, and having a brand in position to meet it can provide the manufacturer with an opening to establish his brand in a strong position within the market. For the consumer, a first and satisfactory meeting with a brand can be of significance and often develop into a lasting association. Once a brand has been tried and well accepted by a consumer, he can become firmly attached to it. To bring about a change a competitor will have to offer more than marginally better value.*

Research of the current position can often yield information showing an opportunity to expand the market through increased usage of the product. In exploiting this opportunity advertising, showing the benefit of heavier usage, or suggesting additional usages, can be helpful. The introduction of larger sizes can also often help increase consumption.

The requirement is that the manufacturer should firstly be aware of the opportunities that are available to expand the market, and secondly be aware which brands within the market have the ability to exploit these opportunities and are likely to carry this through during the operating plan period.

Price influences

One of the most important influences on the development of a market is the level of the prices which apply within it. Price is one of the *key* factors within the *best-value* concept. Price movements up or down, can have a material effect on the consumer's evaluation of the product or brand concerned. A price movement down acts to increase value and is therefore likely to increase demand and expand the market. A price movement up reduces value and is therefore likely to reduce the level of the market. The price movement needs to be considered on a relative basis – if all prices increase then there has not really been an increase in any one.

These observations on price and market movement are generally correct. Of course, they are subject to such limitations as the elasticity of demand for the particular product or brand. Given a low elasticity the market movement will tend to be a small one and with high elasticity the movement is likely to be relatively large. It is also possible that in certain of the 'emotional' markets skilled and extensive presentations can have a material effect on a brand's value, and this can outweigh any value change made by a limited price move.

■ *Most consumer goods markets start with price at a relatively high level, and with demand restricted in part by this price. However, as demand develops and knowledge of the product/brand and the benefit it delivers becomes more widespread, a stage is reached where the potential of the market becomes much clearer. The economies in unit cost that large-scale manufacture and distribution can provide become evident. To get these economies sales volume needs to rise, i.e. the market needs to expand. To get this expansion advertising and promotion may be necessary, but in particular unit price needs to fall.*

Judging correctly just when a market reaches this position is extremely difficult. An analysis of the current market, of consumer attitudes and views, of production and distribution costs, and extensive consumer price testing, these and other studies can help. In the final analysis a sound feel of the market will also be most valuable.

The important fact is that the manufacturer who judges this market development correctly, has a brand which is well positioned and the facilities and resources to finance the necessary operation, can mount a move for market domination. If he is successful he can dominate the market on through its maturity and decline. As a dominant market leader his position should ultimately be a very profitable one.

The decision to make such a move is clearly a strategic one, and yet it requires considerable 'input' from operations. The timing of such a move is crucial, and the detail for this must rest with the operators.

There can be periods when a knowledge of the market movement, of the competitors who compete in it, and of the level of price elasticity which applies within it, can signal that a price increase could prove highly profitable. This can often apply when a market reaches maturity or is in decline.

Market potential

It is always important to assess the potential of a market, and to up-date this assessment every time the operations plan is formulated. Within the assessment a time plan is also necessary.

The potential size of a market should provide a guide to the level of profit that can eventually come from it. In effect, it can provide a guide as to the prize the winner in the market will ultimately be able to claim. The timing plan can indicate the period that is available to reach, and hold, the required position.

Arriving at a worthwhile assessment of the potential of any market is always difficult. Much of the research and analysis discussed in the paragraphs above should be helpful. If the assessment is carried out at regular intervals then, with experience, a high degree of accuracy should be possible.

A statement of market potential, corrected as appropriate from time to time, should avoid the opportunity cost of a major business concentrating too heavily on a small market, or the possible danger of a very small business attempting to dominate a particularly large market without the appropriate preparation.

THE MARKET: THE OPERATIONS PLAN

The manufacturer needs to bring together the various facts and viewpoints contained within the reasoning of this chapter, to arrive at an estimate of the market and its various sectors for the period of his operations plan. The estimate should be set out on a time basis through the period.

It is suggested that he support this estimate with two further figures. The first one should show his view of the 'upside' of the market – this is the upper level it is likely to reach if a major propor-tion of the possible developments favourable to growth actually come to happen. This could mean a total market estimate of, say, 15 per cent above the operating plan estimate.

The second set of figures should provide a market estimate on the 'downside' – this is the lower level the market is expected to reach if a major proportion of the possible developments fail to materialize.

Given these estimates the chief executive, or the manager to whom he has delegated the appropriate authority, can decide where he wishes to position his volumes, market shares, etc. for his brands.

Should he decide to go for the higher level he will be able to include the higher revenue he can obtain, and the prize available to him in terms of market share and profit contribution should he be successful. He will also be able to appreciate, and assess, the additional costs he is likely to incur with items such as higher stock levels in both raw materials and finished product.

If he uses the lower level market for his plans then he needs to be aware of the risk he runs should the market take-off and he is unable to meet the increased demand.

The final decision on the probable market size is one of judgement. There is no formula that will provide a guaranteed estimate. Whichever way the decision goes, there will be a degree of risk involved. Of course, it is always possible to take a form of insurance against undue risk – for instance, by carrying additional stocks or by having vacant plant capacity – there will be a cost involved in the insurance, but it may be worth taking.

Key points

1 The business gets its revenue from the market. It must have a satisfactory level of revenue if it is to live and prosper. The market, its size, its value, its current position, and its probable development over the period of the operations plan are all vitally important considerations to the business. A sound basic rule is that you build brand share during the growth stage of the market, and then take a profitable ride through maturity and decline.

2 The brand plans for sales volumes, market shares, support investments, and ultimately brand profitability, should all be greatly influenced by the size and potential of the market. Of particular importance is the development and potential of the various market sectors.

3 There are always opportunities in the market. They may be in terms of greater penetration, increased consumption, or possibly better value in terms of a lower price – the opportunities have to be searched for, but they are always there waiting to be exploited.

4 If the market estimates are greatly in excess of the actual levels recorded then additional costs in the form of excess stock levels, both for raw materials and finished stock, could be high. Investment and effort could be badly misdirected.

5 But it is vitally important not to miss an exceptional growth break in the market for this could provide an outstanding opportunity for the manufacturer who is prepared, and able, to exploit it to the full. It could provide a brand with a significant competitive advantage for the life of the market. To miss an opportunity of this kind could prove very costly. Big opportunities of this form, once missed, rarely ever return.

6 Good forecasting is of great importance, it can set the scene for a competitive advantage; inspired forecasting can lead to a significant competitive advantage. If you already have good forecasting make sure you keep it. If you haven't got it then you should take immediate action to get it.

5

◇

Competitors

◆

The plan for the new brand was good, very good. It was well designed, and the timing appeared to be perfect. Everything was set for a successful launch operation. The brand margins were very satisfactory. The first year was expected to be a break-even year, with a small profit in the second, and a very acceptable level of profit in the third. And then it all happened! It was a competitor who caused the trouble. He came rushing in ahead of the launch date. His brand price was low. His product very good. In just a week the whole game changed. The break-even in Year 1 was definitely out and so was the profit in Year 2. It was now a bitter fight for life – all caused by that most inconsiderate person, the competitor!

The free enterprise system works satisfactorily only when there is strong and vigorous competition. Out of strong competition everyone can benefit – most importantly the consumer gets a *better-value* buy.

The requirement is that the manufacturer must meet those opportunities which he has chosen for his brands more effectively than his competitors. In those sectors where he has decided to compete in earnest he must win – he must outpace and outmanoeuvre his competitors. The big prize is reserved for the winner.

Clearly it is of great consequence to the manufacturer to know who his competitors are likely to be, and how they can be expected to perform, before he decides that a particular opportunity, or series of opportunities, is one in which his brand can expect to have a competitive advantage and go on to win.

An assessment of competitors and their strengths and weaknesses is an important part of the business strategy formulation process. It is an equally important factor within the planning and formulation of the operations plan.

In strategy it is always possible to decide against entering a particular market or, if appropriate, to make a withdrawal. In operations the need is to pursue the selected opportunities in the market effectively and efficiently. It follows that the information on competitors required by the operator will differ in certain respects from that required by the strategist. Perhaps it would be more accurate to say that there will be a difference of emphasis.

The probable reaction of a competitor to a particular market-place confrontation can clearly be of consequence for the way the manufacturer handles the position himself. It follows that a detailed analysis of each competitor can be of special value in operations in that it should provide guidance for:

1 selecting those opportunities which are most suitable for exploitation;
2 deciding which is the most effective way to carry out the exploitation;
3 deciding how to defend a market position when a specific competitor is about to attack.

In essence, the requirement is a statement of each competitor's (or potential competitor's) strengths and weaknesses in a number of relevant fields. The basic reasoning is that your chances of success will be greater if you attack where your competitor is weakest. And you should have your defence prepared in advance in those areas where he is strong and likely to attack you. This assumes that the areas concerned are of consequence in the specific encounter.

It is suggested that the manufacturer needs to gather detailed information on his existing competitors, and on those companies who are expected to become competitors, under a number of headings: (see figure 5.1)

1 ownership and management
2 finance
3 operating ability
4 capacity
5 brands and market position

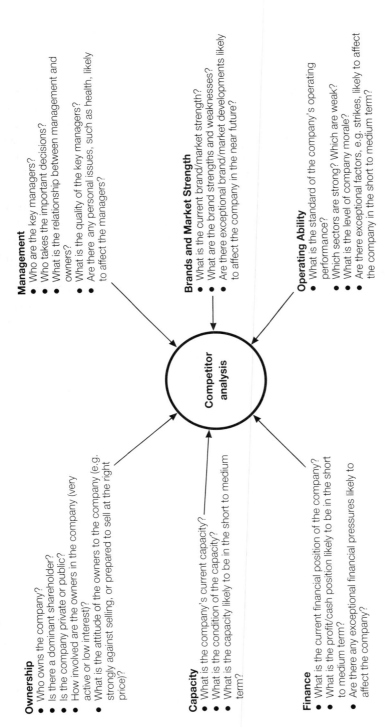

Ownership
- Who owns the company?
- Is there a dominant shareholder?
- Is the company private or public?
- How involved are the owners in the company (very active or low interest)?
- What is the attitude of the owners to the company (e.g. strongly against selling, or prepared to sell at the right price)?

Capacity
- What is the company's current capacity?
- What is the condition of the capacity?
- What is the capacity likely to be in the short to medium term?

Finance
- What is the current financial position of the company?
- What is the profit/cash position likely to be in the short to medium term?
- Are there any exceptional financial pressures likely to affect the company?

Management
- Who are the key managers?
- Who takes the important decisions?
- What is the relationship between management and owners?
- What is the quality of the key managers?
- Are there any personal issues, such as health, likely to affect the managers?

Brands and Market Strength
- What is the current brand/market strength?
- What are the brand strengths and weaknesses?
- Are there exceptional brand/market developments likely to affect the company in the near future?

Operating Ability
- What is the standard of the company's operating performance?
- Which sectors are strong? Which are weak?
- What is the level of company morale?
- Are there exceptional factors, e.g. strikes, likely to affect the company in the short to medium term?

Competitor analysis

Figure 5.1 Competitor analysis

Ownership and management

Who actually owns the competitive business? Is it a public company quoted on the local Stock Exchange? Is it a subsidiary of a company listed on one of the overseas exchanges? Is it a private company?

These and similar questions covering the ownership may prove to be of consequence in later answering the key questions: 'What is the competitor's financial position?' and 'Who manages the competitive company?'

Ownership can have a major effect on the shorter-term pressures on the business particularly with profit levels and dividend payments. A public company needs to keep its profits at a reasonable level and to maintain its dividends. Failure under this heading can have a material effect on its share price level.

With a subsidiary company it is always important to know the position of the parent. Frequently, for instance, if the parent has liquidity problems the subsidiaries could be under pressure to produce cash without too much regard for the possible loss of brand market share.

With a private company the financial position of the owner or owners will almost certainly reflect on the business. If they want a constant flow of high level dividends then the company will be required to deliver this and, on occasions, the demand may have very little regard for the position of the business.

The ownership of a competitive business can be of consequence; of even greater significance is its management.

Sometimes the owners *are* the senior managers. In such a case it is vitally important to know of the training, experience, and personality of the people concerned. How much does the business really mean to them? Are they ready to sell? Are they so vitally interested in developing and progressing the business that they may be prepared to forego shorter-term returns? These and similar issues can be of vital importance in business operations.

When the business is owned and managed by one man his contribution will often be a dominant one. His personal approach will be crucial. If he holds certain well-known views, e.g. 'I will never be under-priced', it can be of great value to know of these when competing with him.

When the business is a subsidiary company it is important to know just how much authority the local management has. Do they have to refer back to head office just to enlarge a brand's promotional investment? Can they mount a counter-attack for a brand without referring back to head office? Are they likely to have to withstand a long series of meetings with head office staff managers before defensive action can be mounted?

These can be questions of significance, and the answers can have a material effect on operations. On occasions the head office may insist on a brand following a particular approach in its development. To break with the routine would require a most exceptional reason. Clearly it can be important to know of the form and timing of the routine.

Where a local manager has the full confidence of the head office, and is given a wide authority, a very different position applies. In this case he may run the business almost as a sole owner. Here it is most important to know of the experience, training, and personality of this controlling manager.

■ *It could prove very worthwhile to maintain a detailed record of the ownership, and the management of all competitors. In particular the record should contain details of the senior people, of their training, experience, their business views, and their personalities. If they have been successful with a specific form of operation this should be noted – most people are inclined to repeat their successful operations even when the new conditions are not exactly the same as those which applied previously.*

Finance

Is competitor A likely to find it difficult to finance the launch of his proposed new brand? Would he find it difficult to raise the money to defend his leading brand if it came under heavy attack? Questions of this kind could lead through to worthwhile opportunities if, in fact, the competitor was likely to encounter a finance problem.

Finance is, of course, linked with ownership. It can be difficult to find out exactly how a competitor is positioned financially over the shorter term. His published balance sheet will provide an indication, but it can often be late in appearing. There will be a need to use other means of checking the position – mutual suppliers can sometimes comment on their experience with the competitor and this may provide a lead; banking and financial circles can on occasions provide information which is helpful.

If a competitor has financial problems it could provide a very worthwhile opportunity. It can be worth taking considerable trouble to check the position thoroughly if there is any indication that a money problem is probable.

Operating ability

How good an operator is the particular competitor? Is he very good right through his business? Is he good in marketing and selling yet weak in development and production? Do you have reason to believe that the management has 'gone over' and the supply of young men coming through is of poor quality?

Performance in the market-place, and personal observation of the people, their approach, and their business behaviour should help to provide answers to this form of question.

If the competitive management is weak then it must be put under pressure. It may not remain weak over the longer term – while it is weak there could be market share and brand volume to be gained cheaply.

Some companies are quick on their feet; they can move to take an opportunity with speed, or they will face up to a problem rapidly and clear it. Others are slower, more cumbersome, and invariably need time to change. The management sets the pace and attitude of the business. It is very important to know what kind of managers control the competitor businesses.

Capacity

If you compete in markets where capacity is no problem, where new capacity can be added at very short notice and at limited cost, then there is unlikely to be any point in researching in depth the capacity position of your competitors.

However, in by far the majority of markets capacity is a factor of importance. It frequently requires a lengthy period of time to build and prepare for production. The plant may have to be purchased in certain sizes, and it could be very costly.

Given that capacity is a significant factor in your markets then it is of consequence to know who has capacity, its extent, and its condition.

If a competitor runs short of capacity as a market begins to take off then he has provided a valuable opportunity. If a competitor's capacity is old, inefficient, and expensive to operate, then he can be vulnerable in a rapid expansion of the market.

If it is known that a competitor is short of capacity then it may be worthwhile to stimulate market growth with advertising, promotional investment, and competitive pricing.

Brands and market position

Information under this heading is of fundamental importance. There is a need to know the current strength of competitive brands in terms of market share, sales volume, sales revenue, advertising and promotional expenditure, product cost and profitability.

In particular there is a requirement to provide guidance as to the real strength of each competitive brand. What is the brand's price elasticity? The answer to this question can often provide a guide as to the brand's real strength with its established consumers.

If it is accepted that its brands are the very base of a company's strength, it follows that any statement attempting to cover the strengths and weaknesses of a competitor must consider in detail his current brands, and his possible new brands.

It is not proposed to consider the competitive brand and market strength position in any detail here. The subject is examined very closely in other chapters of the book.

■ *The basic aim of competitor research is to build a comprehensive statement covering each competitor. It should highlight the strengths and the weaknesses of each one. The statement must go beyond the appropriate figure data. In particular it should consider the people who manage the competitive businesses, outlining their training, their experience, their successes, their personalities, and the business activities they are known to like or dislike. In the final analysis the competitive battle is primarily with the people who manage the competitive businesses.*

DISTRIBUTORS

Distributors are customers, and they are also competitors. They are a special kind of competitor, and so they warrant particular consideration.

The term 'distributor' is used here to describe the various wholesale and retail businesses that distribute manufacturers' brands and products to consumers. In this respect they are manufacturers' customers.

Many of these distributors manufacture, or have manufactured for them, a series of products which they sell to consumers, through their stores, under the brand name of their store or wholesale group. These brands are known as 'distributor' or 'own label' brands.

Many distributors have been particularly active in the marketing of distributor brands over recent years. In a number of categories in the UK it is quite common for a distributor's brand to hold as much as 30 per cent of the particular market through the distributor's own store.

In chapter 14 the distributor in his role as a customer is considered in some detail. Here we are concerned with him as a competitor.

It will be necessary to consider each distributor individually as they tend to differ widely in their approach to distributor brands. Some think of the brands merely as a means of obtaining extra business at the cheap end of the market. The product is frequently of poor quality and the price is probably the lowest available in the store in the particular category. At one time this seemed to be the general approach followed in the majority of stores.

Over recent years there has been a marked change in the approach used by many distributors, and this has been most evident with the major multiple chains and the leading wholesale groups. As these organizations have developed, so their management has become more and more professional in its approach. They have realized that the distributor brand represents the distributor's business. Its quality and its presentation reflect on the distributor. A shoddy brand can be damaging; a good product and presentation can be beneficial. This has meant that in many stores, in many categories, the distributor brand has become of real significance.

The requirement is to consider each distributor and to record his approach to the marketing of his own distributor brands. Is he keen to widen and develop his brands? Has he decided to restrict his distributor brand activity? As with other competitors it is important to know the managers concerned, and to be aware of their views on this particular subject.

The distributor's activity with his brands in particular markets, and within specific market sectors, should be analysed and studied within the marketing department's detailed approach to the opportunities available in the various markets.

■ *Distributor brands are competitors in the same way as other brands, except that they can be expected to have certain advantages, such as pricing and in-store merchandising. The fact that the distributor may be an important customer should not be allowed to cloak the fact that he can also be a competitor, sometimes one of considerable substance. As with other competitors, the requirement is to beat him.*

'GOOD' AND 'BAD' COMPETITORS

There is a view which argues that some of the competitors in a market are 'good' and others are 'bad'. The view reasons that the 'good' competitor 'knows his place' within the scheme of things. He wants to improve his market share but does not attempt to do this at a ridiculous cost. He wants to earn a higher level of profit, but accepts that this is more likely to result from a steady and risk-free approach.

The 'good' market leader has an approach which allows others in the market to make a *reasonable* level of profit. He provides a price umbrella which is very helpful to his smaller competitors; to a considerable extent he is responsible for keeping them in business.

The 'good' competitor gives and receives market signals. He does not make vigorous and unannounced movements. He plays by the established rules of the industry. He understands the costs which go into his products and he avoids cross-subsidization of his brands.

The 'bad' competitor has none of these so-called 'acceptable' traits. He does not accept his position, and in fact he continually tries to change it, frequently by using price aggressively.

The 'bad' market leader is not prepared to provide an umbrella – he is more likely to drive the smaller manufacturer toward bankruptcy with his squeezing of margins. Occasionally he appears to have forgotten about the need for shorter-term profits so keen is he to gain market share.

This whole question of 'good' and 'bad' competitors is discussed in some detail by Michael E. Porter in his book *Competitive Advantage* (New York: The Free Press, 1985).

Competitors are both a blessing and a curse. Seeing them only as a curse runs the risk of eroding not only a firm's competitive advantage but also the structure of the industry as a whole. A firm must compete aggressively but not indiscriminately. (p. 228)

The reasoning I follow in this book is that all competitors are enemies and they have to be beaten, and beaten on a continuous basis. Of course, it needs to be appreciated that beating a competitor does not necessarily mean destroying him.

It is the responsibility of each chief executive to manage the development and progress of his business in a direction and manner to ensure it achieves its objectives. This could require him to be very selective in his operations against his competitors. In Year 1 he may attack competitor A and postpone any action against competitor B until Year 3. He may be happy to take high margins from his brands in market Z, and have low margins and aggressive pricing in market Y.

He should always manage his business in his own best interest. Sometimes his competitors may benefit from his actions, but this will be incidental and not the objective for the action.

There will be periods when the competitive businesses are well managed, and periods when some are badly managed. The badly managed may cause problems through the shorter term; but over the longer term, unless they improve their management, they are likely to be losers. The well managed competitors will always pose a problem. Their managements will have made plans aimed at ensuring they make progress; the challenge is to out-think, outmanoeuvre, and eventually beat them. After all, this is what business strategy and operations are all about.

There can be a position in a market where everyone appears to be a winner. Where there has been market growth and an upward trend in brand margins all competitors can claim higher volumes and higher profits. But this represents only a partial victory; a real win requires the winner to make progress and his competitors to lose.

■ *It follows that all competitors are enemies and must be beaten. This does not mean that a manufacturer should always behave in a combative and aggressive manner toward his competitors. It does mean that he should always be vigilant and plan to use his resources in the most effective manner possible for his business. This may well mean that on occasions some of his competitors will get hurt; better they get hurt than that they should prosper and eventually take over his business.*

Key points

1 A careful study of competitor's strengths and weaknesses should bring forth a number of possible opportunities. They can take the form of a competitor with a financial problem, or one with an organizational/personnel difficulty. When a series of senior managers leave a competitive business and are replaced by men who are inexperienced in the market an opportunity could be available. A take-over bid involving a competitor can divert his management's attention from the market-place battle. These are just a few examples of the form of opportunity that competitor analysis can highlight.

2 There is clearly a need to link the competitor analysis under this heading with that carried out by marketing for the brands and markets. When the two are joined a full appreciation of competitor's positions and the opportunities they present can be obtained.

3 A competitor who has weak brands and is experiencing financial problems can provide an opportunity for market share to be gained cheaply. A financially strong competitor with an aggressive management and worthwhile brands is likely to attempt a major move forward – be prepared for this; with skilful manoeuvring he may be distracted from making an all-out attack where it will hurt you most.

4 Competitors are the enemy and they must be beaten. There is no such thing as a 'friendly' competitor. A competitor will want to improve his business, and he has a responsibility to his owners to do this. Make sure he does not succeed at your expense.

5 A skilled competitor is unlikely to attack all the time. He may be pleased to accept a period of peace, to gather his resources and prepare for future action. A competitor who wants peace should receive particularly close attention. The probability is that he wants peace to develop, or to cover, his own position and certainly not to help yours. If you are skilful you may be able to give him peace and at the same time take his business.

6 The aim should be to get your brands and your business into the positions you consider most desirable without your competitors being aware of what you are doing.

Good analysis of competitive businesses, their managers, their finances, their brands, and their market positions can help in this manoeuvre. It can also help to ensure that you are never caught unawares by a shrewd competitor's manoeuvring.

PART III

6

◇

Business Opportunities

◆

Creating and developing opportunities is at the heart of successful business management. It is a difficult yet challenging and exhilarating part of the management task. For real success it is necessary to go beyond merely commissioning the right research, although this in itself can be of significance. An approach which is both systematic and entrepreneurial is required.

The systematic approach should ensure the search covers the whole area of potential, and that nothing that has possibilities is missed. The entrepreneurial contribution brings an ability to see beyond the bare facts of the research and analysis. It senses the additions that are required, the relatively small refinements that bring the 'extra' the consumer values and is willing to pay for.

The big opportunities, those which can warrant a new brand or provide an existing brand with a major re-launch, would normally have been planned for within the strategy formulation process. But there will be opportunities which have not been foreseen by the strategy and which arise in the course of operation. Sometimes these operational opportunities will develop into major ones.

Irrespective of the source of the opportunity, within operations it requires assessment, evaluation, selection (or rejection), development, and then action in the market. This process is considered in this chapter. The actual development and exploitation of opportunities receives more detailed attention in the chapters which follow.

■ *At the start of this section on business opportunities it is worth repeating the basic and very important point – a business can make progress in the shorter term by putting right its problems.*

89

Cost reductions, changes in organization, improvements in productivity, are all good examples of this. But if it is to make real progress over the longer term, the business will need to create, develop, and exploit new opportunities.

TYPES OF OPPORTUNITY

The opportunities the business is likely to encounter in the operating period may be classified under four headings (see also figure 6.1):

1 strategic operating
2 operating
3 provided by competitors
4 provided by chance

Strategic opportunities

These will have been outlined in the strategic plan formulation. They will be at various stages of development depending upon the time of their first introduction into the plan and their subsequent development.

The operating task is to progress the strategic opportunities as rapidly and effectively as possible, within the agreed priorities of the business, to a position where they are ready for a successful market-place introduction.

Once the opportunity is in the market-place the operational task is to exploit it, again within the agreed priorities of the business, as effectively as possible.

The task of 'progressing' an opportunity will cover all those developments which are necessary to bring the opportunity to fruition. This will include the development of such factors as the product formula, processing, production, packaging, advertising, and promotion. In particular it will be concerned with the development of the competitive advantage which is to be used in the exploitation.

There should be a planned programme for every project and the need is to ensure that the programme is met. This may mean using additional resources to speed up a development, or if a project is ahead of its plan and the business is not ready for this, possibly transferring resources to another project for a period. However, if a major

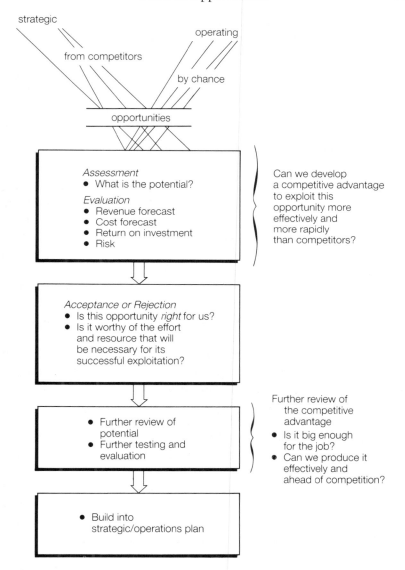

Figure 6.1 Business opportunities: acceptance for operation

project is moving ahead of plan and moving successfully, every effort would normally be made to help it on its way.

■ *Within the progressing, from time to time and on a planned basis, a check should be made of the project's potential, of its competitive position, and of its cost and profit-earning prospect. In effect, periodically the project should be re-evaluated and re-assessed.*

The requirement is to be as sure as is possible just what the potential for the project is, and in particular to be aware of any change. If it is growing this may mean that the priority for the project should be promoted within the company plans. If the potential has declined it may be appropriate to drop the project.

The competitive position refers to the developments, both outside and inside the market, that competitors are known to be working on. In particular, the timing of any possible competitive activity can be of significance. If a competitor has been able to make an adjustment to one of his existing brands which in part provides the consumer benefit of the new project, then clearly the prospects for the project will have changed. If a competitor is known to be working on a similar project, reliable data on his progress will be invaluable.

Information on competitive progress may spotlight a need for the company to put more resources behind its own development.

The difference between being first or second to market with a new brand or a major new development for an existing brand can be immense, even if the time difference is just a few months.

The costs incurred on development projects can easily run away if they are not closely controlled. This in itself is a good reason to have a periodic expenditure review. On a wider front there is the need to be aware of the profit-earning potential of the project and how this is moving as the development progresses.

It will be argued that the project's earnings potential is an extremely difficult forecast to make with any confidence. This is normally correct, but there is a need to attempt the necessary estimates, and to monitor their change as the project develops.

An approach that has merit is one that pushes forward and gets a worthwhile result in the research and development work. When the desired result has been achieved an attack on the various cost items is mounted with a view to achieving reductions without making a major change in performance. If this approach is followed it is very important that allowance is made within the plans for the time period that may be necessary to achieve the cost reductions – it can prove a difficult exercise.

Operating opportunities

These arise during the course of business operations. They are not included in the strategic plan but as the business follows through in its operations, particular opportunities can develop.

Operating opportunities tend to be smaller than the strategic variety. In the development department a chemist tests a new chemical ingredient, and he finds that it has a beneficial effect on performance if it is mixed with another chemical before it is injected into the product. The cost of this operation is very low, and so a series of checks are made to confirm the development. As a result of this the product formula is changed to allow for the new ingredients, and the performance is enhanced slightly. The advance could represent a competitive advantage. This is an example of a typical operating opportunity.

Similarly, the sales department may find that a retail chain, not normally a stockist of the brand or of its competitors, is prepared to stock the company's brand and is able to make very worthwhile sales. While the chain declines to stock competitive brands the company has a competitive advantage with this retailer.

Operating opportunities can be of significance in that while they may make only slight differences individually, in total they can come to represent a significant competitive advantage.

Opportunities provided by competitors

Opportunities of this kind arise during operation, but they are of a special kind and worthy of separate consideration.

A competitor may have a brand that has been selling successfully with a formula which meets a specific consumer need. His advertising has, over a number of years, linked the brand name to this benefit. Suddenly the competitor decides to move away from the benefit. In a re-launch for the brand he uses a new formula aimed at meeting a new need. His advertising also changes the benefit it promises from the brand.

Can the manufacturer make appropriate adjustments to his brand and its advertising and promotion so that he is able to attract customers of the competitor who do not wish to change benefit? And can this be done without disturbing the loyal customers of his own brand? If it can, there is an opportunity available which has been provided by a competitive move.

Similarly, an opportunity may be available if a competitor decides to stop the distribution of a particular pack size of a brand, or withdraws the brand from distribution in a geographical region, or from distribution through a specific class of retail outlet. These are all examples of opportunities provided by competitors.

■ *Of significance are the opportunities that can arise where a competitor moves into a test market for a new brand and gets it wrong. It may well be that the competitor has correctly diagnosed an opportunity within the market but his timing is wrong, or he has made a basic error in his brand presentation, or failed in a particular part of operation, e.g. by failing to get adequate store distribution. Pricing errors can often cause failure in test markets, particularly with completely new products.*

The opportunity to analyse a competitor's test market, to highlight his failures, and then to enter the market with a brand that avoids the mistakes and gets it right, can be a most valuable opportunity.

Of course, a tactic often employed is for a company to deliberately set out to confuse a competitor's test market. It may engage in particularly heavy competitive advertising, very strong promotions, and/or aggressive pricing. The aim can be to delay the competitor so that the company can open its own test market and catch up in timing, or it may be to dissuade the entry of a brand into the market. This would be a major tactical operation and any opportunity arising from it would really have arisen as the result of the company's action rather than that of a competitor.

Opportunities provided by chance

New laws can often provide opportunity. For instance, a particular form of manufacture may be outlawed, providing an opportunity for a company with an alternative method of production available, or an alternative product that supplies the necessary benefit.

Equally the introduction of a new law can act to create a new need.

In the UK the demand for safety belts in motor cars was clearly greatly developed by the change in the law which made their use compulsory.

Opportunities by chance will often arise on a local basis by an act of nature. For instance, a period of particularly warm weather in a region can bring an exceptional demand for ice cream and similar products.

In practice, really worthwhile opportunities by chance tend to be few in number. Occasionally a change in the law will be made at very short notice, but normally a law change will be discussed and reviewed well in advance of implementation. The opportunities the change provides will often be included as strategic or operating opportunities.

PROCESSING OPPORTUNITIES WITHIN THE BUSINESS

All opportunities, irrespective of their source, should pass through a similar process. Firstly, it is essential for the opportunity to be assessed with great care. To find an opportunity and then to let it pass because its potential is not appreciated can be particularly annoying, and very expensive.

Clearly, on occasions the assessment will be a difficult exercise. To be correct always in the assessment of potential opportunities would be superhuman. However, a favourable record in spotting the really valuable opportunities is essential for a business that aims to produce superior results. This is back to the very basic point – in this field of activity management judgement, that is sound judgement, is vitally important.

All opportunities require evaluation, selection (or rejection), and as appropriate, inclusion in plans for action. While all opportunities should pass through a similar process, clearly there will be differences in the time the process takes, the place where it fits into the business procedures, and the degree of detail considered appropriate.

For strategic opportunities the evaluation and selection will have been covered in the strategy formulation process. Plans will have set out forecasts for such factors as market growth, competitive actions, formulation costings, etc. With operational planning it is necessary that these forecasts should be checked, and corrected as appropriate.

Normally, any correction can be expected to be of a marginal nature. The market may be growing slightly faster than expected, costs may be falling below the levels forecast, and so on.

Operating plans can usually take care of these adjustments – making sure a slightly bigger opportunity is not missed, or ensuring that a weakness is suitably guarded against. No major change in company strategy is likely to be necessary, and the next strategic review will be able to consider the movements and build appropriate adjustments into the strategic plans.

From time to time the operating planning will bring forward a need for a correction which can be of significance and which may require at least a strategic review, and possibly a change in the strategic plans.

When a significant change in strategy is shown to be necessary, it should be faced and not merely put off until the next programmed strategic review. New operating plans may be required following the strategy changes.

Operating opportunities also need to be evaluated. In the main they will be covered by the review sessions that prepare the company operations plan.

The evaluation of operating opportunities is always a difficult task. Rarely will time be available to carry out the more detailed research that could provide real guidance. Frequently action will of necessity have to be based on judgement decisions. The important requirement is to expose those opportunities that initially have appeared to be highly remunerative but which, when placed under closer scrutiny, are shown to be heavy consumers of resources and provide only limited return.

The evaluation of strategic opportunities can be in terms of absolute profit potential and also in terms of the expected return on the resources they are likely to need for development and exploitation. A measure in terms of profit is rarely possible with operating opportunities. Frequently the need would be to express the value of the opportunity in terms of, for instance, cost per home sampled or cost per unit produced. While the fulfilment of the opportunity may ultimately result in an advance in profit, the cost per unit form of measure is often better suited for the comparative cost statements that will be necessary.

■ *Selecting the* right *opportunities for action is a vitally important executive management responsibility. With strategic oppor-*

tunities the selection task is certainly one of the most significant that faces the chief executive. Getting it right *is vital for the survival and prosperity of the business. Getting the selection* right *is also of great importance with operating opportunities. While the cost of incorrect selection may not be as high as with strategic opportunities it can be substantial. And of course, getting it* right *can be highly beneficial to the business.*

TIMING

A key factor in deciding which opportunities are to be scheduled for action should centre on the ability of the business to produce a competitive advantage to meet the opportunity. With operations this can often mean having the ability to meet the opportunity faster than the competition. The first man into the market with, for instance, a particular sales promotion may be able to attract the consumer and excite the trade. The man who follows with the same promotion is likely to have much less success with both the consumer and the trade. Again, it may be advisable to be first, for instance, with a promotion at a cost of 10p per unit rather than second with a cost of 7p per unit.

Basically the question to be asked in considering operational opportunities is: How can we handle this opportunity in such a manner, and at such a time, that we gain a competitive advantage over our competitors? The follow up questions should be: What is the cost? What is the return? What is the risk?

Frequently there will be a need to balance the extent of the proposed competitive advantage with the time, and cost, required to produce it. A significant competitive advantage must be the aim – but not at any cost or at any time into the future. If the advantage cannot recover its cost within a reasonable period of time then it will not rate as a competitive advantage.

Within the formulation of operating projects the important factor is that the opportunity has been identified, and the *key* factors involved in its exploitation pin-pointed. In particular the competitive advantage aimed for should be clearly designated. This will often require the concentration of effort and resource on a limited number of *key* considerations, and the enforcement of a strict discipline to meet an agreed timing plan.

■ *Frequently, good operating requires that the ideal approach in terms of detailed preparation is foregone, and appropriate short cuts are taken. There is, of course, a very considerable skill in ensuring that the short cuts are the right ones to take, and the detail foregone is not of vital importance. The requirement is to know when judgement should be used and to have good reason to believe the judgement will be correct.*

Key points

1 Successful businesses make and take opportunities. Creating and developing opportunities is a vitally important part of the management task. It requires skill, effort, and again the all-important *right* attitude. Consumer and other research can be helpful, but the truly successful operators invariably have an ability to look beyond the research. A perceptive imagination is often an advantage, and an astuteness to appreciate a lead, or even a weakness, in the structured research and analysis may be necessary. It also helps to have the determination and stamina to keep going when the going gets really difficult.

2 This is, in part, the entrepreneurial side of the business. Good sound systems and well contrived methods will be of consequence. The computer, with its ability to accumulate and analyse facts rapidly, can also play a valuable part. However, this is an area of operations where the people involved in the creation and development of the opportunities will be all-important. Their expertise, their astuteness, and their enthusiasm will be the key to real success.

7

◇

Brands, Marketing, and Competitive Advantage

◆

■ *Successful business is about making and taking opportunities, and the most important of these are marketing opportunities.*

A marketing opportunity is a consumer need or requirement not met adequately by an existing brand. Within the business marketing is the function primarily responsible for the creation of customers. It is the function concerned with the discovery, development, and exploitation of marketing opportunities.

Marketing meets these opportunities through its brands. It works directly with the brands and should be one of the most fertile areas for the development of significant competitive advantages. Beyond this, marketing, as it goes about its task of creating customers, should be deeply involved in the exploitation of the developed competitive advantages.

WHAT IS A BRAND?

In brief, a brand may be described as firstly a name. Over time this name will come to represent the fulfilment of a specific purpose or the provision of a particular benefit. The name will also come to denote a standard of performance in delivering the benefit. Finally, the name will come to represent a personality, something that is often referred to as a 'brand image'. This personality is the picture, or impression, and feeling for a brand which has developed in the consumer's mind.

■ *Where a manufacturer has done a good branding job, over time, the mention of his brand name will immediately bring to mind, in words and pictures, the purpose the brand meets, its perform-ance standard, and a feeling about the name which reflects the brand personality.*

The establishment of a brand is normally a longer-term exercise. Its positioning and development are strategic considerations.

Operation is concerned with the shorter-term brand development. In effect, it is concerned to make the strategic brand plans actually happen.

The *key* development factors for a brand are contained within the *best-value* concept. They are purpose, performance, price, and pre-sentation. It is around these factors that operation is concentrated over the shorter term.

■ *A brand is clearly a complex phenomenon. All sections of the business, and many contributors outside of the business, are concerned with its establishment.*

Marketing opportunities should be developed and exploited by brands. Where the opportunity warrants this should be by a new brand; on other occasions by an existing brand.

Within the business strategy the marketing opportunity should have been identified and the competitive advantage necessary to exploit it defined. But the task of actually creating, develop-ing, and exploiting the competitive advantage, whether it be a new brand or a suitable addition to an existing brand, rests with business operations. Figure 7.1 shows the brand marketing circle.

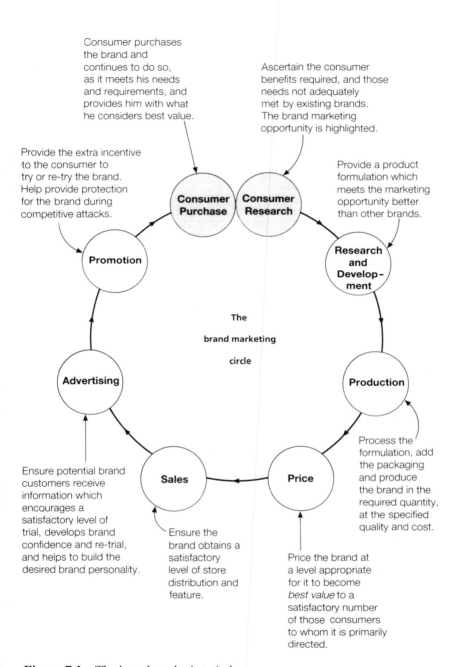

Consumer purchases the brand and continues to do so, as it meets his needs and requirements, and provides him with what he considers best value.

Ascertain the consumer benefits required, and those needs not adequately met by existing brands. The brand marketing opportunity is highlighted.

Provide the extra incentive to the consumer to try or re-try the brand. Help provide protection for the brand during competitive attacks.

Provide a product formulation which meets the marketing opportunity better than other brands.

Consumer Purchase

Consumer Research

Promotion

Research and Develop- ment

The brand marketing circle

Advertising

Production

Ensure potential brand customers receive information which encourages a satisfactory level of trial, develops brand confidence and re-trial, and helps to build the desired brand personality.

Sales

Price

Process the formulation, add the packaging and produce the brand in the required quantity, at the specified quality and cost.

Ensure the brand obtains a satisfactory level of store distribution and feature.

Price the brand at a level appropriate for it to become *best value* to a satisfactory number of those consumers to whom it is primarily directed.

Figure 7.1 The brand marketing circle
Successful brand marketing requires that the circle is completed, and that the whole operation returns a satisfactory level of profit.

MARKETING

If we define the purpose of the business as creating and satisfying customers then we must say that the whole business is about marketing. Within a truly successful business this does, in fact, apply – everyone throughout the business is conscious of the customer, of his requirements, and of the need to meet them in the most effective manner possible.

While everyone in a business should be conscious of the significance of the brands and should make every effort to assist their progress, clearly there is a need for this effort to be directed and co-ordinated. There is a need for someone to take a specific responsibility for each brand's health and progress, and with this responsibility should go the necessary authority to ensure the appropriate action is co-ordinated and progressed. The authority clearly needs to extend over departmental and functional barriers as the brands are of the whole business and not of any individual part of it.

Given the importance of the brands to the health of the business it can be argued that the responsibility for their progress should rest directly with the chief executive. There is some logic in this suggestion, and in, for instance, a one-brand business, it can be reasoned that the chief executive should be the brand manager. Indeed, even in a multi-brand operating business, a chief executive who does not maintain a close overview of his brands could be accused of having his priorities wrong.

However, while the chief executive should be involved in the key decisions affecting his brands, it is usual for him to delegate the on-going management to his marketing director who, certainly in a larger company, would have marketing managers actually managing the day-to-day operations of the brands.

The marketing director heads the marketing department which is responsible for the development and progress of the brands. Marketing starts and ends with the customer. By means of research it attempts to discover the product the customer wants. It works with applied research, basic research, and production, with a view to ensuring that the product manufactured conforms to the customer's requirements. It endeavours, by the use of salesmen and other means, to maintain adequate stocks of the brand with the traders through whose hands it must pass on its way to the final customer. By the use of advertising and promotions, it attempts to create and maintain customer demand for the product.

In some companies the term 'marketing' is not used and the management of the brands is carried out from within the sales or advertising department, or possibly in a special section known as the brands management. The name of the department is not necessarily of significance, the important factor is that managers of an appropriate level, and with the necessary authority, have the responsibility to view each brand in total and to ensure that it is progressed effectively.

This is not to say that the marketing department should have an executive authority over other departments in the business. However, it does require that the business has an organized structure, and that within the organization procedures are followed whereby marketing plans for brand action can be discussed, decisions for action taken, and progressed.

■ *If the marketing department is to perform its important task satisfactorily it will be essential that it earn the respect of every other section of the business. It can do this by building a record which shows it is effective, a record that shows it gets the required results, and also by showing a judicious respect for the contributions of the other sections.*

Marketing should liaise with the various other departments of the business to ensure that the functional competitive advantages which have been developed are applied to the brands as effectively and as rapidly as possible. Marketing also has a major role to play in ensuring that the competitive advantages gained through the development of company projects are introduced and exploited effectively.

However, it is in the creation and development of opportunities and of competitive advantages, which apply directly to the brands' value in the market-place, i.e. to the factors directly concerned in the best value concept, that marketing can make its major impact in the development of a brand-significant competitive advantage.

BRANDS, THE BEST-VALUE CONCEPT, AND COMPETITIVE ADVANTAGE

The *key* factors within the best-value concept are very directly concerned with the consumer's assessment of a brand's value. It follows that any positive move in any one or more of the factors, as applied to a particular brand, can have a marked effect on the brand's value and represent a competitive advantage.

Marketing has the responsibility to review, on a continuous basis, every aspect of the brand's best value equation. This requires that each one of the *key* value factors, as applied to the brand, should be considered individually and also together with the other factors.

In many cases the actual development work will be carried out by other sectors of the business, or by outside agencies, but the drive and the leadership should come from marketing. Marketing should always be better positioned than others to appreciate the real value to the brand of any proposed change. Marketing should be able to see the change in terms of the *whole brand* and not merely as, for instance, an advance in performance or a change in presentation. And marketing should have available the necessary information to evaluate the change in terms of revenue, costs, and brand-profit contribution.

The brand management approach, whereby one manager is responsible for the health, strength, and well-being of a particular brand, gathers part of its value from the fact that it allows the manager to concentrate his whole time and effort on the creation, and development, of brand opportunities, and of the competitive advantages so necessary in their exploitation.

In operations, the brand manager would be expected to work within an agreed brand strategy. Indiscriminate competition between brands within a company would be wasteful – there is little point in a company having two very similar brands directed at meeting exactly the same consumer need. However, within the bounds of the agreed strategy, competition between brands in the development of competitive advantages should act to bring about a more effective total operation.

BRAND PURPOSE

The discovery of a new consumer need or requirement which is not serviced adequately by the brands currently in the market is the discovery of a marketing opportunity. An outstanding way to gain a competitive advantage is to discover a marketing opportunity before your competitors, and then to develop and exploit it successfully.

Marketing opportunities within this heading are usually discovered under one of three approaches:

1 direct from consumer research;
2 as the result of new ingredient developments;
3 following developments in other markets.

Consumer research

Progressive companies are continually meeting and talking with consumers. They check the consumers' view of existing brands, of their likes and dislikes, and beyond this they try to get an indication of the consumers' unsatisfied needs and requirements.

Research of this kind is really a part of strategy formulation. However, frequently it will also be part of operations for as the operators work to open up the strategic opportunity they will need to go back to the consumer to verify details and to check their developments.

Getting worthwhile results from research of this kind will depend very much on the skill of the researchers in both setting up and organizing the actual research study, and then in interpreting the results. This is a form of research which requires very careful preparation and highly skilled execution. It can also require considerable patience as the opportunities frequently need time to mature.

There are two broad approaches that the company can take under this heading. One is to make a broad sweep of selected consumers on a regular basis. In this way the manufacturer will have a developing record of consumer views and requirements. The second is to mount a specific research project looking at a particular field of consumer activity. Of course it is quite normal for a manufacturer to apply variants of both approaches.

Ingredient developments

New chemicals, new food ingredients, new perfumes, and similar developments are continually coming forward. They can add materially to the performance of an existing brand, or be a key factor within the formulation of a possible new brand. If they are to be successful the new items must have a value to the customer. They must either enhance an existing benefit or provide a new one.

It can be argued that these new ingredients are merely providing a solution to the unfulfilled needs contained within the consumer researches. In many cases this will be true. But on limited occasions the ingredients will come first – they will bring the new consumer need into existence. On these rare occasions the new ingredients can form the basis of what could be a significant competitive advantage – this requires, of course, that the ingredient and knowledge of the need it creates is obtained by the manufacturer ahead of his competitors.

Other market developments

Developments in the markets of other countries can often form the basis of a marketing opportunity. This applies particularly where the country in question has higher living, social, and economic standards than the manufacturer's home country.

If the manufacturer wants to gain a competitive advantage under this heading then he will need to ensure that he receives suitable information of new developments taking place in the countries which he believes can provide the lead to the new opportunities.

The competition between manufacturers within his own country to obtain an early indication of a possible opportunity is likely to be intense, and it will probably be too late to wait for the development to appear as a new brand or as an adjustment to an existing brand in the overseas market. Details of regional test-market performance may be necessary, or, if possible, details of the consumer researches which have preceded the test marketing.

The multi-national groups clearly have a lead position in obtaining competitive advantages under this particular approach. This applies especially to those groups whose operations are widespread with major units in the more advanced areas such as the USA, and parts of Western Europe. Frequently they will have local operating companies which can be used for collecting and distributing information on competitive developments. They will, of course, be able to provide their associates with immediate and detailed information of their own activities.

There are a number of ways in which manufacturers without a direct international connection can gain access to the development information. They can form a link with a similarly placed manufacturer in the selected country and agree to exchange information. Or if the flow of information is one-way they can arrange a payment basis.

There are a number of commercial agencies that specialize in providing information on new brands and new developments on a regular basis. The information is frequently for sale on subscription terms, and a follow-up service for sending actual products, as requested, is also provided.

■ *Sound and fast information on new developments in the markets of other countries has a double value – it can provide the manufacturer with the basis for a new brand or existing brand improvement, and secondly it can act as a warning of what he might expect his multi-national or other competitors to launch against him.*

For the operator, the first requirement is to decide whether or not he wants to invest in buying the information. For the very small business the answer may well be 'No', but for the bigger business the answer is likely to be 'Yes'.

Given that he does want to know what is happening in the other countries, the requirement is the basic one of ensuring that the investment is worthwhile and that it is cost-effective in terms of his information requirement.

An approach which provides for a wide coverage without undue detail, but which also gives a rapid follow-up on any interesting item, is one that is likely to be the most satisfactory in terms of cost-effectiveness.

Some 'overseas' ideas for brands and brand developments travel well, others do not. A slow, half-hearted reaction to a new development can mean the loss of a valuable opportunity and possibly a gain to a competitor. A hasty, ill-planned, rush into a development can be equally costly if the home consumer rejects it.

Clearly a means is required to differentiate between those overseas developments which can be expected to enjoy a successful introduction and those which are likely to be failures.

Skilfully designed consumer research can be helpful. A regional test market could be used – this will require careful preparation, satisfactory investment backing, and an adequate period of time in the market. Of course, there are arguments against regional test markets. The manufacturer will need to decide for himself what is the best approach for the particular item, and for his business.

■ *Discovering a new purpose that is not adequately covered by existing brands can be one of the most productive first steps for bringing into existence a significant competitive advantage. Frequently the strategy formulation process will have focused on the opportunity within the markets and will have defined the consumer need. The requirement of operations is to flesh-out these outlines, and to spell out the consumer benefit in specific terms.*

Adroitly designed consumer research will be important and a close, well tuned link with research and development could be of significance. There will be a need to ensure that the product brief, that is the brief issued to those responsible for the actual development of the proposed product, is both clear and specific. Similarly there is a great need for clarity and precision in areas such as briefing for advertising.

BRAND PERFORMANCE

Talk with a marketing manager on the subject of competitive advantage and he will almost certainly refer to product performance. This is, in part, understandable, for a performance advantage which is demonstrable is normally one of the most exploitable of competitive advantages. Often it will lend itself to comparative advertising, and respond well to sampling and other aggressive promotions – all very much to the liking of the marketing manager.

Performance improvements are always worth having providing they can be obtained without excessive effort and expense, and they can be passed to the consumer without a major movement in brand price.

Normally worthwhile improvements in performance follow investment in research and development. Improvements in performance are always obtainable, and the important questions leading to it tend to be:

- What particular part of performance is of consequence to the customer?
- What degree of performance improvement is achievable?
- What will the improvement cost in terms of time and money?

The requirement is for the manufacturer to decide which particular part of the product performance he wishes his research and development effort to concentrate on. His consumer researches should provide him with guidance.

Should he concentrate on the main benefit or should he go for one of the subsidiary benefits? Much will depend on the positioning of his brand, and on the time and investment necessary to achieve a satisfactory performance development.

If his brand is a 'niche' player, i.e. a brand that has a speciality benefit, then his first priority should be to ensure that he leads in his speciality. If his brand is the leader of the main sector of the market then his priority will be to ensure that his brand delivers the main benefit at a satisfactory level.

Of course, the main market leader may want his brand to also cover a particular subsidiary benefit. And if the niche brand is to move into the main market and eventually challenge for leadership, then it will require at least a satisfactory level of performance in its delivery of the main benefit.

Deciding just where the manufacturer should make his main effort is a strategy consideration. But it is also an operating point because so much will depend on the prospects of achieving a successful outcome, in given periods of time and with given levels of investment.

The strategy may have foreseen an opportunity for the speciality to broaden its appeal and to challenge for market leadership. But if in operation the time-period needed to attain the necessary improvement in performance proves unduly long, or the cost involved unduly high, then the brand may be well advised to change strategy and to concentrate further on its speciality.

■*With performance improvements three factors are always of importance:*

- *How significant is the improvement?*
- *Can it be demonstrated to the customer?*
- *How much will it cost?*

Normally, if the market leader is to be overtaken as the result of a brand-performance development then the attacking brand will need a significant advantage over the leader. A minor advantage is unlikely to be enough. Ideally the significant advantage should be easily recognized, and should be capable of competitive demonstration.

Minor performance advances can be of value to brands. To the market leader they make it that much more difficult for a competitor to mount a successful performance attack. For the contending brands they narrow the gap with the leader, and make a significant advantage a little bit easier to achieve at a later date. But a minor advance alone is unlikely to be satisfactory as the centrepiece of a major attack.

It is vitally important that the operator should be sure just how significant the product-performance advance his brand has achieved really is to the customer. Not to the chemists or other researchers responsible for its development, but to the customer. In effect the operator needs to know whether he has a significant competitive advantage or merely an advantage.

■ *The immediate cost of giving a strong backing to a significant competitive advantage can be very high. There will always be a degree of a risk. But the opportunity cost of not backing it could be considerably higher. The important requirement is to be sure that it really is a significant competitive advantage in the view of the consumer, and that the company has the ability to manage the exploitation with the necessary skill, resources, and drive.*

BRAND PRICE

A brand can have a price advantage in the market-place, and this can be very effective in improving its sales volume and market share, but the advantage may not be a competitive advantage within the definition used in this book. Here a price advantage is only accepted as a competitive advantage if it is backed by a unit cost advantage.

This definition of a competitive price advantage is important, and the difference from merely a price advantage can be of considerable consequence. We are, in fact, talking of a unit cost advantage for an equivalent quality and quantity of product.

■ *With a competitive price advantage a brand could sell at a lower price than its competitors and still have a higher unit contributory margin. With only a price advantage the brand would have a lower contributory margin per unit, and if prices should be moved down it could move into a unit loss position before its competitors.*

Of course, a business can have a unit-cost advantage which it does not use on price. It can take the advantage into additional margin and use it on advertising, sales promotion, or on one of the other avenues open to it.

There are three ways in which a brand may obtain a significant competitive price advantage:

1 by effective and efficient operation;
2 by having a higher volume;
3 by skilful price adjustment.

The first two approaches are directly concerned with unit cost. The strongest position is to have both; indeed only if a manufacturer has both can he really be sure he has a unit-cost advantage.

The third approach is concerned with his skill in positioning, and moving, his brand price in its market-place operations.

Normally, a significant price competitive advantage can only come when a manufacturer has both 1 and 2. If he can add 3 then he should most certainly have a significant advantage. If he has 3 alone he could have a shorter-term advantage, and in certain circumstances this could be particularly valuable, but it is unlikely to rate as a significant competitive advantage.

The skilful adjustment of brand price in the market-place is really part of the operation of the marketing manager. Price is one of the marketing *tools* and needs to be used with great care and skill. This whole subject is discussed in more detail in chapter 13.

BRAND PRESENTATION

Brand presentation, in its widest form, has three major tasks:

1 to encourage potential customers to try the brand;

2 to provide existing users with assurance, confidence, and encouragement to continue buying;
3 to help develop the desired brand personality.

Under this heading a competitive advantage can be gained by carrying out each of the tasks more effectively than competitors. As advertising is normally a major part of brand presentation it is discussed in greater detail in a later chapter.

An aspect of presentation which can be of major significance to a brand is concerned with its personality development. Before a brand is launched, before work commences on its advertising, before its package design is considered, before any of the basic presentation work commences, it is necessary that the manufacturer should have decided what kind of personality he wants for his brand.

■ *It is vitally important to the brand that the right personality should be chosen at the start of its life, and then developed. Changing a brand personality is both difficult and risky – much better to get it right from the beginning.*

What is the *right* personality? This will depend on such factors as the brand's purpose, how it is to fit into the market, where it is to be positioned in terms of performance, its position in the market's price order, its point of difference, and the consumers who are expected to become its main customers.

The manufacturer needs to ask himself how he wishes his potential customers to think about the brand, the impression that he would like to form in their minds when they hear and/or see the brand name mentioned.

In the future this may be of major importance to the brand. There may be competitive brands which have basically the same purpose, performance, and price, and then the brand's personality will be a key factor in the customer's purchasing decision.

Consumer research clearly has a major role to play in helping the manufacturer to decide what form and kind of personality he should give his brand. He will need to be sure that his brand has the ability to match the chosen personality in performance. The desire may be for a personality that can come to represent a high level of efficiency in use, but if the brand is, in fact, a very poor performer the desire is unlikely to be achieved. Similarly a rough, tough personality is unlikely to develop, irrespective of the skill and expenditure on advertising, if the brand is a weak performer.

■ *The manufacturer should set out clearly just what personality he wants for his brand. The need is to be clear, specific, and coherent. He must avoid the temptation of trying to make the personality all things to all people.*

A definition of the desired brand personality should be set out in a straightforward and simple manner. Everyone engaged in preparing the brand presentation should have this statement in front of him – where necessary it should be explained and further developed to ensure clarity and avoid misunderstanding.

When once the manufacturer has firmed in his view of the brand personality he desires then he should ensure that every piece of brand presentation material (pack designs, television advertisements, posters, showcards, etc.) plays its part in building the chosen brand personality.

He would be well advised to check with appropriate research that the presentation material prepared does, in fact, contribute to building the personality he requires. And he should check with consumers to ensure that the desired personality is forming within their minds.

The manufacturer will need to accept that the firm establishment of a brand personality will require time. He may need to exercise patience and discipline in his approach. The temptation to attempt short-term changes in brand personality should be avoided.

A wise personality selection followed by skill, discipline, and patience in application, are likely to be fully rewarded. A well established and favourable brand personality can come to represent a significant competitive advantage.

Key points

1 The business makes progress through the discovery, development, and exploitation of marketing opportunities. These are satisfied and exploited through brands.

2 The business is as strong as its brands. Through its brands it meets its customers. Through its brands it generates the revenue necessary for its survival and advancement.

3 Marketing is the function within the business which has the specific responsibility for the maintenance and development of the brands. Marketing should be at the heart of the business and its influence should permeate every part of it.

4 To do its job properly the marketing department needs the help of every other section of the business. It needs to earn the respect of the other sections – it must develop a record that shows it can build successful brands.

5 If it is to become truly successful a brand needs a significant competitive advantage. Marketing should take the lead in the development of this advantage – the most productive areas for its efforts are likely to be those which centre on the *key* factors within the best value concept, that is brand purpose, performance, price, and presentation.

6 Once a brand-significant competitive advantage has been developed it should be exploited to the full.

7 The market will always provide opportunities but they have to be worked for. They have to be discovered, developed, and exploited before they can be recorded in terms of revenue, and ultimately profit. The big opportunities in the market are exploited by brands. Strong brands should mean a strong business.

8

Opportunities and Brand Development

◆

Within the business there should be a continuous attack on the level of product costs. The administrative expenses should be reviewed frequently and kept at an acceptable level. Moves of this kind will be essential if the business is to make progress. However, if real success is to be enjoyed, certainly over the longer term, the business must go beyond this; it must win in the market-place.

This is a very basic and fundamental rule. Cost reductions and changes in organization can help to put problems right, and ensure a better performance through the shorter term. But real progress over the longer term requires the business to develop and exploit opportunities in the market.

In the two previous chapters we have discussed business opportunities, their nature, their form, and their significance. We have also considered the importance of marketing opportunities and the development of competitive advantages to exploit them.

This chapter will consider how the marketing opportunities which have been selected for action can be linked to the brands and moved forward to a successful exploitation. The achievement of this vital link can be greatly assisted by the use of an approach which utilizes the brand development plan.

BRANDS AND OPPORTUNITIES

Every brand should have its own development plan, normally covering a period of three or four years. The period will need to vary from business to business depending upon such factors as the research and development lead times which apply.

Responsibility for the formulation of the brand development plan should rest with the brand manager, or marketing manager, within the marketing department. Essentially the brand development plan plots the future progress for the particular brand over the periods ahead. It is the *tool* which is used to co-ordinate and activate both the development and exploitation of the brand.

In formulating the plan for his brand the manager should start by outlining the timing of the marketing opportunities that he sees opening up for the brand through the period covered.

For this purpose it is reasonable to consider the opportunities under three headings: strategic, major, and minor.

The *strategic* opportunities will, in almost all instances, have been foreseen during the strategy formulation process. They will be opportunities thought to be of great significance to the brand.

Major opportunities will also be of importance in the brand's development. They will include the periodic re-launch activities which the brand will need if it is to keep its performance at a satisfactory level and its presentation up-to-date within a competitive market.

Minor opportunities will normally be shown specifically for the earlier part of the programme only. They will be concerned with such operations as the improvement of store distribution, or a new pack size introduction.

While a three-heading classification of brand opportunities has been used here, in practice it will often be very difficult to differentiate between, for instance, a lower-level major opportunity and a very strong minor one. It is always possible that an opportunity may change during its development, starting as a minor one and, over time, becoming of major significance.

Nevertheless, it is necessary to attempt to classify the opportunities available in order of significance, as there will be a need to allocate resources and priorities to meet them. There should be competition among the brands for these resources, and in deciding priorities the significance to the brand of a particular opportunity will clearly be of consequence.

It is also necessary for the major opportunities claimed for a brand to be described and explained in detail, and backed by suitable research data and other appropriate support information.

As the timing of the opportunity comes closer, so the need for a detailed and specific statement increases. The important requirement is that the opportunity should be based on facts and not just enthusiasm. But, of course, if there isn't the *right* form of enthusiasm then there is unlikely to be a successful operation.

COMPETITIVE ADVANTAGE

The brand development plan sets out the marketing opportunities it believes the brand should be progressed to exploit. It should also set out the competitive advantages the brand will need if it is to carry out the exploitation successfully.

■ *If the brand development programme is to be of real significance it must go beyond merely setting out the competitive advantage desired. It must go on to outline just how the advantage is to be developed and exploited. Reviews of the programme should set out progress against the requirement, highlighting problem areas and, where appropriate, calling for additional resources to overcome bottlenecks.*

The resources required to develop a particular competitive advantage will vary widely depending upon the content and extent of the advantage. For instance, a requirement to deliver a specific performance benefit from the product may require an extensive development section investment, but a need for improved store distribution is primarily a matter for the sales department with only a limited resource investment.

FORMULATION OF THE PLAN

In drawing up the basic proposals for his brand the manager concerned should have access to all the available research data on the market, its development and segmentation, on the consumer, the trade, and so forth. He should be looking for marketing opportunities for his brand and taking soundings within the business as to the possibility, and probability, of producing competitive advantages that meet the opportunities.

A very close liaison between the marketing managers and their research and development colleagues will be essential. Marketing, from their researches and knowledge of the likely market growth, should be clear as to the brand product and packaging developments that are desirable. Marketing should also be aware of the timing and cost position desired.

Research and development managers can help turn the marketing thinking into a realistic approach. The product improvement that marketing wants tomorrow may be three years away – but a compromise, almost as good, could be available within twelve months. The new packaging material will be available next month at a very high premium in price, but within a year a new plant should mean that this price will be halved. This is the kind of reasoning, discussion and argument, that is likely to take place as the brand development programme takes form.

The development managers will often be able to contribute thoughts on the use of new ingredients, or new packaging, which may become the basis for a brand's competitive advantage. For the shorter-term items within the plan liaison is likely to be necessary between sales and marketing personnel.

Frequently the way a brand's performance advance is presented, in particular where and how it is presented, can be of vital importance. For strategic and major brand developments, presentation is invariably a significant factor requiring close liaison between development, marketing, and advertising personnel.

Proposed activities of this kind need to be included in the brand development plan. Additional resources may be needed to carry them through effectively. They invariably have an important timing contribution – it could prove very costly if a significant product advance is delayed into the market because the presentation is unsatisfactory and late.

In a company which has more than one brand competing in a market there can be a question as to which brand should exploit a particular opportunity. Given a keen and positive group of brand managers it will not be uncommon for an attractive opportunity to be claimed by more than one.

There may be occasions when it is possible for more than one brand to exploit a particular opening. However, it is unlikely to be acceptable that more than one brand should attempt to exploit, for instance, exactly the same consumer benefit. Where the opportunity is considered of strategic significance then the strategic plan should clarify the position. In other instances the decision as to which brand should take the opportunity would, in most companies, be the responsibility of the marketing director.

BRAND DEVELOPMENT, STRATEGIC, AND OPERATING PLANS

While the brand development plans may be constructed independently of either the strategic or operating plan, they must be suitably co-ordinated with these plans. In effect, they act to bring together strategy *and* operations, for they cover both strategic and operating activities (see figure 8.1).

The strategic plan covers the direction of the total business effort. The brands are central to the business effort – if the strategy is to be successful then the brands are sure to play a major role in the success.

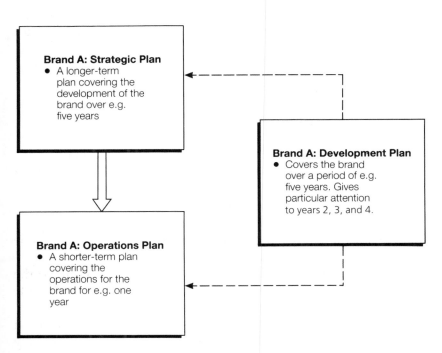

Figure 8.1   The brand development plan: a link between the strategic and operations plans

The brand development plan will follow through on the strategy planned for the brand. It will be concerned with greater detail than the strategy and will be more specific with, for instance, such items as formula improvements, packaging requirements, and advertising developments.

The brand development plan will provide a lead into the brand's position in the company operations plan. Once the operational plan is agreed for action then the brand development plan should be adjusted to fit with the requirements. Normally, the adjustments should be minimal. Changes in the timing of particular promotions may be necessary, and adjustments to cope with competitive activities in the market-place.

■ *The brand development plan occupies a position between the strategic and operations plan. It should help to bridge any gap that may inadvertently appear between strategy and operations.*

Much of the work contained in formulating a brand development plan will be closely aligned with that which will be needed for strategy and operational planning. There will be some extra work, but it should be very limited.

WHOSE RESPONSIBILITY?

The two key plans for action within the business should be the strategic plan and the operational plan. The brand development plans are within these two plans. They detail aims and requirements within the positioning and actively required by the two key plans.

In those companies having a marketing department and employing a marketing approach, the brand development plans should be the responsibility of the marketing director.

The brand development plans are particularly important to the marketing department, as this department is primarily responsible for the health and well-being of the brands.

The plans can act as a form of progress check for each brand within the business, and also as a means of concentrating attention on any special requirement of a particular brand. They can also act as a means of informing other departments and managers within the business of the progress of the brand concerned and of any action, and in particular the timing of the action, required from them to keep the brand progress moving at a satisfactory pace.

In a branded goods company the chief executive and his directors should review brand progress on a regular basis. The brand development plans can act as a basic progress report and become an important part of this review session.

Key points

1 Marketing opportunities are developed and exploited by brands – either new or established brands. Within the business it is the marketing department that has prime responsibility for the creation, development, and exploitation of the brands.

2 The brand development plan is a *tool* of marketing. It can play a valuable part in ensuring that everyone associated with the brand is aware of the development planned, and of the part they are expected to play in it. It can also act as a brand review report which highlights where additional resources and effort are required if satisfactory progress is to be maintained.

3 The brand development plan, and the progress reports associated with it, can be helpful management *tools*. But the most skilfully compiled plan does not provide the necessary skill, effort, and enthusiasm to get results. Results are generated by the operators who turn the plan into action.

4 Marketing is the function within the business at the very centre of brand development. Managers within marketing have a vitally important part to play in planning, co-ordinating and leading the brand development and exploitation process. They need to be skilful in their planning, sensitive in their application, and their attitude must always be positive. Their enthusiasm for the brand and its progress is crucial. A sensible degree of enthusiasm can be infectious – it can spread through the business and become a great stimulant to a better performance.

PART IV

9

◇

Research and Development

◆

The product is at the very heart of the brand. If the product fails to meet the customers' needs, if it fails to deliver the benefit it promises, then the brand is unlikely to ever become *best-value* for a satisfactory number of customers.

Over the longer term the cost of the product is sure to play a major part in arriving at the brand price. In the shorter term it is always possible that the brand price can appear to disregard the product cost, but if the brand is to live and prosper into the longer term, its price will need to cover its product cost by a satisfactory margin.

This means that for business success, that is success in terms of volume, market share, and profitability, the product must fulfil its purpose, at a satisfactory level of performance, and at an acceptable cost.

The product, its performance, and its cost should concern everyone in the business. All sections of the business have a contribution to make to the product within the brand, but in particular it concerns research, development, and production. In this chapter the contribution of the first two of these departments is discussed. The chapter which follows considers production and product costs.

The term 'research' is normally used to denote the original laboratory work involved in developing new products or processes. It is usually considered under two headings: basic and applied.

Basic research concentrates on the more fundamental issues of scientific discovery. *Applied* research works on the known developments coming from the basic research. Many universities engage in basic research as do a number of large-scale businesses.

Applied research is conducted in most universities and, on a very much wider basis than basic research, is practised in many businesses.

'Development' is a term often used to cover what is really an aspect of applied research. Development bridges the gap between research and the consumer. It takes the output of applied research and forms and packages it in a manner which is acceptable to the consumer (see figure 9.1).

While many manufacturing businesses choose not to engage in research, very few are without a development department.

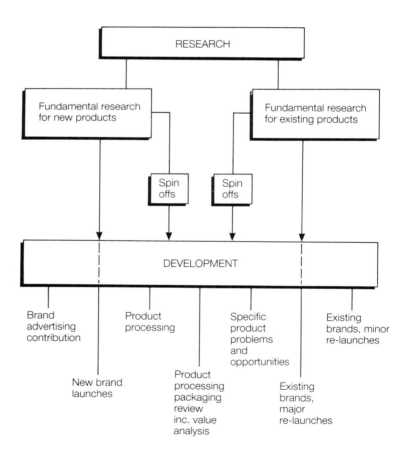

Figure 9.1   Research and development

RESEARCH

The decision to have a research department is a strategic decision, as is the decision of how much should be invested in research, and where the investment should be directed. Indeed, the department is unlikely to feature directly on the company operations plan, although the results of the research investment programme could appear in the form of products for new brands and for relaunched established brands.

A skilfully directed and well managed research department can be the base from which a stream of competitive advantages flow. Funding and staffing will be important, with skilful direction a vital factor. Research is normally very much a *people* resource. It follows that leadership and management are also of great significance if the department is to be truly successful.

Skill in all the fundamental management approaches, especially those in the management of people, are necessary within research if the results are to be satisfactory. Effective researchers are invariably people with a very high level of skill, an ability to persevere despite difficulties and disappointments, they also have the ability to follow a systematic approach and bring to it a special form of creativity.

■ *If the research effort is to be successful it is necessary that the researchers be selected with great care, equipped satisfactorily, and be well motivated. It is most important that everyone associated with the research effort should be clear that the value of the department to the business is measured in terms of the ultimate success of the products it produces in the market-place.*

The association of the research department with shorter-term operations needs to be handled with great care. On the one hand it is important that research personnel should get a feel of the market-place, of the success that a well developed product can bring, and of the significance of the profit to the business. However, it is also most important that their concentration on achieving the necessary breakthroughs on their research projects should not be disturbed. A skilful balance is required.

Links between research, marketing, and development

The main link between the researchers and the operators should come through two channels – marketing and development.

The direction of the research investment is a vitally important strategy consideration. The final decision on this direction should be taken by the chief executive, and he should receive advice from both his marketing and his research staff. Marketing to provide guidance on the likely customer requirements into the future, and research on the areas where they can expect to produce results.

Similarly, at the periodic review of research projects the marketing contribution should be of consequence.

Normal contact between research and development would come under three headings:

The transfer of a project

When a project is due to leave the research department for development, and, eventually, the market-place there will be a need for very close research–development liaison. It may well be worth a research team actually moving with the project to ensure a smooth take-over.

Meeting a specific problem

Normally product problems which arise in operations would be taken care of by development. But if the problem is of a special nature and there is a researcher who has a particular skill in the problem area, then it would be sensible to use him.

Research–development review sessions

It is most important that there should be periodic sessions when the researchers and development staff have the opportunity to meet and consider their mutual progress.

In particular the development staff should be given access to any possible 'spin off' benefits from ongoing research projects.

('Spin-off' benefits normally take the form of technical advances which have been developed on research projects and which can be used to benefit existing brands and processes.)

The research–development link is a vital one. A first-class research result can be lost, or delayed for an unnecessary length of time, through lack of appreciation and understanding in development. The feedback from development into research is also of major consequence. Development staff should have an intimate knowledge of the production process, and they are also nearer the market-place. They should have much to offer the researchers.

Key points

1 If it is well managed and satisfactorily funded, the research department should be the source of a continuous flow of product competitive advantages. Research is primarily concerned with strategic issues. Its link with operations is normally via development.

2 Among the key research factors are:
a Researchers need to be selected with great care. Good ones have the rare mixture of a high level of skill, and an ability to follow a disciplined approach with a suitable degree of creativity.
b The research effort must be directed and concentrated on the *right* projects.
c Good research people are like most other good people in business. They respond to effective motivation, and they want to be active members of a winning team. Skilled and well motivated researchers create product competitive advantages.
d The research–development link is vitally important. Possible product competitive advantages must not be lost or delayed through misunderstandings and technical opinion differences.

3 It is said that when accountants get together they love to argue over concepts and values. Chemists and scientists are in this respect just the same as accountants. Their arguments may possibly have some benefit; the important requirement is that they must not be allowed to delay progress.

DEVELOPMENT

The manufacturer must question whether or not he should have a research department. In many instances, and particularly for the smaller business, the answer will be a clear 'No'. However, there is unlikely to be any question as to whether or not he should have a development section; here the answer will almost certainly be 'Yes'.

The development task can be described under five headings:

1 Taking product innovations from research and forming and packaging them so that they may be marketed to consumers. (This will also include taking developments from outside research bodies, such as universities, where the business uses such agencies for research purposes.)
2 Working with marketing to formulate and develop products for new brands.
3 Working with marketing to formulate product improvements for existing brands.
4 Handling any specific product opportunities and problems that arise during the course of business operations.
5 Maintaining a continuous review of product formulation and processing costs with a view to making acceptable changes as appropriate.

■ *There is a view that the very bright chemist or scientist should be placed in research; one who is not quite so bright can go to development. A manufacturer who accepts this view will be making a great mistake. Of course he needs proficient people in research, but he needs equally proficient people in development. And further, the effective person in development could well be worth as much, and possibly more, to the business than his colleague in research.*

The really good development man will have all the necessary technological skills, and in addition he will have good commercial sense. Development is nearer the market and the customer. The good development man will have the chance to appreciate the marketing opportunity available and he is well positioned to make a positive contribution to meeting it. He will have a good grasp of product costs, and an appreciation as to how performance and costs can be effectively balanced.

Competitive advantage may be gained under each one of the headings set out above and which cover the development task.

Product developments

The need for a close and effective working relationship between research and development has already been mentioned. Frequently, a new chemical or other scientific discovery will be available to a number of competitors in a market. They may have all mastered the fundamentals of the discovery in research terms. From then on it becomes very much a development matter as to which competitor reaches the market first with a satisfactory product in an acceptable form. The competitor who wins this race should certainly have gained a valuable competitive advantage.

The development contribution that can be made in terms of the product form and processing should not be under-estimated. Does the customer want the liquid to be thick or thin? Would he prefer a cream to a liquid? Or would a powder be the most acceptable form? It is possible that every one of these product forms could, with suitable ingenuity, be produced. The good developer will deliver the product in the form which is preferred by the potential customer.

In these remarks the term 'product' includes packaging. Here development will have a special part to play. The manufacturer may have a research department which covers his own product field, but he is most unlikely to also cover packaging in its many forms.

Part of the development task will often be concerned with simplifying complex research approaches so that they can be understood and appreciated by the shop floor production personnel. There may also be a need to ensure that the research recommendations are practical; where they are not practical there will be a requirement to liaise back into research, and ensure that a suitable approach is developed.

New products

Not all new brands are based on research discoveries. Sometimes a new brand can come from marketing development. Marketing research may have uncovered a consumer requirement which is not serviced adequately by any existing brand. To meet this requirement a relatively simple product development is necessary, e.g. to change the form of a product from liquid to cream.

In cases of this kind development would work directly with marketing, producing a product that fits as closely as possible to the consumer requirement.

In many respects work under this heading will provide the development man with an opportunity to demonstrate his positive approach effectively. There may be a small brand in the market which is struggling, but if it were given a specific product improvement and marketing support it could make a major stride forward. It may be possible to buy the brand and work on it; if this is considered impractical then the development man can formulate an appropriate new product. There have been a number of successful brands which have come through to market success in this manner. They have the great advantage that they avoid any major research investment.

Product improvements

In any particular market, major new product developments are unlikely to appear more than once every ten years or so. In markets where research investments is especially heavy and the field relatively unexploited new discoveries may be more frequent, but a ten-year period would seem reasonable for a typical consumer goods market.

However, there will be improvements coming through for the performance, form, etc. of existing products. These may be spin-offs from research projects, or they may come from specific activities within the development department. Sometimes they can be of real consequence and possibly worthy of a new brand. More frequently they will contribute to the re-launch of an existing brand.

Developments of this kind can be of major significance to an established brand in the market-place battle. From time to time the brand will need to go back to the consumer for re-trial, to combat new developments in competitive brands, and to ensure that existing users remain loyal. One of the best ways for a brand to meet these various requirements is by a worthwhile improvement in performance.

Marketing and development should agree a programme of product improvements for each active brand within the company portfolio. There will be periods when it is vital for a brand to have something new to offer the consumer. It may be, for instance, a new perfume, a new packaging development, or a new performance ability. Product innovations of this kind can often play a valuable part in helping to exploit a growth period in the market.

Marketing and development have a responsibility to ensure that a flow of suitable innovations of this kind are available for the company brands. Used astutely within the market-place they can bring a competitive advantage. Not to have the innovations will almost certainly provide an active and positive competitor with an opportunity.

Product opportunities and problems

From time to time there may be changes in the law, in the environment, or in some other area which is not planned, and which has a material effect on the marketing of the brands in a particular market. Such changes may cause problems for existing brands. Of course, to the positive operator the changes will equally provide opportunities.

Often the particular change will require a development in product formulation or in packaging. He who gets the new development in his product first, and gets it *right*, is well positioned to win the advantage.

The successful exploitation of opportunities of this kind require an ability to foresee the 'problem' arising. To have a little more time in preparation over competitors will also be most valuable. It is necessary to have the skill to formulate or construct a solution to the problem, to ensure the solution is *right*, and then to prepare it so that it may be produced in quantity at the specified standard of quality, and in good time.

This is very much a task for marketing and development. It is where good development people can pay for their keep and provide a handsome return.

Reviewing costs

The cost of the various ingredients contained within the brand formula will change from time to time. Some of the ingredients will be fundamental to the formula and to the product performance. They should not be changed without detailed checking with the consumer. There will be some ingredients which should not be changed except in the most extreme circumstances.

However, there will be other ingredients for which highly suitable substitutes are available. Detailed consumer research may have already shown that the substitute can be used without any recognizable change in the product or its performance.

In some instances the changes in performance may be of a very minor nature and not linked to the brand's main promise.

By monitoring the various ingredient prices the development section will be well placed to recommend formula changes that can bring worthwhile cost savings without materially changing performance.

It is not recommended that the development section should have authority to change brand formulas. The brand product is so important a factor within the brand that any proposed changes in formula should be referred to executive level management. But the development section should make recommendations and accompany these with appropriate justifications.

CONFIDENTIALITY

Time is always of importance. On specific occasions, it can be one of the most valuable factors in the business. With adequate time a major project improvement can be developed, a new production process can be introduced, and new packaging can be designed.

One way of ensuring that your prospects of winning the competitive battle are greatly improved is to keep your competitors short of the time they need to combat your new brand launch, or your existing brand product improvement, or whatever innovation you are introducing. Ideally they should get to know of the innovation when it actually reaches the market-place and not before.

■ *If an existing product improvement, or new product development, is to enjoy full success it is necessary to get ahead with the formulation work, ensure that it is right for the specific market-place opportunity, do this ahead of your competitors, and keep your innovation and its progress strictly confidential. If you do this you should have time to introduce your brand to its prospective customers, encourage them to try it, go back for a second trial promotion, and all before your competitor is able to counter your attack with his own brand improvements.*

The need for strict confidentiality applies to every sector of the business; it applies particularly to research and development.

If a competitor gets to know what your research laboratory or your development department is doing today, he will have a very good idea of what you are likely to be doing in the market tomorrow. He will be able to get his own research and development team working, and if he is smart he may even beat you into the market with the innovation.

Everyone in the business should be made fully aware of the need for strict confidence in all business plans and activities. This applies particularly to research and development personnel. The desire to read a paper at a university, or to address a professional society, on a particular topic must be foregone if the content is likely to assist competitors. Similarly, articles in magazines and learned journals should be sure to avoid any information which may assist competitors.

Great care is necessary in placing consumer tests. Normally such tests have a significant part to play in the progress of a new innovation. It is important that they should be placed in a way which ensures their results are worthwhile in terms of accuracy. But if the tests are allowed to attract publicity, or are concentrated in a particular area, there is always the possibility that they will be picked up by competitors.

There is a need for strong leadership from top management on this issue. All employees should be made aware of the requirement for strict confidentiality – and the message should be repeated frequently.

The converse of this is that the manufacturer should take a very active approach to obtaining information on the research and development activities of his competitors. Again all employees should be involved and all should be encouraged to look for, and report, any sign of competitive action. All brand developments should be reported, but again there is a particular importance attached to product innovations.

The salesmen of suppliers may make a mistake and let slip details of the latest competitive raw or packaging material purchases; a store buyer may mention the latest pack he has been requested to test, a salesman's friend may mention that his home has been selected for a consumer test, and so forth. Small pieces of information of this kind, when brought together, can give a lead on the new innovation a competitor is developing. This could prove most valuable in constructing a counter-attack or in providing for a move which supersedes the competitive effort.

DEVELOPMENT AND ADVERTISING

In most advanced countries there are now advertising authorities, sometimes backed by the law and in other instances maintained by the advertising industry on a voluntary basis, charged with the task of ensuring that advertising is truthful and not misleading.

The normal procedure followed by authorities of this kind is that if a manufacturer wants to make a claim for the performance of his brand, particularly a claim which is in any way contentious, he is required to prove his point. This can be of importance to a manufacturer where he is making a competitive claim within his brand advertisement and, for instance, comparing the performance of his brand with another in a particular circumstance.

There is no doubt that the ability of a brand to make a superlative claim, one that places it above all others in a particular aspect, can be of significance to the brand in the battle for the consumer's custom. There is much more than a small difference of two words in the claim, '*the* most effective stain remover' as against '*one of the* most effective stain removers'. The first claim sets the brand above all others in terms of stain removal, the second accepts that it is one of many. But before the claim can be accepted for use the authority is likely to require that it be justified. There is always the possibility that a competitor may challenge it and require its removal.

There can be a considerable skill involved in ensuring that a product is tested in the right way, in the right context, and at the right time, to justify a particular product performance claim. Of course, the tests must be truthful and in no way misleading. If the requirement is to justify a competitive product performance claim in, for instance, a television commercial, then the skill required can be at an even higher level.

Advertising, marketing, and development managers have a responsibility to ensure that their brand is given every opportunity to show itself in its most persuasive manner within its advertisements. Frequently this will mean a feature of the performance of the product within the brand. The development manager is likely to have a very significant contribution to make toward the successful completion of this task.

DEVELOPMENT, OPERATIONS, AND COMPETITIVE ADVANTAGE

It has been argued that the researcher is concerned with strategy considerations. Normally his contribution comes in the form of a project which takes a long period, often a number of years, to make its mark. The development manager is seen much more as a member of the operating team. His work is more concerned with the medium and shorter term. His contribution is closely linked with current results.

This simple analysis of the research–development position is basically correct, although researchers do, on occasions, become involved in operations, and development managers can most certainly have a part in strategy formulation.

For the large, multi-national company with a substantial investment in research, an effective development department is of marked importance. The successful research projects have to be turned into practical business propositions.

For the small or medium-sized operator, frequently without a research unit or at best a very limited one, an effective development department is of vital importance.

In those companies with effective research units, development has the key function of bringing the new innovation to the market-place. The skill, and the speed of operation, of the development manager can come to represent an important contribution to the competitive advantage the manufacturer should gain if his innovation is *right* and he is first to the market. In this form of company, a skilled and positive development contribution can also help to build competitive advantages in brand re-launches and special activities.

It should be appreciated that many companies have research units which cover only a limited number of their markets, in those markets where they compete without a research service they rely solely on their development department to support their brands.

However, it is in companies that do not have a research unit at all that the developent department really comes into its own. In most markets companies of this kind are in a large majority. Here the brand products are entirely in the hands of development. It follows that if the brands compete in truly competitive markets and they want to make progress then a fully effective, entrepreneurial, development dcepartment is essential.

Such companies usually have brands that hold a special position in their markets. They are often referred to as 'niche' or 'speciality' brands. While not necessarily in direct competition with the main market sector they are affected indirectly by the innovations introduced by the leading brands. There is also always the possibility that one of the major operators will invade their segment.

Development has the task of keeping these niche-brand products up-to-date, ensuring they keep pace in their speciality performance, and in other respects as suitably effective. The speciality performance will be a major part of any competitive advantage they may have – if they lose it, they are likely to be lost.

The need is for personnel who can maintain a close monitoring of the developments taking place in other parts of the world, and also have a well-tuned feel for what is happening in the research units and development departments of their major competitors in the national market.

They require an ability to differentiate between those innovations which are likely to be of significance to their brands and those that are of passing interest only. When they move they may need to move rapidly, possibly concentrating the whole resource of their department on to one project. And the move must be *right* for their brand for they are unlikely to get a second chance.

Development departments of this kind need to be equipped satisfactorily. But the key to their success rests very clearly with their people. A high level of skill is of importance, but beyond this there is a need for an ability to sense a technological opportunity and to appreciate whether or not it can be met satisfactorily with the limited resources that are available.

Key Points

1 Finding able scientists, chemists, or technologists, who have a *feel* for the market-place, and a good commercial sense, will always be extremely difficult. But it is worth making an exceptional effort to locate them, and when you get them making sure they are well motivated and rewarded. This type of individual should make a particularly effective development manager.

2 Frequently the innovation that gives a brand the vital competitive *extra* with consumers will not be based on a fundamental discovery; it will be a relatively simple development that has been added to an established position. Thickening a bleach, putting stripes into a toothpaste, making a tablet dissolve more rapidly are all examples where relatively simple developments have made a major difference in the market-place. These are examples of effective development work.

3 An active and able development section is essential to the small manufacturer who has no research unit. The section may do some innovation, but much of its time is likely to be concerned with adjusting brand products in an effort to keep pace with market-place developments. For the small manufacturer with a 'niche' brand, the development section must ensure that the lead in its speciality is maintained – without the lead the brand could be lost.

4 For the big international company with a major research unit supplying a flow of innovations, the requirement is to win the race to turn the successful research project into a product acceptable to the consumer and the market-place. It can be more than just frustrating to be first with a research breakthrough yet be beaten to the market. A good development section will be sure to win the race.

10

Product Costs

♦

Research and development may have arrived at what is considered the ideal formulation to meet the brand's consumer benefit. Marketing may be happy that the formulation meets their requirement and justifies the advertising proposed for the brand. But the product costs have to be faced, they cannot be ignored. And if they do not make a business proposition possible, then adjustments will be necessary.

■ *You ignore product costs at your peril. In many of the big consumer markets product costs can amount to over 50 per cent of the final trade selling price. Any major variation from the optimum level of product cost, up or down, can mean a worthwhile competitive advantage with substantial profit or a disadvantage that can bring failure.*

Product costs are in part dictated by strategy considerations. The investment in a new plant is a strategy factor, and it can make a major difference to unit costs. But product costs are also very much linked to effectiveness and efficiency in operation (see figure 10.1).

In this chapter product costs are considered under five headings:

- raw materials
- packaging
- processing
- production overhead
- the experience curve

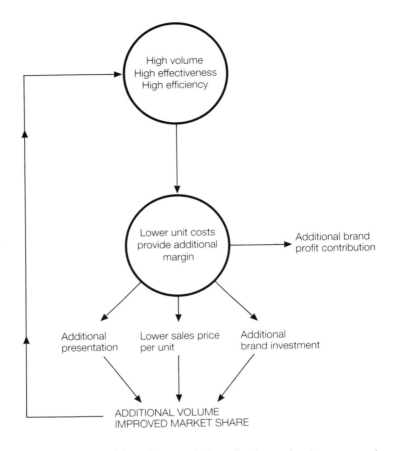

Figure 10.1   Competitive advantage in brand unit-production costs: volume, effectiveness, efficiency
A lower brand unit-production cost can lead to a competitive advantage, possibly a significant one. The additional margin the lower unit-costs provide can be taken into additional profit or used to generate additional volume through a lower unit-sales price, extra presentation, or other form of brand investment.

- A satisfactory level of volume with competent effectiveness and efficiency can bring a competitive advantage.
- High volume *without* competent effectiveness and efficiency can bring a competitive disadvantage.
- High level effectiveness and efficiency can bring a competitive advantage without high volume, but it will be difficult to obtain unless competitors are inefficient.
- High-level volume (i.e. higher than competitors) with high-level effectiveness and efficiency can bring *a significant competitive advantage*.

The chapter opens with a short section on what is termed 'The Optimum'. This is an approach which can be helpful to the manufacturer in his quest for a competitive advantage in this area of operation.

THE OPTIMUM

It is strongly recommended that the manufacturer should have constructed for each of his brands a statement showing the 'optimum' unit-cost of production.

This statement accepts that the product formula should be as specified by the development section and agreed by marketing. It provides for the purchase of raw materials and packaging at what are the most advantageous prices.

Within the statement, allowance should be made for production to take place on the most modern and effective plant, with a full capacity. The number of personnel allowed within the statement should be the minimum necessary to maintain an effective operation. Allowances for wastage should be at the level of a highly efficient production process. Breakdowns, maintenance and other down time should be included at a level considered appropriate for a very well managed plant.

The product unit cost arrived at from the statement should be known as 'the optimum'.

This exercise may appear to be unduly theoretical but it does, in fact, have two very practical uses. Firstly, it can act as a target against which the actual performance of the business is measured. In particular, when detailed comparisons are made of the actual against the target it will show clearly where effort should be concentrated and what are the likely returns from the effort.

Is the problem a shortage of volume? Is the problem excessive labour costs, or a wastage level that is far too high? Is there an excess overhead problem?

This is the form of questioning the comparison can encourage.

It is important to point out that this is a comparison with optimum and not with a standard. The standard provides, for instance, for the plant that is in operation. It allows for the condition of the plant. Comparison against standard can provide an indication of management effectiveness in the circumstances which currently apply.

Comparison against optimum has a different purpose. It provides guidance of the cost levels that could apply with the very best plant and with a full capacity. It shows what would be achieved if the appropriate investments were made and the volumes and efficiencies achieved (see figure 10.2).

	Optimum	Standard
Formula	As specified by R&D	As specified by R&D with any approved adjustments
Processing	With equipment which provides for the most effective and efficient operation.	At a level which is acceptable using the equipment available.
Formula and packaging costs	Most advantageous level possible	A practical level in current circumstances
Plant capacity	Full level	Practical level given current volume
Plant operating speeds	Maximum possible	Practical level in the circumstances
Operating efficiency	100%	Practical level in the circumstances
Wastage allowance (varying with each item)	Approximately 0.5%	Approximately 1%
Breakdown maintenance time, etc.	Minimum allowed	Practical levels
Personnel times and costs	• Fully qualified staff. • Competitive rates. • Hours necessary for full capacity	Practical levels
Plant condition	• Modern • Fully effective	As in position

Figure 10.2   Product costs: optimum v. standard
The optimum and standard levels used in this figure are intended to provide an illustration of the optimum approach. In practice the levels used may differ from those shown, depending on the approach of individual managements to the setting of standards.

In terms of management performance the optimum provides something to be aimed for, but without the investments and volume, something which it would be unreasonable to expect management to achieve.

■ *The optimum figure also has another very valuable purpose. It shows the level of unit cost attainable by a competitor should he make the necessary investment, gain the volume, and achieve the required efficiency level in operation. In effect, it shows the importance of winning in the market place and having an effective and efficient operation, in terms of product unit costs.*

RAW MATERIALS

Competitive advantage can be gained under this heading in three main ways:

- Obtaining better value in purchasing;
- Effective use of the raw materials in manufacture;
- Movement control so that capital tie-up is kept to a minimum.

Obtaining better value

The price at which ingredients are purchased hinges primarily on the skill of the buyer. He negotiates the purchase contract for each item with an appropriate supplier.

The brand formula requirements will be set out in the agreed specification. The production schedules will set out the required quantity and the necessary timing. The buyer's task is to obtain the ingredients at the right level of quality, at the right time, in the right quantity, and at the right price.

In his bargaining with suppliers the buyer will have a number of tools to help him. He will be aware of the quantity he is proposing to buy and he will know just how valuable such an order may be to a prospective supplier. He will be aware of the supplier's competitors and he will know of their quality and of their prices. He will also be aware of the supply position, quality, and price of any suitable substitute ingredient.

While the buyer will be concerned to maintain good business relationships with his suppliers he should always be working to get the
best possible deal for his company. He may need to be very tough in
his approach and in his negotiations, but it is always possible to be
both tough and to maintain good relations. The supplier will also be
interested in getting the best deal for his business while maintaining
a relationship which will provide for further business into the future.
In his particular way he will also need to be tough in his approach.

The buyer should be interested in obtaining the best deal for his
company – this does not necessarily mean the lowest price, although
price must always be an important factor within the negotiations.

The buyer's skill centres on his ability to judge correctly the movement in the price of the major raw and package materials his brands
require. He also needs to know his suppliers well enough to be sure
of their quality standards and of their ability to deliver on time.

■ *In his negotiations the buyer needs to have a feel for just how far he
should push his suppliers. And this applies for price, quality, and
delivery. It isn't clever to drive such a hard bargain with your best
supplier that he goes bankrupt. Nor is it clever to support a supplier
who is unlikely to ever become fully competitive.*

Records, computer readings, and a fast supply of relevant market
information are among the services which can help the buyer. Very
good buyers are invariably shrewd characters with a special feel for
their materials and their markets. It can be of significance that raw
material costs, usually treated as completely variable in product cost
presentations, can on occasions be only partially variable or even
fixed with volume. This can apply when volume-buying discounts
operate, and where special and expensive forms of transport are
necessary.

Effective use of materials

Here we are concerned with the use of the raw materials in the production process. Essentially the issue is how can we keep wastage to
a minimum? Or, for those processes where the material can, in effect,
be expanded, how can we be sure to get the maximum level of output?

Each production process will tend to have complications of its own. Each will require special considerations. The need is to set a standard against which actual results can be measured. The standard needs to be a practical one and the important consideration is the trend of actual performance against it. With experience the trend should show a continuous improvement.

In reading and acting upon the results of these comparisons it is always important to keep in mind:

- The quality of the output. The requirement is that the quality of output should be in line with the specification. Certainly not below, for this could mean an inferior product, but also not above the specification. Output at a quality above the specification can be wasteful and expensive.
- The quantity of the output. If the only way to achieve an acceptable material wastage level is to run the processing equipment at a very slow pace, then the cost of this control could be very high.

  If there is a relationship between the level of wastage and the rate of processing it is necessary that this should be highlighted and appropriate action taken.
- When considering the level of wastage, it is important that both the percentage level and the value of each item should be considered.

  A three per cent level of wastage may be acceptable for a relatively inexpensive item, for an expensive item it should certainly not be acceptable.

Movement control

Excess capital tied up in stocks or work-in-progress is idle capital. It can be very costly.

The aim must be to manage the business with as little capital tie-up in stocks as is commensurate with an efficient operation. The aim can go further than this, in that it could be possible to run with stocks that are passed through the business and on to the customer before they need to be paid for. From the manufacturer's viewpoint this form of stock control, sometimes known as 'just-in-time' control, is an ideal position. It requires very close liaison with suppliers at the receiving end, and very close liaison with customers at the distribution end. It is an ideal position and something to aim for (see figure 10.3).

Of course, just-in-time control can carry considerable risk. A single ingredient late in supply or of faulty quality could hold up the whole

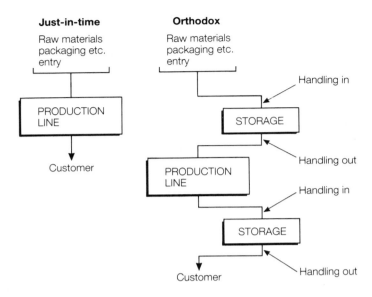

Figure 10.3   Just-in-time v. orthodox approach

production process. Advocates of the just-in-time approach claim that the detailed review of procedures and the establishment of a positive attitude toward quality which it enforces are an important part of the total value it provides. They believe that the ultimate savings the approach brings, when it is applied effectively, extend well beyond the savings in capital and handling. They argue that savings in direct production costs and in capacity are generated by the improved quality levels that are developed through the whole process.

All members of staff should be made fully aware of the cost of capital and just how much capital they are holding and using. They also need to be given every assistance to control and conserve the capital they use to produce a fully effective performance.

PACKAGING

The remarks set out in the previous paragraphs for raw materials apply equally to packaging. Costs in packaging also start with the brand specification and the actual consumption can be measured against an acceptable standard.

Packaging tends to be much more a part of brand presentation than are raw materials. In costing packaging it is important to attempt an estimate as to how much of the cost is for presentation and how much is for straightforward product packaging. For instance, if the carton has six-colour printing to provide more effective presentation than the usual four colours, then the excess cost is for presentation. Of course, the extra expenditure may well be very worthwhile. The point is that it is important to know what it is costing so that it may be evaluated.

It is a fact that the cost of a well-designed carton, bottle, or other container is not necessarily any higher than the cost of a badly designed one. It is always possible for the good design to cost less.

PROCESSING

Here we are dealing with the costs incurred in the process of production. With many of the products in the major consumer goods markets the concern is with the processing of the raw materials, bringing them together, and then placing them in packets, bottles or some other form of container. In modern plants the operatives are primarily concerned with the direction of electronic and other mechanical equipment which carries out the actual processing and mixing. The production lines are also primarily automatic in operation.

In contrast, there remain many small production units which rely heavily on manual operatives. Normally the volumes are very low, or there is some special requirement that cannot be easily mechanized.

In the first case the three factors of greatest influence in determining unit cost levels are a) effectiveness and efficiency in operation, b) capital investment and c) volume.

In the second case the *key* factor is effectiveness and efficiency in operation. Capital investment has limited impact – although it is most important to differentiate between lack of investment because the capital cannot be made to work satisfactorily, and lack of investment because of the manufacturer's inability or reluctance to invest. Volume is normally at a relatively low level and does not affect costs materially.

A comparison of the make-up of product processing costs under the two cases brings out the very basic factor that in the high-volume situation the bulk of processing costs can be classified as fixed over the short to medium term.

With the low-volume situation the bulk of process costs are likely to be variable in the short to medium term, although in many instances personnel costs may become fixed over the shorter term. Whether a business has high or low volume it needs to ensure that it is effective and efficient in its process operation. Clearly the processes employed will vary from plant to plant depending on the product produced. Where the pace of production is set by the operatives there are many studies and proven approaches available which can help ensure high level productivity. A suitably skilled and well motivated work-force will be necessary if productivity is to move near to the optimum level.

Even in the highly mechanized plants people remain of great importance. They service the machines, keep stoppages to a minimum, manage the change-overs, and keep the production lines running smoothly. They also need to be suitably skilled and well motivated albeit in a different manner to the operatives in the low volume plant.

In high-volume production the investment in plant is likely to be substantial and probably the *key* factor in determining unit processing costs. A very general rule would be that the higher the volume the greater the degree of mechanization possible in the process production.

The decision to invest in plant is a strategic decision. The size of the plant to be purchased is usually of major significance. If the manufacturer is able to buy a plant and then add to it at regular intervals with small additions, and for this exercise to be an economic one, then he is very lucky. Usually he will be required to buy his plant in blocks of a given size, and with a specified level of capacity.

The operator is concerned with running the existing plant in the most effective manner possible. If the plant is an extensive one with a very substantial capital investment then the 'fixed' cost coming from it will be high. If the unit cost of production is to be reduced to its lowest possible level then the plant may need to run for seven days each week and for 24 hours each day.

To keep a plant running at this level is rarely practical. Down time for maintenance and repairs will be necessary. Nevertheless, it is important that the manufacturer is clear as to the maximum capacity of his plant, and also its capacity given various working arrangements, e.g. three eight-hour shifts per day, two shifts per day, seven-day working, five-day working, etc.

Shift and seven-day working can attract a number of extra costs. Running the plant for lengthy periods without full maintenance can also attract extra costs. It is necessary for the manufacturer to have estimates of these extras, as their extent will influence his decision as to which are his most suitable operating levels and also his wider decision as to when to invest in new plant.

When planning the development of his processing plant the manufacturer will need to face the important question of whether or not he should plan for what is known as 'dedicated' processing facilities, or accept facilities which are universal.

A 'dedicated' plant is one that is set up to produce one product only. A 'universal' plant is one that can, with adjustments, handle a series of products and a series of different containers.

The dedicated plant should be capable of high efficiencies in operation. It avoids the constant changes of filling and weighing equipment, of size adjustments, and the slow running periods that invariably follow each change. The personnel become experts in running a dedicated plant. The numbers required will be fewer and they should develop great skill in knowing and handling the plant. But such a plant will necessitate much higher capital investment.

To justify the investment in dedicated plant the manufacturer will require a satisfactory level of volume. It is important that cost estimates should be available to show the comparative costs of dedicated and universal plant at given volume levels and with various levels of changeover. A manufacturer with a fully effective dedicated plant could have a very worthwhile cost advantage over competitors forced to employ universal plant providing he has the volume to keep it working for an economic period of time.

The way production is planned can have a major effect on the efficiency of facilities. A plant that is able to engage in long runs is likely to be much more productive than one that is required to make frequent change-overs. Similarly, a plant that suffers from recurrent hold-ups in the supply of component parts will be less productive than one that has a well-planned continuous supply of the parts.

PRODUCTION OVERHEAD

As plants become more automated in their operation, and more capital intensive, so the level of cost recorded under the heading of 'production overhead' will tend to increase. Much of this overhead will be of a fixed nature, certainly over the short/medium term, and will be out of the direct control of the operating management.

The requirement is that the highly automated plant should contribute at the highest possible level of efficiency. This means that it must receive a well co-ordinated level of service in terms of component supplies, fuel, maintenance, and trained personnel. The problem facing management is to ensure that this service is available and at the same time keep a close control on the level of overhead incurred.

It is essential that within the production unit there should be staff who maintain constant liaison with the development section. How the product is to be processed, how it is to be structured and formed, can have a marked effect on its quality and production cost. In particular, it can materially affect the rate of processing and the capacity of the plant. This last item can be a cost of great significance and it is not always clearly visable on the normal control statement.

THE EXPERIENCE CURVE

The experience-curve concept was introduced into business management by the Boston Consulting Group. The concept is one of principle. Originally researched back in the 1960s it has been tested widely in many industries over the years. It has certain similarities with the widely accepted learning-curve approach.

In *Perspectives on Experience* (1968), the Boston Consulting Group have summed up the effect of the experience curve as follows:

Costs appear to go down on value added at about 20 to 30 per cent every time total product experience doubles for the industry as a whole, as well as for individual producers. (p. 12)

Business men may argue with parts of the detail of the experience-curve approach but they would certainly appear to agree with its main conclusions.

The use of the experience curve in strategy formulation has been stressed. If it is accepted, then it can be helpful in forecasting the movement of costs with the development of a market. This can clearly be of assistance in forecasting such factors as market development, levels of profitability, and competitive positions.

The experience curve can also have a use in business operations. It is probably too broad a tool to be of real assistance in estimating unit cost movement through the shorter term, but it can be used:

1   As a general target for production management;
2   As a constant reminder to everyone concerned that costs do not move down the experience curve automatically, they need to be pushed by operating management.

■ *It is important to note that the experience curve refers to the accumulated product experience, and this can increase without growth in the size of the market. The experience curve argues that costs should go down even if the market moves into decline, for the accumulated product experience will still increase.*

During a period of rapid market expansion unit costs should fall. The faster the climb in total market volume the more rapid should be the fall in costs. Costs go down for reasons such as people getting better at their jobs, more specialization, additional investment in more productive plant. In effect, costs go down under the pressure of good operating management, investment, scale and competition.

It may prove difficult to get production managers to accept the reasoning of the experience curve, particularly when their own production volume is in decline. But there is a lot of evidence that substantiates the reasoning, and there is always the possibility that competitors may have discovered a way to reduce costs even when it appears impossible.

Key points

1 The product is at the heart of the brand.

   If the brand is to meet the consumer's need and stand a chance of being a success in the market its product must deliver the brand promise at a satisfactory level of performance. And if the brand is to be a success in profit terms the performance must be delivered at an acceptable level of cost.

2 Product costs are always of major importance. In many markets and particularly the big consumer markets, product costs can exceed 50 per cent of the brand trade price – you ignore them at your peril.

3 Product costs start with the brand formula. It can prove very expensive to have a formula which under-performs and fails to deliver. It can also be expensive to have a formula that over-performs and is more costly than it needs to be.

4 Every ingredient in the formula should play its part in enhancing the product performance. Beware of ingredients that the consumer does not appreciate and which are included primarily to justify advertising claims – in the final analysis they are rarely ever worthwhile.

5 Volume can be a key factor in determining process unit costs. If you are more efficient than your competitors the more volume you have the greater your advantage. If you are less efficient your extra volume could prove a major disadvantage.

6 The financial rule book may say that plant should only be replaced when the new investment can show a satisfactory rate of return. But out-of-date plant can prove very expensive in terms of both direct and indirect costs. And new replacement plant is normally a low-risk investment.

7 If you accept the experience-curve reasoning then you accept that, in effect, costs on added value should never stop going down. This can be a tough target for the production manager to face, particularly if his volume is static or in decline, but the experience curve has extensive research to back it. Of course, costs do not go down the curve automatically – they have to be pushed, they have to be moved down by effective management.

11

◇

Sales Promotion

◆

A manufacturer should always be trying to sell his brands or products. When he mounts a sales promotion he is making a special effort to make sales. He is directing extra resources to achieve a particular sales objective.

Often thought of as one of the 'poor relations' of the total marketing operation, sales promotion is, in fact, a particularly important and effective weapon in the hands of a skilled operator.

Sales promotion has a significant part to play in strategy formulation. A well-judged, skilfully developed strategic promotion, can play a vital part in the longer-term development of a major brand.

■ *Sales promotion also has a vital part to play within operations. Shorter-term market share gains, frequently the result of good promotion, go together to make longer-term market share growth, and ultimately the sales volume which is so vitally important for brand strength and profit contribution.*

Successful sales promotion requires skill, effective creativity, and good judgement. Timing can often be crucial, as also can the level of investment used to support a specific operation. There are times when the promotion should be strong and penetrating, and others when a more conservative holding operation is wise.

■ *Wherever skill and judgement is of great importance there is sure to be considerable opportunity to gain a competitive advantage. Sales promotion is certainly no exception to this general rule.*

155

'LET'S HAVE A PROMOTION'

'The market is dull, we need some excitement, why don't we have a promotion?' This suggestion, or one very similar to it, will often be heard within an operating company. It is a suggestion which completely underrates the whole value of a sales promotion within a well-managed and effective operating business.

A sales promotion should be a special effort to achieve a specific objective. Within the operating plan it acts to co-ordinate the efforts of the whole organization in its drive to achieve the objective.

The number of special efforts the business can mount over a given period of time will be strictly limited if resources and effort are to be concentrated; and concentration will certainly be necessary if optimum results are to be obtained.

There is always some way in which a brand can improve its performance, and this applies even to the most dominant market leader. It may be by greater penetration, it may be by heavier consumer consumption, or it may be by more widespread trade distribution – there is always a better position to be reached, there is always a better way. Sales promotions are concerned with moving brands forward to better positions.

■ *With only a limited number of special effort priority positions possible within the operations plan it follows that there is a most valuable opportunity cost associated with each one. A wasted priority is a waste of a valuable opportunity.*

In a well-managed business sales promotion proposals receive the most careful preparation and are backed by detailed and exacting research wherever possible. They are subjected to the same degree of rigorous analysis and check as any other investment proposal.

In a well-managed business the idea that a valuable priority position within the company operations plan should be used because 'we need some excitement' would be summarily dismissed. Sales promotions are positive marketing tools. Out of them can come significant competitive advantages; they can be very much a

Stage 1:   Review the brand's promotions objectives for the period.

Stage 2:   Develop a first draft brand promotions programme for the period which sets out to achieve the brand's objectives. Claim the priority positions within the operations plan that are considered necessary (by the brand).

Stage 3:   Negotiate the first draft programme with the operations plan executive (i.e. the person/s with the authority to decide the formulation of the plan).

Stage 4:   Formulate a second draft programme that utilizes the priority positions actually allocated to the brand by the executive in the negotiation. Build into the programme estimates covering the expenditures and revenues expected to result from the adoption of the second draft.

Stage 5:   Pass the second draft for comment to those managers within the business who will be primarily responsible for ensuring the programme is met and that it delivers the desired results.

Stage 6:   Note any comments, build in appropriate adjustments, and negotiate the second draft with the executive. (This includes the negotiation of the expenditures necessary to mount the second draft programme.) Build into the programme any adjustments coming from the negotiation.

Stage 7:   Issue the agreed brand promotions programme for the period to appropriate managers within the business.

Stage 8:   Review the progress of the brand through the period. Negotiate any necessary adjustments in the programme.

Figure 11.1   Formulating a brand's promotion programme for the period of the operations plan: an eight-stage approach

part of winning in the market-place, and also a part of improved profitability (see figures 11.1 and 11.2).

PROMOTION: A CHANGE IN VALUE

At this early stage in the consideration of sales promotions it is worth reviewing the basic way in which they work within business operations.

Stage 1: Define the prime objective for the promotion.

Stage 2: Select the promotional type best suited to achieve the prime objective.

Stage 3: Carry out a preliminary rough assessment of the proposed promotion, its likely effect, and its cost, to ensure that it has the ability to form a 'business proposition'.

Stage 4: Develop an effective creative approach for the proposed promotion. Wherever possible test the approach with a suitable sample of those consumers to whom the promotion will be primarily directed.

Stage 5: Draw up a draft brand promotion advice giving full details of the proposed promotion. The advice should include a statement of the objective, the volumes involved, timings, costs, and responsibilities. Circulate the draft for comment to responsible managers.

Stage 6: Make any adjustments considered necessary from the comments. Submit the draft to the operations plan executive (the person/s with the authority for the formulation of the operations plan) for inclusion in the plan.

Stage 7: Distribute the approved brand promotions advice to all appropriate managers. The advice is now a plan for action and should include details of objectives, timings, costs, and responsibilities as agreed.

Stage 8: Progress the actual development, production and distribution of the promotion. Also progress any support factors that form a part of it. Work to ensure the promotion is launched into the market with skill and enthusiasm.

Stage 9: Make any adjustments that are shown to be appropriate, and possible, by the early market experience.

Stage 10: Prepare a report on the performance of the promotion, including details of the results achieved and the costs incurred.

Figure 11.2   Formulating and managing a brand sales promotion: a ten-stage approach

A sales promotion provides the manufacturer with a means of making a temporary change in the value of his brand or product. For instance, if the price of a brand is reduced for a period its value to the consumer is enhanced. Similarly, if an extra 25 per cent of the product is offered at the same price as previously applied for a standard amount, in effect the price has been reduced and the value enhanced. If a free gift is provided with the brand then for some consumers the brand value will be increased.

It is important to appreciate that the promotion allows this value change to be made on a *temporary* basis. The promotional price reduction only applies for a limited period, or if the reduction is marked on the pack it applies only for the number of special packs issued. This means that it is possible for the reduction to be considerably higher (thereby providing a much greater short-term change in value) than would a permanent price change.

This *temporary* factor is one of the promotion's great merits in operations. New, or re-launched, brands invariably require sampling – they require a temporary period when their value can be greatly enhanced. This way they are much more likely to become *best-value* to the consumer and get the vitally important trial.

Similarly when a brand is forced to defend itself against a new competitor which has certain innovative advantages it needs to adjust its value quickly, particularly during the period of the main opening attack of the new brand.

Promotions are exceptionally well suited to meet these, and other similar brand-value change requirements.

It follows that before a promotion is developed there are three basic questions which should be asked and answered:

- To whom is the value change directed?
- How should the value change be presented?
- How much should the value change be?

The answers to these questions will clearly be closely linked. The first question in effect asks 'What is the prime objective of the promotion? If it is to sample men, then are they to be young, middle-aged, or older men? Are they to be men who live in the north or in the south? Are they to be wealthy, or from lower-income groups?'

The second question looks for the best way to appeal to the selected group. The best approach for older men may differ from that for younger; men in the north may react differently to a particular kind of offer than those in the south, and so on.

The third question asks how extensive the value change needs to be to achieve the desired result. For instance, is a reduction of 10p per pack enough to motivate the men concerned, or will it be necessary to go to 20p, or even 25p? Is an expensive gift required, or can an economy item be used successfully?

■ *Promotions work by changing the value of a brand or product for a temporary period. For success they need to be accurately directed, the presentation form of the value change needs to be skilfully developed, and the extent of the change should be enough (but not too much) to ensure that the objective is achieved.*

THE OBJECTIVE

Before any planning or creative work is undertaken for a promotion the question: 'What is the prime objective for this promotion?' should be asked, and answered.

■ *Every sales promotion should have one prime objective. It may also have a number of subsidiary objectives – but only one prime objective.*

Promotions that have a number of major objectives run the great risk of spreading their fire and failing to achieve any one of them satisfactorily. It is against the expected achievement of its prime objective that the promotion's estimated cost should be appraised – and when it is completed it is against the actual achievement level of this objective that its success or failure should be judged.

Wherever possible the prime objective should be stated in quantifiable terms, e.g. to increase the penetration of homes in the UK from 1.5 million to 2.5 million or to improve brand distribution through the independent section of the grocery trade from 10,000 to 20,000 stores. If the prime objective is stated clearly and specifically, it should be easier to direct the promotion accurately, and the business should be able to derive better value from its investment. With brands where the purpose is aimed at providing a more specialized benefit, the direction of a sales promotion can be of very major significance – if your hair cream is specifically suited to women with blonde hair, you may waste much of your investment if your promotion is directed to women generally.

THE PROPOSAL

Before a sales promotion is considered for action within the business operations plan it is important that it be assessed, evaluated, examined in detail, and, if appropriate, adjusted.

A major sales promotion is likely to affect every section of the business. It is necessary for managers of the various sections to have the opportunity to comment on the proposed promotion. In particular they should be able to comment on how their particular section is expected to handle it, and how this could be improved. Beyond this it is necessary for the whole promotions proposal to be costed as accurately as possible, and a comprehensive timetable for operation prepared.

■ *A document which sets out full details of the proposed promotion is required. It is suggested that this document should be known as the draft promotional advice, and that it should be prepared by the responsible brand manager.*

The suggestion is that the document should start as a draft, that it should be discussed by the section managers within the business and any appropriate improvements incorporated.

The proposal should then be submitted to a review body for inclusion in the business operations plan. If accepted, it would become part of the plan and passed for action.

The review body should be chaired by an executive such as the marketing director. Other members of the review body could be the company planning manager (representing production and distribution) and the sales director. A member of the commercial section could also be in attendance. Ideally the body would be of a limited size, say three or four people, with responsibility for every promotion admitted into the operations plan, and with authority to make alterations to proposals as considered appropriate.

The advantage of an approach of this kind is that the draft proposal can contain all the details such as the main objective, the type and form of promotion proposed, the research information backing the proposal, production and distribution data, selling dates, pricing proposals, and a cost and revenue statement.

Very importantly, the draft should carry a timetable for action covering the key dates for each section, and against each action should be listed the name of the individual responsible.

The review body would have the authority to approve or reject the proposal for action. Once accepted, the document becomes an action plan for the business and every section will be expected to meet its responsibility under the plan.

The brand manager acts as a form of progress chaser for his proposal. He smooths its way through the business and eventually into the market-place. Quite often he will be able to settle minor problems with the sectional managers concerned, but with major problems he may need to return to the operations plan review body.

This approach may appear unduly formal and overladen with paper. In fact, it need not be too formal as the brand manager can clear much of the detail with the section managers as he compiles the proposal.

Some paperwork is necessary and there will be a need to ensure that it is kept at an 'essential working' minimum level. The proposal may well cover an extensive investment and, clearly, proper records should be maintained. A prime requirement is that all the various back-up reports should be kept as brief as possible; if appropriate reference could be made to a more detailed report held centrally and available to those who really need it.

In a small business it should be possible to keep the proposals to a limited content and with a restricted circulation. But if unnecessary mistakes and complications are to be avoided it will be essential to maintain adequate records.

COMPETITIVE ADVANTAGE

Having selected the prime objective for his promotion, and specified it clearly, there are four main factors with which the manufacturer must be concerned if he is to build a competitive advantage into his sales promotions:

1 In the selection of the promotion type he uses;
2 In the creativity he builds into the promotion;
3 By the amount of investment he is prepared to place behind the promotion;

4   In the level of effectiveness and efficiency at which he manages and carries out the promotion.

Of course, the aim should be to produce a significant competitive advantage and for this it will certainly be necessary to get the selection right, to have a high and effective level of creativity, the right level of investment, and an execution which is of the highest standard.

Selection of the promotion

In these notes sales promotions are considered firstly under two headings:

- *Strategic promotions*   These normally require substantial investment and resource backing and are used to attain objectives which are of major significance for the longer-term progress of the brand.
- *Tactical promotions*   These are used from time to time to attain certain specific brand tactical objectives. They usually receive only a limited level of resource backing.

Strategic promotions

Strategic promotions can, in turn, be considered under two headings:

- *Offensive*   This type of promotion invariably has the basic objective to encourage consumer trial. The promotion aims to give the consumer an extra incentive to put the brand to his own personal *best value* test.
- *Defensive*   These promotions are usually involved in protecting their brand from competitive attack. In particular, they are often directed to stop a competitive brand gaining access to their brand's regular users.

Tactical promotions

Tactical promotions are also frequently considered under two headings:

- *Consumer*   These are promotions aimed primarily at the consumer, i.e. the ultimate customer.
- *Trade*   These are promotions aimed at prompting some form of

action from the traders through whom the brand passes on its way to the consumer.

Promotional types and forms

Under each one of these headings there are a whole series of promotional types and forms.

Sales promotions have probably been in use since trading began. Over the last twenty years they have certainly been used in a more systematic and organized manner. More detailed research records of the effect on brand sales, volumes, etc. of each of the various promotional types have been maintained, and it is now possible to predict with a reasonable degree of accuracy the more general results they are likely to achieve. It should be added that the predictions are certainly not foolproof, and exceptional skill in design, and a high level of effective creativity in presentation can always bring exceptional results. Beyond this the amount invested in the particular promotion will clearly have an effect on the results achieved.

Promotional types in frequent use in current markets include:

Household sampling

a sample of the brand is delivered direct to the home
One of the best examples of an offensive strategic promotion. Can be used nationally, regionally, or by households of type, social class, etc. Can be highly effective when used in the right circumstances. In particular when the brand has a significant performance advantage over its competitors which is readily appreciated by the consumer. When used at the wrong time, and in the wrong circumstances, can prove very costly. Household sampling requires heavy up-front investment.

Special introductory pack

the brand is packed in a specially printed carton showing an attractive price, e.g., 'regular price 50p – special trial offer pack 25p'
This can be an effective sampling promotion. Not as easily directed as a household sample. Difficult to prevent multiple purchase by bargain hunters.

Extra product pack

an extra quantity of product is included in the pack without a price adjust-ment e.g., '15 per cent extra free'

Normally an effective defensive promotion. Particularly attractive to existing users – acts to 'stock up' the consumer.

Reduced price pack

e.g., a special pack for the brand is marked '10p off'

When mounted on an established brand this is a defensive pro-motion. In the main, attracts regular users. But can be used to attract switchers in certain circumstances.

Household coupon

a coupon, redeemable against a specified brand, is distributed direct to households or distributed via newspapers, magazines, and other publica-tions, though these tend to have a lower drawing power than those delivered direct to homes

An offensive promotion – can be effective in sampling. A major and costly problem is mal-redemption – the coupon is redeemed against the total grocery bill and not against the specific brand.

Free gift give-away

a free gift is attached to the brand as an incentive to purchase

An offensive promotion. Its degree of success tends to depend on the attractiveness of the free gift. Can be expensive to mount – the gifts have to be purchased and attached to the brand.

Cash-back offer

the consumer forwards a number of box tops, say three or four, and in return receives a sum of money, say £1

A defensive promotion, acts to 'lock-in' existing users.

Self-liquidating offer

an item, e.g., a cookery knife, is offered at an attractive price – the applicant must include the price plus a number of box tops – the price covers the cost, hence self-liquidating

A defensive promotion – unlikely to attract new users. Inexpensive to mount – but is normally lightweight.

Consumer competition

e.g., consumer is asked to estimate accurately the number of people in a picture – entry forms must be accompanied by a specified number of box tops

Tends to be defensive. Normally lightweight – but an outstanding creative presentation can make a material difference to the results of this form of promotion.

'Buy one, get one free'

consumer buys specially printed pack, sends the top to a redemption office and receives coupon for a free pack

A defensive promotion – aims to hold existing users. Cost depends on the level of redemption and the value of the coupon.

Trader gift

a free gift, e.g., a bottle of wine, is given to every trader who purchases a given number of cases

A tactical trade promotion aimed at getting smaller traders to stock the brand, or to build trader stocks. Would normally be used with independent traders, and often operated through cash-and-carry warehouses.

Trade coupon

a coupon, redeemable against a case of the brand, is distributed direct to each trader

A tactical trade promotion. Used to get store distribution for the brand.

Special sample pack

a special sample pack – normally a small size and retailing at a very attractive unit price – is placed with retailers

An offensive sampling promotion. Difficult to direct, and there may be many multiple purchases. Normally much less costly than a direct household sample – but more limited in effect.

On-pack coupon

a coupon is printed on the pack – it is redeemable against the next purchase of the brand

A defensive promotion. Attractive to regular buyers. Acts to tie-up consumer for two purchases – the coupon can be the subject of mal-redemption.

A sweepstake

e.g., the consumer is given an entry ticket with a number. Winning numbers can be checked at the store. Purchase of the brand is not required

This can attract new users, but is normally a lightweight promotion.

It is always possible to use more than one type of promotion in a single operation e.g., to have a 'special introductory offer pack' also carry an on-pack coupon.

It is also possible to add strength to a promotion, and change its effect, by giving it additional publicity. If the consumer is informed directly in his home that his local store is featuring a particular brand promotion, he is more likely to take advantage of the offer. In this way, it is possible to give a defensive promotion certain offensive values.

The need is for the manufacturer to be sure what his main objective for the proposed brand promotion is, and then to decide which promotion type is best suited to achieve the objective.

■ *When the right promotional type is selected, effective creativity added, and a satisfactory level of resource backing provided with fully competent operation, then the promotion will have good prospects of achieving its main objective.*

Initially the aim should be to get the right promotional approach. Later, as the financial and other aspects of the promotion are considered, adjustments may be necessary. But for an opening, selecting the promotional type best suited to achieve the particular main objective should be the aim.

Selecting the *right* promotional type

The first essential requirement is to be clear on the main objective of the promotion. This needs to be spelt out in detail and it needs to be specific. A bland statement that, for instance, the brand wants sampling is not good enough.

The requirement is to identify clearly the potential customers at whom the promotion is to be primarily directed, and to outline any characteristics they may have.

The second important consideration is the manufacturer's full awareness of the strengths and weaknesses of his brand. He should know just how strong his brand's competitive advantage really is.

For instance, all new brands need sampling, they need to provide the consumer with the opportunity to put the brand to his personal *best-value* test. But a new brand would be unwise to go to the expense of a widespread household sample unless it had a significant performance competitive advantage. A marginal performance advantage alone is unlikely to be enough to mount a successful challenge through a household sample against an entrenched leader.

Similarly, a widespread sample is unlikely to be worthwhile if the brand's competitive advantage applies for only a limited number of consumers who form a small section of the market. A special cleaner that works only on carpets made of a rare mohair fibre is unlikely to create the right impression if it is sampled generally and used by people who have the more usual woollen carpets.

In one of the very big consumer markets, one where the majority of households in the country have an interest, a new product development that is worthy of the 'big investment approach' comes along very rarely, but when it does come it is important that it should be recognized, developed, and exploited.

In this instance, the requirement would be a significant competitive performance advantage in the main sector of the market, and one that is obtainable at a reasonable cost. Such a brand could possibly be worthy of the most aggressive of offensive strategic promotions – a national household door-to-door sample.

For new or re-launched brands directed at special market sectors sampling remains most important but it clearly needs to be specifically directed. For this type of brand it may be possible to use a directed product sampling, e.g. direct to higher income homes, via coupons in selected magazines.

Frequently, the main objective will have certain time requirements attached to it. When a brand is under attack in the market, a three- or four-week delay in getting the promotion into the market can be most damaging. This could narrow the choice of promotional type.

Similarly when a new or re-launched brand is anxious to beat a competitor into the market time could be of the essence in reaching consumers with samples. This could also narrow the choice of promotional type.

The manufacturer will have four main sources for guidance as to which is the most suitable promotional type for his particular requirement:

- His own previous experience; the results obtained by promotions mounted over recent periods should provide valuable guidance.
- The experience of other manufacturers in his markets; he should be aware of how well promotions mounted by his competitors have performed.
- The experience of other manufacturers in similar markets; detailed information under this heading may be more difficult, but not impossible to obtain.
- His testing experience; if the manufacturer is proposing to mount a major strategic promotion he will be well advised to arm himself with suitable experience. This could, for instance, take the form of a series of consumer in-home tests, or a series of tests carried out in retail stores – whichever testing approach is most suitable should be used.

Testing will not necessarily provide results which will be repeated completely on a wider basis, but it should provide guidance which will avoid a failure in the market-place, and also show where the promotion promises to deliver outstanding results.

If he keeps his major objective clearly in mind, is aware of his brand's strengths and weaknesses, makes use of the four main sources of guidance mentioned above, and makes a preliminary check of the estimates of the various promotion costs and revenues, the manufacturer should be able to reach a sound decision as to which promotional type is best suited to his particular requirement.

Creativity in promotions

Competitions are competitions. They may get attention, they may attract a limited amount of consumer interest, but they are understandably considered lightweight in the promotions world. And yet, once in a while along comes a consumer competition that gets large numbers of people interested, gets traders excited, and brings a major uplift in sales. Why? What competitive advantage does this particular competition have over the others?

In circumstances of this kind the competitive advantage is invariably an outstandingly high and effective level of creativity, which turns an ordinary lightweight promotion into something special.

The Oxford Dictionary defines 'creative' as 'inventive, and imaginative'. And clearly, a high level of effective creativity can make a significant contribution to any promotion. The literature that is delivered to the household with the sample, the message that accompanies the coupon, even the coupon itself, can be either dull and boring or bright and interesting.

■ *The important consideration is that the creativity should be 'effective'. Creativity that merely develops excitement is not enough. The creativity must be directed to developing interest and activity that means the recipient takes positive action to follow through as required by the particular promotion. Beyond this the results of the creativity must be of a kind that enhance the brand personality.*

How do you get a high level of effective creativity into a promotion? This is indeed a difficult question and of the same nature as one which asks: 'How can you be sure to get a high level of effective creativity into your advertising?'

There is no simple and guaranteed answer. Those who have studied the subject, and have had some success in practice would seem to be agreed that you should set a straightforward and clear brief. You should keep your limitations to as few as possible, but where you have them they should be clearly stated. If you have points which you feel are of significance then make sure they are also noted at an early stage. The important requirement is to avoid producing a series of limitations after the creative team has been working and has produced proposals.

Most important of all, get very good people working on the project, and be sure to work with them in a constructive and positive manner.

If you follow this approach there is still no guarantee that you will get a high level of effective creativity. But you should at least get a very competent execution. You should avoid the more elementary errors that can easily occur if your approach is unprofessional. This is important. If your promotion is going to 10 million homes the difference between a 25 per cent and a 35 per cent effective take up rate is 1 million homes, and if your repeat rate is say 30 per cent, then you could have 300,000 extra regular buyers. Over time these extras can make a major difference to your sales volume and to the brand profit contribution.

How much to invest?

This question goes beyond the one promotion and extends to the brand promotional investment programme for the period.

A particular promotion

If we consider a particular promotion, there are two key considerations:

1 The need to achieve the main objective for the brand contained within the promotion;
2 The investment required, its place in the brand promotions programme, its affect on the brand's profit contribution, and the profitability of the business.

The first requirement is to get an indication of the costs and revenues expected to arise if the promotion is mounted in the manner considered most likely to achieve the main objective. The two key figures are normally the cost per objective unit and the total number of objective units reached.

With a strategic promotion there is a requirement to compare estimates of brand volumes and revenues with appropriate costs, with and without the promotion, over an agreed period of time.

These are always very difficult estimates to prepare with confidence – many factors, including competitive activity, can affect the figures. There is also the question: 'How long a time period should be used?'

However, it is necessary to make an attempt at getting a realistic estimate. A time period of six months would seem reasonable for most major promotions. However, it is accepted that this may vary with the market and the particular brand circumstance, for instance, for a big investment such as a door-to-door sample a longer time may be fully justified.

■ *A financial estimate of the costs and revenues to be generated should be included in every promotional proposal. The estimate will have limitations, but it should have a value in helping to sift the very good promotions proposal from the very poor. It will also impose a discipline and remind everyone concerned that market share and volume can be of great significance, but* not *at any price.*

It is also important that an understanding of the fact that promotions can be heavy consumers of 'indirect cost' should be appreciated within the company. Throughout the business, from production through to sales, promotions invariably take up considerable management time. In particular, within the sales and distribution set up they are normally very heavy consumers of personnel time and effort.

It follows that every promotions proposal should be closely examined to ensure that the main objective of the promotion can be achieved at an acceptable level of cost.

■ *It needs to be fully appreciated that the most expensive promotions for the business are those which are unsuccessful. They take up all their direct costs, a proportion of the indirect costs, and they fail to make a worthwhile return. Indeed an unsuccessful promotion with its additional administrative and customer liaison problems, invariably takes up more than its proportion of the indirect costs.*

Tactical promotions aimed at achieving objectives such as independent store distribution, can sometimes have outstanding importance. A major consumer promotion backed by an extensive investment can fail without an adequate level of brand-store distribution. However, it is important that a tactical promotion should not be allowed to outpace a major strategic promotion in the attention and effort it gets from the various indirect personnel, and in particular from the sales force.

With tactical promotions the key consideration is to keep them simple and easy to handle. It can be an economy to make a tactical promotion sensibly generous so that it may be sold without undue time and effort, and thereby ensure that the strategic promotion has the lead position.

There can be occasions when it is wise to over-invest in a promotion rather than run the risk of under-investing. The launch of a new brand or a major re-launch of an established brand can be a good example of this. At the time of its launch a new brand must get a satisfactory level of sampling; it must ensure that a satisfactory number of potential consumers get the opportunity to try it for themselves. This applies particularly where the brand has achieved exceptionally good consumer test results that give it a significant performance advantage over its competitors.

At launch the brand has a special position; one that may never return again. At this time it may be better to over-invest and ensure adequate sampling rather than run the risk of missing out on the potential and then having to return, probably at much higher cost, later.

Frequently the cost per household covered in a promotion decreases with volume, e.g. the cost of sampling 2 million will be lower per unit than the cost of sampling 1 million. It is important that factors of this kind should be considered in the financial section of the promotions proposal.

Further cost factors which are not necessarily covered by a conventional costing approach but which nevertheless are of consequence are:

1   Who currently 'holds' the market?
2   Who has capacity?

If a manufacturer holds 40 per cent of a market or market sector, and decides to launch a new brand into it, he will almost certainly sample and convert many of his existing customers to his new brand. If a manufacturer is entering what is for him an entirely new market, or new market sector, then his sampling activity will affect only his competitors' customers. Clearly a different cost position applies.

When a plant has been specially erected to produce for a new brand to enter a particular market a number of costs will be incurred whether or not the plant is used. For certain purposes it may be appropriate to reason in terms of a marginal cost for production coming from the otherwise vacant plant.

At the other extreme, if production of the new brand means plant over-loading and the withdrawal of an existing brand a further cost has been incurred.

The financial section of the promotions proposal is of major importance. It has a valuable 'control' role, but beyond this, if used in a positive manner, it can help to ensure the promotion makes good commercial sense.

A brand promotion programme

Within the normal operational planning the brand promotional investment programme will cover a period of say, one year forward. Figure 11.1 at the beginning of this chapter outlines an eight-stage approach to the formulation of a brand's promotional programme for the period of the operating plan.

The strategic plan will have covered the promotional investment in more general terms. For a new brand it may have allowed for an initial launch promotion, e.g. sampling, and possibly followed this with say two other sampling type promotions. The plan may have provided for a given investment level rather than specifying the use of a particular promotions type. The operations plan is concerned with turning the strategy into market-place action.

For promotions this requires:

- A review of the strategic plans;
- Proposals to correct any under-performance;
- Proposals to exploit any exceptional opportunities that have developed;
- The formulation of an effective brand promotions programme.

The review of the strategic proposals will be concerned with checking that there have been no new developments which warrant a change in strategy: Has the market suddenly shown dynamic growth? Has a major competitor taken very aggressive action?

If it is appropriate, the strategic plan should be revised. There is no point in staying with a strategy that no longer makes business sense. A new strategic plan with a new promotional investment plan within it, will be necessary. Where the strategic plan for the business is reviewed in some detail once each year, the brand promotional investment plan is more likely to need adjustment rather than complete revision.

Adjustments are usually made to cover one or both or the two approaches – the correction of under-performance, and the taking of exceptional opportunities. Promotions are frequently well suited to meet these requirements.

Under-performance can take a number of forms. Inadequate consumer penetration is an obvious one that promotion can be used to rectify. Trade distribution problems, regional sampling limitations, the ineffective introduction of new pack sizes, these are all deficiencies that effective promotion can often correct.

A market which expands rapidly, or a brand that proves more popular than originally perceived, are both examples of exceptional opportunities that should be taken. Promotion can often be the most cost-effective means of meeting these new opportunities.

The proposed promotional investment programme for the brand should include proposals for meeting the basic strategic plan, for correcting under-performance, and for taking exceptional opportunities.

The promotional investment plan will need to be incorporated into the overall plan for the brand and then into the total company plan. These plans may need to be reviewed and adjustments made, as company profit objectives are considered.

Competence in operation

The need for a high level of competence in handling each promotion applies from its initial inception through to its eventual move to the consumer. The manufacturer has control of a very large part of this chain of movement. If he is skilful in his management of the promotion he will greatly enhance his prospects of gaining a competitive advantage from the total operation.

The design of the promotion pack and material has already been covered under the heading of creativity. The product and its packaging should clearly be maintained in first-class order right through the operation.

The promotional volume should be available at the right time and in the right quantity. This will require careful planning and possibly a willingness to carry an above normal level of stock. If the promotion is to be advertised it is essential that the appropriate stock of the brand is available so that the consumer can purchase it in his local store when responding to the advertisement.

The quantity of the promotion pack to be issued is clearly linked to the level of investment. If the promotional objective is to be achieved there is an elementary need to ensure that a sufficient number of packs is issued to make this possible. For instance, if the objective is for the special pack to penetrate to say 20 per cent of households, and this represents say 3 million homes, then a minimum of 3 million packs must be issued. Indeed, if the operation is via the retail trade then considerably more than 3 million packs will be needed to take care of the double- and treble-pack purchases that are bound to occur.

With promotions that involve special packs there is a considerable skill required of the sales force in placing these packs so that the objective can be met.

There is also a need to make the special promotional packs 'work'. The promotional pack will normally tempt the consumer by its specially attractive price, or the gift item it carries, and so on. The skilled sales force will use this 'special attraction' in their negotiations with traders. The packs should move rapidly through the stores and so there is a case for the retailer to give them prominent display with an advertising feature. Beyond this the retailer may be persuaded to add a further price-cut of his own to make the packs that much more attractive.

PROMOTION AND THE BRAND PERSONALITY

The rule is that any activity on a brand will have an effect on its personality. Promotions are certainly no exception to this rule. It follows that the manufacturer should use great care to ensure that his promotions reflect well on the brands which use them.

The manufacturer should use promotions which fit well with his brand personality. If he is prepared to work at it he will find that attractive items that link with his brands can be found. Even a simple price reduction of say 20p can be presented in a way that is both tasteful and effective. However, there is another important requirement – the promotion invariably involves an extensive investment backing and it must work; it must achieve its objective.

■ *What should be the priority – brand personality building or an effective promotion? Referring back to the ideal, the aim should be good personality association and an effective promotion. But it may prove very difficult, at times almost impossible, to find the ideal. What should then be the rule?*

It is suggested the rule should be to find a promotion that works and then test it for personality associations. If it is favourable, use it. If the association is neutral and harmless, then it can be used. If the association is in any way harmful the promotion should not be used.

PROMOTIONS AND BRAND ADVERTISING

In chapter 12, a number of views on advertising appropriation fixing are discussed. One view accepts that the appropriation may vary in size depending upon the needs of the brand, and also accepts that at times the advertising may be primarily concerned with reminding the consumer of the brand's basic promise.

If this view is accepted, and it is accepted within this book, then it can be further argued that promotions can carry out part of the reminding task. The leaflet that accompanies the coupon, the entry form for the competition, these and other similar documents will carry pictures of the brand and of the benefits it can provide. These are brand reminders.

This means that the brand promotional programme can be used to support its theme advertising investment. During appropriate periods a substantial saving in the brand advertising appropriation could be possible. In fact, if the approach can be made to work satisfactorily, it should provide a means of extending the brand advertising appropriation.

A TRADE-LINKED PROMOTIONS PLAN

This chapter has so far been concerned with a promotions plan which is based on the needs of each individual brand. In particular the plan has concentrated on the direction of major promotions toward the ultimate customer, i.e. the consumer. It has accepted the importance of the trade in providing the vital link with the consumer but the proposed promotions plan has been very much brand-consumer orientated.

Over recent years, as the retail chains have grown in size and strength, an alternative approach to promotional planning has gained a degree of acceptance.

This alternative approach accepts that a very limited number of retail chains control outlets which cover a major share of the total business. It goes on to reason that the key consideration for the manufacturer should be to ensure that he maintains access for his brands with the consumers who are serviced by the major retail chains. In this way he will keep contact with a major part of the market.

From this reasoning, the promotional programme is drawn up in terms of each one of the limited number of 'key' retail chains. Thus, in the UK the manufacturer might reason in terms of say six major retailers, and two wholesalers. The brands are then fitted into the plan. For example, the plan would provide for major retailer A to promote brand X in January, May and November with major retailer B promoting brand X in February, July and December, and so on with the other retailers. Each retailer having his solo period for promoting brand X.

Advocates of this 'trade-linked' promotions plan* would claim that:

- It is realistic. It is merely recognizing the fact that in many countries a very limited number of powerful retailers control access to the consumers who make up a major part of a particular market.
- It enables the manufacturer to achieve his sales volume and market share objective in a less costly manner.
- Acceptance of the approach does not preclude the manufacturer from maintaining direct contact with the consumer through other channels, e.g. advertising.
- The manufacturer can always mount strategic, or tactical, promotions on a national or regional basis outside of the trade-linked programme.

---

* In certain countries the law forbids the manufacturer having promotions which are specially tailored for individual traders.

In such countries a trade-linked promotions plan could not be employed. However, in many countries it is legal to provide individual traders with special personal promotions and this is the position which currently applies in the UK.

These claims would be strongly contested by the advocates of the brand-orientated promotions plan approach. They would argue that his brands are among the most important assets the manufacturer has, and anything which acts to transfer power from the brands to the trader is not in the manufacturer's interest.

They would also argue that the approach can be risky for the manufacturer in that it hinges on the trader accepting the promotional offers. When once the trader appreciates the strength of his position he will want even more generous terms, and beyond this he will accept only those promotions of the type and value which fit with his immediate requirements.

As traders grow and become more powerful within their markets they are likely to attempt to move manufacturers toward the trader-linked approach. On balance this approach does tend to strengthen the trader's bargaining position. Beyond this it acts to take the trader out of direct competition with other traders on the feature of a particular brand.

For the manufacturer much will depend on the strength of his brands. If he has strong brands, brands which are leaders or very near the top of their markets, and these are big markets, he is likely to be particularly keen to maintain a brand-orientated plan. His bargaining position with the trader will be a comparatively strong one.

For the manufacturer with a list of middle-of-the-market brands the position is much more difficult. If he does not engage in some degree of trade-linked operating he is unlikely to get any of his brands featured, and in many cases he will not get his brands stocked.

However, the middle-market brand manufacturer would not be well advised to put all of his promotional effort into a trade-linked approach. He could run the risk of having his brands entirely dependent on trader goodwill for their existence – this is most certainly not a position that any manufacturer would consider satisfactory.

For the small manufacturer with small brands, the position is very different. Here the problem is crystallized in the question: 'How do I live?' For this manufacturer the problem is: 'How do I get, and keep, distribution?' A feature is a big, big bonus.

The small manufacturer will be watching carefully to spot any opportunity to fill a feature position in the retailer's programme. He will bend over backwards to meet the major retailers' requirements. He will produce a special pack at short notice, and he will accept terms that are tough.

The important requirement for the small manufacturer is that he does not accept the retailers' very tough terms on a brand that is doomed to fail. If he accepts harsh terms the aim should be that there will be sampling and longer-term growth for the brand concerned. If there are no real prospects of the growth then the shorter-term deal – no matter how attractive – is unlikely to be of real value.

The requirement for the small manufacturer is that he works to ensure that his brands have a special appeal, a competitive advantage with a section of the market, probably a minority section, and that the feature he buys with the major multiple will enable him to sample potential buyers and that a satisfactory number will repeat purchase.

Key points

1 Promotion is one of the most powerful of the marketing *tools*. Used effectively it can play a major part in raising the demand for a brand rapidly, and then holding it at the higher level, so that the economies of high-volume production and distribution can be exploited. Equally, the skilful use of promotion can greatly reduce the impact and effect of a competitive brand attack.

2 There is a limit to the number of brand promotions the business can mount effectively during the period of its operations plan. A promotional priority is a valuable opportunity – it is important to the brand, and the company, that it should be used effectively.

3 Every promotion should have one prime objective stated specific-ally in its promotional proposal. There may be other subsidiary objectives, but the achievement of the prime objective is what the promotion is really all about.

4 For a successful promotion it is necessary to select the *right* type for the particular occasion, build into it effective creativity, back it with the *right* level of resource, and ensure it is managed effectively.

5 Dull and boring promotions cost as much to mount as those that are bright and interesting. It is worth working very hard to build in the *right* effective creativity.

6 The costs and revenues a promotion is expected to generate should always be assessed and calculated before it is accepted for action. Every promotion, as every other investment, should have its budget and should be expected to meet it.

7 Promotions tend to be heavy consumers of indirect costs. Be wary of proposals for small or lightweight promotions – their indirect costs can be high and they can act to hinder the important major promotions – they are rarely ever worthwhile.

8 Remember that promotions can play a significant part in developing the brand personality. The presentation of the promotion must always be *right* for the brand's personality.

9 The most important thing about a promotion is that it should work. It should achieve its prime objective at an acceptable level of cost. The most expensive promotions are those which fail. They waste a valuable opportunity, cause a monetary loss, and invariably incur heavy indirect costs.

10 Promotion, *successful* promotion is a powerful marketing *tool* – used skilfully it can play a major part in building and exploiting competitive advantage.

12

◇

Advertising

◆

In a well-managed company every one of the component parts of the proposed operations plan will be challenged. Each one will be questioned in detail. However, by far the strongest and loudest questioning will almost surely be reserved for the brand advertising appropriations.

Everyone sitting around the table when the appropriations are considered will have a knowledge of advertising. They will see it on their television screens, in their magazines, newspapers, and so on. They will all know which advertising works for them – and they are likely to have very definite views on the advertising used and proposed for the company brands. They will certainly have a view as to which advertising is wasted and on which brand extra investment should be made.

This position is, in part, understandable. Advertising is the kind of subject which invariably attracts discussion and it is a subject on which strong emotional views are often held.

The success or failure of a particular advertising campaign will often be clear after a short period of exposure; however, evaluating a campaign in advance of exposure is a very different proposition.

Judging proposed advertising is a particularly difficult assignment. To do it with confidence requires considerable skill and experience. Estimating its effects with accuracy is even more difficult, particularly when it is appreciated that it is the marketing effort as a whole, including the product, its promotion, and its price, which is really responsible for raising brand demand.

Advertising is often a major part of the total marketing effort, however, it is possible to market a brand without using advertising.

There have been successful brands which have not been advertised, but it must be admitted that they are very few in number.

We are concerned in this chapter with brand advertising within the company operations plan. In particular we are concerned with how we can develop and exploit a competitive advantage, preferably a significant one, within the brand advertising investment.

THE TASK

The consideration here is with brand advertising as distinct from special purpose, often one-off, advertising (e.g. an announcement of a public meeting) which tends to be of a different nature.

The job of brand advertising is to help build and maintain brand sales volume. It does this by encouraging consumers to try the brand and by giving those consumers who are already users assurance, confidence, and encouragement to continue buying. In the course of carrying out these tasks it should play its part in building the desired brand personality (see figure 12.1).

The task of brand advertising is therefore threefold:

1 To persuade consumers to try the brand;
2 To provide existing users of the brand with assurance, confidence, and encouragement to continue buying;
3 To play its part in developing the desired brand personality.

While these brand advertising tasks are always present, they are not all present at the same level of intensity all the time. There are times when trial is vitally important, for instance at the brand launch, and there are times when providing assurance and confidence to existing users may be of greater significance. This is a most important consideration for the use of brand advertising and for the level of the investment made in it. The topic receives more detailed attention later in this chapter.

OBJECTIVES

It has been stated that the job of advertising is to *help* build and maintain sales volume. Advertising is frequently held responsible for a lack of sales volume, or given all the credit for a rise in sales levels, such judgements are almost certainly incorrect.

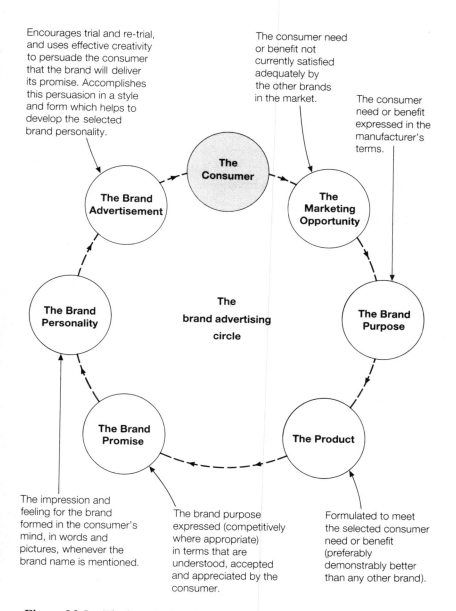

Encourages trial and re-trial, and uses effective creativity to persuade the consumer that the brand will deliver its promise. Accomplishes this persuasion in a style and form which helps to develop the selected brand personality.

The consumer need or benefit not currently satisfied adequately by the other brands in the market.

The consumer need or benefit expressed in the manufacturer's terms.

The Consumer

The Brand Advertisement

The Marketing Opportunity

The Brand Personality

The brand advertising circle

The Brand Purpose

The Brand Promise

The Product

The impression and feeling for the brand formed in the consumer's mind, in words and pictures, whenever the brand name is mentioned.

The brand purpose expressed (competitively where appropriate) in terms that are understood, accepted and appreciated by the consumer.

Formulated to meet the selected consumer need or benefit (preferably demonstrably better than any other brand).

Figure 12.1   The brand advertising circle
Successful brand advertising begins and ends with the consumer.

If the approach of the *best-value* concept is accepted then the other key factors – purpose, performance, and price – clearly have a major part to play in developing sales volume.

The best advertisement possible is unlikely to bring repeat sales if brand performance and price are badly out of balance. Similarly, a brand that has a high performance and a very attractive low price may sell well, even with relatively poor advertising.

On occasions, elementary factors such as a lack of brand distribution can have an adverse effect on sales volume – a highly persuasive advertisement will fail to bring a sale if the brand is not in stock when the consumer wishes to purchase.

■ *It is important to judge brand advertising against its objectives rather than against the objectives of the total brand.*

Brand advertising can act to motivate consumers to try the brand, give consumers confidence, and play a major role in developing a favourable brand personality. It is against objectives of this kind that it should be judged.

Through the years there have been numerous attempts to show a direct relationship of sales volume with advertising. Over a very short period of time it may be possible to show a form of direct relationship, for instance, where there is an outstanding advertising campaign for a new brand. But over the medium to longer term direct relationships are rarely, if ever, to be seen.

COMPETITIVE ADVANTAGE

There are three main areas in which a competitive advantage, and possibly a significant competitive advantage, can be gained from the brand advertising investment:

1 by having a superior advertising campaign;
2 by getting the investment in brand advertising *right*;
3 by investing the brand advertising appropriation wisely.

These approaches are inter-linked, and they can have a material effect on each other (see figure 12.2)

---

1 Produce superior advertising:

- get the *right* brand promise
- get the *right* brand personality
- use effective creativity to produce superior advertisements

2 Place the *right* level of investment behind the superior advertising.

Consider:

- the position and movement of the market in which the brand competes:
  - is it growing?
  - is in maturity?
  - is in decline?
- the position of the brand in the market:
  - is it right in terms of the best-value concept?
  - is it new?
  - is it established?
  - is it strong/weak?
- the quality of the advertising
- competitive activity
- corporate position

3 Invest at the *right* time and in the *right* place:

- a good media buy will show the brand to good effect, to the *right* people, and at the *right* cost

---

Figure 12.2   Competitive advantage in brand advertising

A superior advertising campaign

The discussion here concerns an advertising campaign and not just one individual advertisement. A campaign can be made up of a number of advertisements and continue over many years.

How do you get a superior advertising campaign? If you are sure you have the correct answer to this question then you are indeed a person with a very special ability. Over the years advertising specialists, marketing men, consultants and many others have researched and considered the problems the question poses. None of them have produced a fully satisfactory answer.

The advertising agent employed to work on the brand advertising clearly has a particularly important contribution to make. Indeed, some manufacturers are prepared to turn over the responsibility for their brand advertising completely to their chosen advertising agency.

Advertising can play a vital part in the development and exploitation of a brand. Unsatisfactory advertising can limit a brand's growth; at the extreme, badly directed and executed advertising can completely ruin a brand.

A responsible business management should not pass over the *full* responsibility for its brand advertising to its agency. Its brands are the very heart of a business. They are the pillars on which the business is built – without them there is no business. There are certain *key* decisions concerning the brand advertising which are so important for the business that they should be taken by its management. Indeed, it is suggested that certain of the *key* decisions should be taken by the chief executive.

The company should select its advertising agency with great care. In particular it should verify that the personnel who are to work with the company on the brand or brands are of a satisfactory calibre and experience, and beyond this that they have a positive attitude. It is important that, in their working relationships, the agency and company personnel should be able to build rapidly a mutual respect.

If the agency is to play its full part in creating superior advertising it is necessary that it has access to brand and company data which would normally be considered highly confidential. The company should make this data available and in return the agency should ensure that it is always treated as strictly private.

The relationship between a business and its advertising agency is in many respects a very special one. They have a mutual interest in ensuring the brand concerned is successful. A wise company management will listen very carefully to the advice of its agency; but it will always reserve the right to take certain key decisions itself.

It is suggested that if a brand is to have advertising which is more effective than its competitors, and advertising which will give it a competitive advantage, then it should be considered under three headings:

1   the brand promise;
2   the brand personality;
3   the brand advertisement.

The brand promise

When the *best-value* concept was discussed in an earlier chapter, the brand purpose was considered. The purpose was defined as the consumer need the brand meets, or the consumer benefit it provides.

Every brand should be directed to meeting a particular consumer purpose. The selection of the purpose at which his brand is directed is one of the most important decisions the manufacturer has to make. It is, of course, vitally important for the brand that it should have the performance ability to deliver to the consumer the benefit contained within its purpose and preferably deliver it significantly better than any other brand.

■ *The brand's promise is, in essence, its purpose expressed in terms that can be understood, appreciated, and accepted by those consumers to whom the brand is primarily directed.*

In his strategy development the manufacturer will have decided from his various researches just which marketing opportunities are available to him and he will have selected for action those opportunities which he has reason to believe he can meet more effectively than his competitors. These will be the opportunities where he believes he can develop a significant competitive advantage for his brand.

A marketing opportunity is a consumer need or requirement not met adequately by the brands currently in the market. And so the manufacturer should be fully aware which particular consumer benefit the brand is designed to meet.

He will have described this brand consumer benefit in 'manufacturer terms'. These terms may include a series of technical standards and other qualitative measures. They are not the sort of terms that are likely to be understood and appreciated by the brand's potential consumers.

Within the advertising agency there should be individuals who are skilled in turning complex statements into simple language. Language which is well understood, appreciated and accepted by consumers.

The simple statement should be easily remembered and should be linked with the brand name. In fact, the brand name should be part of the statement.

It needs to be emphasized that there is a very high level of skill involved in creating a simple statement that meets the brand's requirements to the full. Ideally, given that the brand has the necessary performance ability, it should be possible to build into the statement words which portray the brand's superiority in delivering the particular consumer benefit. To do this, and to do it with an economy of words, so that the statement may appear on small packets, or even small bottles, and still be read on a supermarket shelf, requires special writing ability.

■ *The simple statement referred to above, when it is agreed for use, becomes the* brand promise. *It is the one statement that encapsulates the benefit the brand brings to the consumer. It is a statement that should be used in all brand advertisements, on the brand pack, on showcards, on coupons, in fact in all brand publicity.*

Over time, if the manufacturer does a good marketing job for the brand, mention of the brand name will immediately bring to mind, in words and pictures, the brand promise.

It is vitally important for the brand that its promise should be *right* and so it should be tested with consumers. The need is to get their reactions and to ensure that they do understand, appreciate and accept it.

Much has been written over recent years under the heading of 'brand positioning'. A popular definition of the term is 'to decide where in the market a brand is placed'. The placement can be in terms, for instance, of price, of usage or of consumer benefit. The last of these, consumer benefit, would seem to be the one most commonly used. In this respect, the 'promise' approach followed in this book and brand positioning have much in common.

Over recent years there have been a number of other approaches which have gained widespread recognition, for instance the USP (Unique Selling Proposition). The essence of the USP approach is that every advertisement should make a definite proposition to the customer and that this proposition firstly should have distinction, secondly it should be unique, and thirdly it should be of real consequence. It will be appreciated that the USP doctrine has some similarity with the 'promise' approach of this book.

The promise approach has the great advantage that it starts with the consumer (i.e. the ultimate customer) when the particular marketing opportunity is discovered and then selected for action. Product research and development follow until a satisfactory product, one that delivers the purpose as required by the consumer, is developed and produced. The circle is then completed when the brand returns to the attention, (and eventual purchase and consumption) of the consumer via the brand advertising.

■ *The decision for the acceptance of the brand promise is so important for the future of the brand that it should be taken by the chief executive. The decision is one that should be taken only after detailed and careful consideration. When once taken it should not be changed lightly. If well chosen and developed the brand promise will grow in strength and value with use. Its lifetime could well be measured in decades rather than years or months.*

Should a change ever be made? There could certainly be occasions when a change is appropriate. Considerations including developments in the environment, in consumer values, in the performance of the product, etc., can mean that a change may be necessary. But the change should be made only after very careful research and study. And, of course, the brand will need to have the performance ability to deliver any new promise.

■ *The basic rule is: 'get your brand promise right, and then stay with it'.*

The brand personality

No matter how he sets about the task of presenting his brand the manufacturer is bound to make an impression. This applies particularly to his brand advertising. The television commercial can be quiet and sombre, or it can be loud and jovial – the presentation will automatically work towards the establishment of a brand personality.

Clearly, the manufacturer should be concerned with building a personality that is helpful to his brand, one that will enhance its growth and help to secure its standing with the consumer and, in particular, with those consumers to whom it is primarily directed.

The brand personality (often termed brand image) may be described as the picture, or impression, and feeling for a brand, which has developed in the consumer's mind.

There is considerable evidence on record to show that the development of a favourable personality can be a factor of major significance to a brand in its quest to gain and to hold customers. A favourable personality will be valuable at all times of a brand's life, frequently its value becomes even more pronounced as the market moves into maturity and on into decline. It will also have a special value to its brand when competitive brands are able to offer a similar performance and price. In these circumstances a favourable brand personality can certainly represent a competitive advantage.

This means that the manufacturer, well before he puts his brand into the market, should decide what kind of personality he wants for it. This will require very careful study. Clearly, a favourable personality can be directly linked with the brand performance. For a brand that has a high-level performance in any conditions, a strong robust personality may be right; for a brand that is very mild and soft in use a caring personality could be well suited.

The important requirement is that the manufacturer makes the *right* selection for his brand and that he ensures all his brand presentations, and in particular his advertising, is produced in a style and manner to develop and enhance the chosen personality.

The selection of the *right* brand personality should be approved by the chief executive. He may receive guidance from his advertising agency, from research consultants and from his own marketing staff, but the final decision should be his.

The record shows that when a personality has been chosen for a brand, and a series of brand presentations which aim to develop the personality introduced, changing it will be extremely difficult. Indeed, if the presentations have been extensive then without a very major investment a change will be almost impossible.

■ *Again the basic rule is: 'Get the selection of your brand personality right, make sure your presentations deliver it, and stay with it.'*

The brand promise and the brand personality are two fundamentals in brand advertising. They should be always present.

Every presentation made by the brand should be conscious of these two fundamentals. In both cases their value will develop and strengthen over time. The urge to change them frequently should be strongly resisted. When he has got them 'right' for his brand the manufacturer has made a major move toward producing advertising which can eventually give his brand a competitive advantage.

The brand advertisement

Here we are concerned with actually producing a superior advertisement, one that achieves its objectives to the full.

Producing the advertisement is the responsibility of the advertising agency. This should be their great skill and their major contribution. The manufacturer also has a part to play and if he fails in his contribution he cannot expect his agency to make up for his failure.

The position of the particular brand, its strengths and weaknesses, the movement of the market in which it competes, and the activities of competitors, these and other relevant factors will vary from brand to brand and from time to time. It follows that the direction, the form, and the objectives of the brand advertising will need to be specific to the individual brand and to the particular circumstances. It is clear that there just cannot be one set of rules as to how to make superior brand advertising. Nor a set of rules to cover a series of positions.

However, a series of guidelines which if followed should certainly provide valuable assistance in the quest for superior advertising include:

- A written statement, setting out the direction and objectives of the brand advertisement, or series of advertisements, should be agreed between the manufacturer and the agency. This statement should be available to the agency before it starts any work on the particular advertisement.
- The agency should be supplied with full details of the brand, including its market position, formula outline, production details and its development history. In particular, the agency should be informed of any competitive advantage the brand holds and details of its performance in use when compared with competitive

brands. Any available consumer research data and laboratory test results should also be supplied.

(It may well be advantageous to allow agency personnel to meet the research and development staff responsible for the brand and also to met the production personnel.)

- The advertising agency should be given a clear indication of the marketing plan for the brand including details of any promotional and other sales activity proposed. They should also be given a clear indication of the extent of the investment proposed for the advertising campaign.

- If there are any matters of principle that the manufacturer is not prepared to include in his advertisements he should inform his agency before they start working on the account, not after they have produced a considerable amount of work.

- The discipline imposed on the agency by the 'brand promise' and the 'brand personality' should be enforced at all times, but the agency should be allowed full discretion in its creative approach.

- There are a number of advertising tenets that have been established over the years and which normally contribute to the formulation of an effective advertisement. 'The headline is all important; four out of five readers never get beyond it', is one such tenet for press and magazines and the fact that the words 'free' and 'new' can have a special significance in advertising is another. These tenets should be well known to the agency specialists, and they should also have the skill to recognize the exceptional case where the tenet should not apply.

- The manufacturer should set high standards. His comparisons should be with the very best. If he is not satisfied with the quality of work presented by the agency he should make his feelings known promptly – he should not allow his dissatisfaction to rumble on. Equally when the agency deliver first-class work they should be given the appropriate credit. Good advertising people are very similar to other good people in business – they like to be on a winning team and feel they have made their contributions toward the victory.

- There should be an agreed timetable for the production of the advertisement, with the appropriate progress review meetings scheduled.

- All the proposed advertising should be tested with the consumers to whom it is to be primarily directed. The important reaction to the advertising is that of these potential customers, not the personal reactions of people such as other advertising specialists or marketing executives. If the advertising fails to bring the desired reaction from potential customers it will fail.

- A budget covering the production costs of the advertising should be agreed. A manufacturer who gives his agency a free hand on production and then finds the costs are excessive has only himself to blame.

If a manufacturer selects his advertising agency with skill and care, has the *right* brand promise, the *right* brand personality and follows the guidelines set out above, can he be sure his brand will have superior advertising? The answer must be a very firm 'No'. In a field such as advertising where success depends so much on creative skills and human reactions, there can be no guarantees.

However, he should at least obtain competent advertising and this is of real value. His advertising should play its part in helping to ensure that the brand has the opportunity to become *best-value* with those consumers to whom it is primarily directed.

The aim, of course, of everyone concerned must be to provide superior brand advertising for only *superior advertising* will have the possibility of gaining a competitive advantage in presentation for the brand.

■ *Having worked successfully with his advertising agency and produced a superior advertisement the manufacturer should resist the temptation to change it frequently. Those people who are very close to it, often those who have played an important role in its creation, invariably seem to tire of a good advertisement much more rapidly than do consumers.*

A really good advertisement can work well for many years – it can become even more effective with time and exposure.

The manufacturer should beware of the new man, or men, who have just joined the brand and after a quick review want to change the advertising. He should check the position carefully. Change for the sake of change can be doubly expensive – the new advertisements may not work and they will cost money to produce.

Getting the investment *right*

It can be a wise decision for a manufacturer not to invest in brand advertising. He may be able to use his funds to greater effect in, for instance, a sales promotion or a price move. But for most manufacturers the important consideration is not whether he should or should not invest in advertising but how much to invest.

There are a number of formula approaches to the advertising investment problem. The most popular of these is the percentage-of-sales approach. Also very popular is the case-rate method, a similar approach.

It is difficult to build a logic for these methods. What level should the percentage or case rate be? Should it be the same for all markets? Should it differ from brand to brand? What of the age of the brand, should this be a consideration? To these may be added other questions.

However, it is a fact that a percentage-of-sales or a case-rate approach is claimed to be used by many very successful, companies. This, in itself, is a good argument for giving the approach serious consideration.

The approach is really of a defensive nature. It is claimed it acts as a form of discipline on management, it ensures that the brand will be supported at all times and guards against profit-greedy and short-term thinking. In the case of a leading brand, it acts to ensure that the brand is not caught without support if a competitor launches an opportunistic attack. And it is also claimed that the investment acts as an assurance to regular customers and shelters them from competitive advertising – in this way it discourages new entrants to the market.

Further and more detailed examination will often bring to light the fact that in many companies the approach is used as a form of discipline for more junior brand managers, with senior executives reserving the right to adjust the percentage level or case rate at short notice whenever they consider it appropriate.

Percentage levels and case rates can have a mythical effect on some managers. They have been very successful with a brand in a market and have used a particular percentage level of advertising support. And so this approach and the support level of advertising achieve a direct link with success. Such a link can be a powerful one; but it is still extremely difficult to give it any logical recognition.

One of the basic problems facing acceptance of the percentage approach is that it does not appear to be possible to produce authentic research data which shows a direct and continuous relationship between advertising expenditure and sales volume for an established brand. For a new brand launch or a major re-launch of an existing brand, a form of relationship may possibly develop over the shorter term but even in these special circumstances a direct relationship is most unlikely.

There have been many studies of the brand advertising–sales relationship undertaken by major companies, research bodies, academic institutes and others. With the research undertaken by companies, if they have uncovered information of real value on the subject then they are likely to treat it as strictly confidential for it could provide the basis of a competitive advantage.

The various research studies may have provided a series of useful guidelines as to when it is advisable to advertise strongly and when a lower level of investment should suffice. But they would not appear to have given any strong backing to the percentage-of-sales or case-rate approaches.

In this book neither the percentage-of-sales nor the case-rate approach is accepted as the most competent answer to the question: 'How much to invest in brand advertising?'

It is suggested that before reaching a decision as to how much he intends to invest the manufacturer should consider:

The movement of the market

The best time to develop your brand share of market is during the growth stage. At this time new, uncommitted buyers are entering the market for the first time. These new buyers are beginning to form their value judgements on the brands competing in the market – later they will become committed but at the early stage their minds are more open.

The manufacturer may need to invest heavily, but during the market growth stage new triers are likely to cost less per person or per household than at any other time. If his brand is in good shape then during the growth stage it should certainly benefit from strong advertising backing.

In a mature market the brand advertising may take the form of a reminder, and the investment can be at a lower level. The need is more to give confidence and assurance to regular users, although there will still be some new triers who will need to be motivated.

As the market moves into decline so the need for brand advertising should subside. Now the requirement will be for limited reminder advertising. At this time brand margins should be higher and unit profit contribution also at a higher level.

The brand position

Here we are concerned with the use of the term 'position' in two ways:

1   Whether or not the brand is *right* in terms of the *best-value* concept. That the brand should have the *right* purpose and the *right* balance between performance and price is a basic requirement for success in the market. Without these the all-important repeat sales are unlikely to materialize and the brand advertising investment will be substantially wasted. The manufacturer should be sure that he has the brand *right* in terms of the *best-value* concept before he embarks on a major investment in brand advertising.
2   The age and condition of the brand in its market. Is it:

- a new brand?
- a brand about to receive a major re-launch?
- a mature brand?
- a brand in decline?

If the brand is a new one in its launch year it will need all the advertising support possible within the corporate plan. During its first year the new brand makes its position and standing in the market. There is unlikely to be a second chance – in the brand's opening period it may well be cheaper to overspend rather than underspend on advertising.

The need for a strong advertising backing for a new brand would normally extend beyond the first year, certainly into the second year and possibly into the third.

When a brand is to receive a major re-launch, its position with regard to advertising support is very similar to that of a new brand.

It is, of course, most important that the manufacturer should be sure of the strength of his re-launch proposition. A 'lightweight' product development should not be classified as major and given extensive advertising backing – the result of such a move is almost sure to be disappointing in terms of market-share and sales-volume development, and also in terms of brand profit contribution.

The level of advertising appropriate for a mature brand will depend very much on the movement of the market and on the competitive position.

An established brand in a mature or declining market should be mainly concerned with reminder advertising. The unit contributory profit margin is likely to be at a high level and the need is to retain established consumers as long as possible.

With a mature brand this requirement to retain consumers is paramount. If a competitor mounts an attack in the market then the need is to defend vigorously. A well-chosen promotion could possibly be the best defence, but reminder advertising may also have a part to play.

With a brand that is in decline the first requirement is to be sure just why it is fading. If it is because the market in which it competes has gone into a steep decline, then it is probable that the best move for the brand is that it be allowed to decline and to contribute as high a level of profit contribution as possible in the process. So much depends on the brand itself and the reason for its decline. If the brand retains certain basic strengths (e.g. a well developed personality) it may be possible to revive it, and brand advertising is likely to have a part to play in this.

However, it is important that the manufacturer ensures that he does not waste scarce resources and effort attempting a lost cause. Relatively few brands that have moved into a longer-term decline are returned to a growth position with a satisfactory profit contribution.

The quality of advertising available

If the advertising produced for the particular campaign turns out to be of a very poor quality, i.e. it fails to achieve its agreed objectives with those consumers to whom it is directed, then the manufacturer would be well advised not to run it. Better that he save his money until he has produced advertising of an acceptable quality, or use the investment in other places. At the extreme, poor advertising can do real harm to a brand – and if this poor quality concerns the brand promise and brand personality, then the brand may never recover.

Equally, if the advertising produced is shown to be of a superior quality, advertising which is particularly effective in achieving its objectives, then the manufacturer should consider increasing his investment. From advertising of this quality he may be able to obtain a competitive advantage – if he has, then he should be sure to exploit it.

It is always possible that the quality of the brand advertising is competent without being superior. A large proportion of the advertising produced falls into this category. Is the manufacturer wise to invest in this standard of advertising?

The quest must be for superior advertising – and the effort to obtain it should be continuous. However, there may be a need for brand advertising at a given time and it may be necessary to use the competent advertising. This would be a form of holding action until the superior advertising for the brand is produced. As a general rule, the manufacturer should insist on the best and only use the best.

Competitive activity

If a competitor, or a number of competitors, decide to invest heavily in brand advertising through a particular period the manufacturer will need to review his own investment plans. While advertising and sales are not directly linked, good advertising certainly does effect sales. If he does not respond to the competitive activity the manufacturer may suffer.

He should be sure that additional brand advertising is the best way to reply to the competitive action. It could be that a suitably placed promotion or, for instance, a short-term price move would be more effective.

There can be occasions when the lack of competitive advertising provides an opportunity. When a brand is the only one in a particular market that is prepared to advertise then its solo position can give its advertising an extra value.

Corporate position

A manufacturer may wish to invest in advertising at a given level for one of his brands, but before commitment he needs to be aware of his corporate aims and objectives. A need for shorter-term profit and cash may mean that he is forced to restrict investments he may otherwise have made. This subject receives further consideration in paragraphs which follow.

How much to invest?

So far these notes have been critical of the widely accepted per-centage-of-sales approach to arriving at the level of investment for brand advertising. A series of subjects have been reviewed, each one of which is considered to be of particular importance in the decision as to how much to invest, but a clear and simple set of rules has not been outlined. The reason is that a worthwhile set of simple rules is not possible. This is an area where sound business judgement is vitally important.

From the discussion set out in the preceding paragraphs it will be clear there are times when it would be right to invest heavily and other times when the investment should be restricted or placed be-hind other methods of brand support. Getting decisions of this kind *right* can certainly bring a competitive advantage.

As a very general guide, the approach to arriving at the brand ad-vertising appropriation preferred here would start with a detailed consideration of the subjects listed above. The strategic objectives for the brand would be reviewed, and the objectives for the shorter-term operational period agreed.

Work can then begin on the formulation of a draft proposal for the brand advertising investment. This would normally take the form of a statement covering the period of the operations plan and setting out the television space, radio time, press space, and other media con-sidered appropriate to provide the necessary level of consumer per-suasion and brand personality development which will enable the brand to achieve its sales volume objective. When the proposed media schedules are converted into money, allowance made for the various production costs, a 'first figure' for the brand investment will be available.

If the task of building up the proposal is to be met competently an extremely high level of skill is required. The part that advertising is expected to play in the brand activity for the period should be clearly stated. Regional activities need to be outlined and explained. Sim-ilarly any special tests covering varying levels of expenditure need to be specified. The media chosen to support particular operations will need to be reviewed, factors such as the television spot length and whether or not the spots are to be batched or used on a more thinly spread continuous basis, these and other considerations need to be covered.

If a particular pattern of advertising is proposed the reasoning behind the proposal should be discussed. Wherever possible the proposal should be backed by marketing research data which provides guidance on probable results.

■ *It is essential that the brand advertising proposal for the period should be presented with the proposal for the brand sales promotions investment. The two proposals are clearly linked and should be complementary in their use.*

This is an approach which sets realistic objectives for the brand, objectives which are in line with its strategic aims, and then attempts to build a proposal that will provide the necessary advertising support to ensure that the objectives are attained.

The approach should not be confused with one that sets a sales value objective and then calculates the level of advertising such an objective can support after providing for a required level of profit contribution.

It should be clear that the approach outlined for the formulation of a brand advertising appropriation is merely an initial draft. When it has been built into the marketing plan for the brand, the brand profit contribution reviewed, and its place in the overall marketing plan for the business considered, then it can move forward and become a firm proposal for the brand advertising investment.

Review of the appropriation

The brand advertising investment is an integral part of the company operations plan. We have reasoned here of a plan which covers one year ahead, is reviewed at six-monthly intervals, and a new plan covering a further one year ahead follows the review.

It is suggested that the brand advertising investment proposal should be reviewed within the total review of the operations plan.

The policy on appropriation review can be of significance. If there is no review within the one-year period of the operations plan then there will be a temptation for the marketing men to play safe and ensure they have a full budget – they tend to prefer to have too much money rather than too little. This is understandable, particularly if they are held fully responsible for brand market share and sales volume and only partially responsible for profit.

However, there is also the possibility that without a shorter-term review a major opportunity may be foregone. A necessary burst of advertising may be missed or unduly delayed.

Of course, it is always possible that it may be a sensible move to reduce a budget for part of the year - without a periodic review this is unlikely to happen.

A half-yearly review is probably a satisfactory balance, providing it is accepted that exceptional developments may require special action.

Investing the appropriation wisely

A well-designed, highly effective advertisement which is never seen, is of little use. The aim must be to create a great advertising campaign and ensure that it has every opportunity to be fully effective. Potential customers must have the opportunity to see and appreciate the campaign.

The important consideration is that the brand advertising *has every opportunity to be fully effective with those consumers to whom it is primarily directed.* This phrase covers the two *key* considerations in media selection.

Firstly, that the advertising should have the opportunity to be fully effective and this means that it needs a medium where the brand benefits can be shown to their best effect.

Secondly, that the brand advertising should be seen by those potential consumers to whom it is primarily directed. If the brand is directed to young men between 15 and 25 years of age then it needs to use media which provide coverage of this group. In this instance, a magazine for retired people is unlikely to be helpful.

There is, of course, one further factor to be taken into account. There is a limited sum of money available for investment in brand advertising. It follows that the cost of the media is of importance. The aim must be to obtain the desired coverage at the lowest cost.

The product and its performance characteristics will have major influence in deciding which media should be used. Would demonstration be a very strong factor in motivating consumers to try the brand? Television is known to be an effective medium to demonstrate a product, in particular to demonstrate it competitively. Does the product need colour illustrations? Food products invariably look more appetizing when shown in colour – black and white newspapers would have limitations, but colour magazines could be right. Posters can be effective if the advertising message can be expressed simply and with very few words, but if explanation is necessary they are likely to be unsuitable. Clearly there is a skill in selecting the right medium for a brand's advertising requirement at a given time in its development.

Within each medium there are important questions to be answered as to how the advertising should be structured and timed. For instance, should the television advertisement be of 60, 30, or 15 seconds? Should the magazine advertisement be full-page, half-page or just one column? Again the product, the content of the advertisement and the development of the brand will provide the answers to this form of question. At the brand's introduction a 60-second advertisement may be necessary to explain and demonstrate its promise. Later it may be possible to remind the consumer in 30 seconds or even 15. Similarly, a full magazine page may be necessary during the brand's earlier periods, with smaller spaces at later times.

Of course, the coverage provided by the medium will also be a key consideration. The most persuasive of magazine advertisements will not work satisfactorily if the consumers to whom the brand is directed never read the magazine. And a television advertisement is likely to be prohibitively expensive if the potential consumers are a very special group and strictly limited in number.

The media world has been, and continues to be, researched heavily. Details of the readership, in terms of geographical regions, and in terms of sex, income, social class and many other classifications, are available for all the major and many of the minor newspapers and magazines. Similarly details are available for television audiences and radio listening. All the recognized media are covered in this way.

Price-lists are also available for all the various media. And so there is a complex task involved in deciding how to invest the available brand advertising funds so that they may work to the very best effect. It is a field in which the computer can have a part to play in analysing the available data and in searching for the *best buys*. It is also a field where a well-seasoned *feel* for the market and a shrewd eye for a bargain are vitally important if a competitive advantage is to be gained. Sound timing and good judgement are particularly valuable. This is an area where the experienced professionals excel. The really good operator has the ability to read and appreciate the research data, and then to think beyond it.

BRAND ADVERTISING AND PROMOTIONS

There is a view, held strongly by some marketing specialists that the advertising and promotional appropriations should be treated as completely separate investments. Behind the view is a reasoning which argues that the advertising job is primarily of a longer-term nature, in particular the building of the desired personality or brand image normally requires a lengthy period of time. Promotions are viewed as shorter-term *tools* used to achieve specific objectives. It should be stated that this view is held by many successful marketing men.

■ *Within this book it is accepted that, at times, the prime purpose of advertising is to remind the consumer of the brand and of its promise. It is further accepted that brand promotions can play a part in this task. It is reasoned that brand advertising and brand promotions are complementary.*

Acceptance of this reasoning can have a marked effect on the level of both the brand advertising and promotions appropriations and on the way in which they are invested.

Key points

1 The job of brand advertising is threefold. Firstly to encourage consumers to try the brand, secondly to give confidence and assurance to regular users, and thirdly to help create the *right* brand personality.

2 All three tasks are always present but not necessarily at the same level of intensity. During the early periods of a brand's life, consumer trial will be vitally important. Later the reassurance of regular users will be of greater significance. Acceptance of this reasoning can have a major effect on the form of advertising produced, and on the level of investment placed behind it.

3 Select your advertising agency with great care. Ensure they have the necessary skills and resources to produce the form of advertising that your brands are likely to need. In particular ensure that your staff and the agency personnel can rapidly build mutual respect, and a good working relationship.

4 There are two fundamentals for your brand which you must establish before you start working on the creation of your brand advertising. The fundamentals are the brand promise and the brand personality.

The brand purpose, expressed in a manner which is understood, appreciated, and accepted by those consumers to whom the brand is primarily directed, becomes the brand promise. Get your brand promise *right* and stay with it. Equally, be sure to get your brand personality *right* and also be prepared to stay with it.

5 Your advertising agency should bring *effective* creativity to the production of your brand advertisements – this is their major contribution. They should be given wide discretion in the actual construction of the advertising. Be sure the creativity is *effective* – the aim is to produce advertising which achieves its objectives with those consumers to whom it is directed. If it also wins artistic awards they will be welcome, but achievement of the objectives comes first.

6 Test your brand advertising with the consumers to whom it is directed. Test it against its objectives – remember the total brand must pass the consumer's *best-value* test to get the all-important repeat purchases.

7 Be cautious of the formula-type approaches to arriving at brand advertising appropriations. There will be times when your brand needs strong backing, and there will be times when a lighter approach can apply. The requirement is to get the advertising and the investment right for the particular occasion.

8 If you have created a very effective advertisement beware of the temptation to change it too quickly. A really good advertisement can become even more effective over time and with extended exposure.

9 Remember, a media buy can only be a bargain if it allows the advertisement to show the brand to its best effect, and is seen by those people to whom the brand is primarily directed.

10 It is said that advertising always works best for a good brand. There is truth in this statement. Be sure your advertising is effective, be sure it is meeting its objectives – also be sure that your brand has the right purpose, and the right balance of performance and price. This way your advertising can play its full part in helping your brand to build a significant competitive advantage.

13

Pricing

◆

Pricing is often referred to as essentially a shorter-term tactical operation. Items such as advertising and product development are thought to be of a longer-term and strategical nature, as indeed they can be, but pricing rarely receives this recognition. This is probably because a price move can often have dramatic impact over the shorter term on brand sales volume.

In fact, pricing is a particularly important strategic consideration. Skilful management of price can secure a competitive advantage and the longer-term profitability of a brand; careless price movements can provide competitors with major opportunities. Clearly, in formulating his brand's pricing approach within his business strategy the manufacturer will need to exercise considerable skill.

If the strategy is to prove successful in the real live market-place the manufacturer will need to exercise a similar high level of skill, possibly of a slightly difficult kind, in his operational pricing activity. The strategy could have planned for a specific price-level for a brand, but in the market-place competitors may not be prepared for the planned position to materialize; they may have different thoughts as to what price-levels should apply in the market. Handling brand price positions of this kind effectively is just one example of the need for skilful pricing within business operations.

■ *The significant part that pricing has to play in determining company revenue and profitability needs to be fully appreciated. Price is a key factor in setting the level of a brand's unit margin; it is also a key factor in determining a brand's volume, and so it must be of major significance in determining profitability.*

207

PRICE AND THE BEST-VALUE CONCEPT

In chapter 2 the importance of the brand *best-value* concept, and the reasoning behind its application were discussed. Price is a *key* factor within the brand *best-value* concept.

The other *key* factors within the concept are purpose, performance and personality. In one important respect price differs from the other three factors, and the difference is of consequence in business operations.

The purpose a brand is intended to meet is fundamental. It should be decided well before the brand enters the market and the product formulated so that the brand delivers its purpose or benefit. The purpose becomes the brand promise in its advertising. To change a brand purpose is both difficult and risky. The change rarely works completely satisfactorily.

To change a brand performance, certainly to bring about a substantial improvement, would normally require considerable research and development effort. It is an easier move than a change in purpose, but it is not a simple operation.

To change a brand personality is extremely difficult, certainly requiring a period of time, and probably a substantial investment.

■ *Brand price can be changed overnight without any major difficulty. This should not be taken to imply that the brand price should be moved frequently and dramatically. On the contrary, in the main brands benefit from price stability with substantial changes reserved for very special occasions.*

However, there can be times when major price moves need to be implemented at very short notice. Normally they would be part of the strategic plan, but the actual decision on timing and implementation will be with operational management. For instance: a new brand is launched into the market and is an outstanding success. It races to market leadership with a volume well above other brands. Should the brand reduce its price and attempt to close-off the market?

The decision to move the brand price down in this instance would be a strategic one – but its extent and timing will be greatly influenced by operational considerations.

In the case outlined, if a strategic price reduction is considered to be the right move then it will be important that operational views do not delay it until after other new brands have entered the market – the best time to stop a competitor is before he gets started. It could also be important that the price cut be of consequence and that the temptation to hold on to short-term profit be seen in the wider context of the brand holding a longer-term position of market leadership.

Within the *best-value* concept brand price is seen to some considerable extent as a balance to the brand performance. The formula for brand success reads: Get the purpose *right*, get the *right* balance between performance and price, and add the *right* brand personality.

What is the *right* balance between performance and price? In general, a high-level performance relative to the market can command a high price, a low-level performance relative to the market requires a lower-level price. Of course, the measures are not necessarily completely balanced. Frequently, a speciality brand can command a high premium for a relatively small advance in a particular performance factor, but its volume is likely to be limited within the market depending upon the demand for the speciality.

Over the longer term, given that consumers are able to try the various competing brands, the performance–price relationship should become known and be a *key* factor in the consumers' judgement of the *best-value*. Brand personality can affect the balance but its effect is unlikely to be extensive. (With brands competing in markets where buying is more heavily influenced by emotion, e.g. the perfume market, the brand personality can have a much greater influence on brand value.)

■ *The one way in which a manufacturer can adjust the value of a brand in the market-place at very short notice is through the adjustment of its price. This elementary fact is of major significance in business operations.*

If a new brand with a superior performance enters a market at the same price as existing brands, or one of the existing brands in the market receives a major re-launch which provides a better performance without increasing its price, then the relative brand value positions in the market will change. In the shorter term the only way an existing brand can balance its value position in this circumstance is by making a price reduction. It can do this via a special price offer, with other forms of promotion, or it can make a more permanent price-cut. But if it doesn't move, and the attacking brand does a good marketing job, then it must expect to suffer in the market-place with a loss of brand share.

PRICE AND COMPETITIVE ADVANTAGE

It is not possible, in the terms used in this book, to gain a competitive advantage in price without also having a unit cost advantage. This statement is based on the definition of a competitive advantage as an advantage your competitors do not have.

It means that for the same quantity and quality of product you have the ability to produce and distribute at a lower unit cost. This means you can, if you wish, sell at a lower unit price than your competitor without necessarily taking a lower unit contributory margin.

The advantage can be based on effective and efficient operation. However, in all probability brand volume, based on a higher level of market share, will be the key factor behind the lower unit costs. In this respect the retailers' margin should be considered as part of the brand distribution cost.

The classic case of a brand using a competitive advantage in price based on lower unit costs can be seen where the brand has been able to develop a dominant leadership of a market, a leadership which gives it a much higher volume than any other brand in the same market. It uses this position to obtain lower unit costs of production and, because of its leading position in the stores, lower unit costs of distribution. It then proceeds to take a low level of unit contributory profit margin, and this means it has a relatively low level of unit price.

The brand's competitors, with their lower brand volumes and higher unit costs are forced to keep their selling prices in line. In fact, because the retailer may require a higher unit cost of distribution, they may be forced to have trade selling prices below those of the leader.

Obviously the competitors will be squeezed. They will have little money to invest in product development, advertising, or similar activities, to challenge the leader. Their profits, if they have any, will be low.

The leader, even with low unit margins, can make a higher level of total profit as he has high volume.

The very desirable position of the leader given here, a position envied by all the other manufacturers in the market, is one that would normally apply only for a dominant leader. During the periods of market maturity and decline, when consumers are less likely to change brands, the leader may decide to take his advantage in terms of a higher unit margin.

The ability to gain a price competitive advantage of this kind is possessed by only a limited number of manufacturers. They need to have a brand that has the necessary clear leadership in its market, and they need to be effective and efficient in their operation. It is always possible that if the general standard of efficiency of the operators in a particular market is low then one very effective competitor might possibly gain an advantage without his brand having clear market leadership. And, of course, it is always possible to get an advantage by developing a more cost-effective product formulation. Nevertheless, to gain this classic form of price-competitive advantage without a brand that is a clear market leader is extremely difficult.

However, this does not preclude a manufacturer from using price advantageously within his brand marketing, and also using price skilfully in his shorter-term price movements within the market.

Frequently, the use of a high degree of skill in his price tactics will bring a valuable short-term gain, and if this is repeated a number of times through the period of an operations plan it will, in itself, represent a competitive advantage.

Similarly, if a maufacturer decides to use price aggressively, at a time when he does not have a cost advantage, but when his competitors are unable, or unwilling, to compete with him, then his move could bring him an advantage in the market. In these circumstances his investment in price could show a very worthwhile return.

PRICE AND COST

The old adage: 'Price is policy, cost is fact', was often used to bring out the point that price does not necessarily have to be linked directly to cost. This is, of course, true over the shorter term. Through the longer term, however, it is essential that price should be at a satisfactory level above cost.

The fact that a *true cost* is impossible to calculate is conveniently ignored by the old adage. However, a *reasonable* calculation of brand marginal cost should be possible. And a similarly *reasonable* calculation of brand full cost should also be possible, although it must be accepted that this will be of an approximate nature due to the arbitrary allocation of certain items.

There may well be periods when a manufacturer is prepared to sell his brand below the calculated full-cost level. The need to bring a new plant to a reasonable level of capacity, or to take a defensive move against a major competitive attack are examples of circumstances when a below-full-cost price could be justified.

However, for a manufacturer to continue to sell a brand below full cost through the longer term requires some special reason. The case for such a move can be made; a market that has great potential but takes a very long time to get started, for instance, could be such a case, but it does need to be a good case.

Selling below marginal cost is another matter. To do this over the *shorter term* requires a strong justification and to contemplate such a move over the longer term would require a most exceptional consideration.

The manufacturer needs to ensure that his own accounting system provides him with a *reasonable* calculation covering both the marginal and full costs for each one of his brands. Beyond this he should be aware as to how these costs are likely to change with variations in volume. He also needs to make cost estimates for competing brands. It will be difficult to arrive at figures in which he can have full confidence, but it is important that he makes an effort to achieve a reasonable degree of accuracy. Normally it should be possible for his chemists to produce accurate statements of the competitive brand formulas. His purchasing officials, working from their own experience, should be able to provide details of the various material and packaging prices. Again, his own experience should guide him on process costs. Bringing these various factors together the manufacturer should be able to build a reasonable guide to the marginal (or variable) costs for competing brands. Additional estimates of administrative and other costs will be necessary to arrive at a full-cost figure.

The competitive brand-cost estimates should be most useful in providing an indication of the possible competitive reaction to a move up, or down, in brand price. Also, they will provide guidance as to how each competitive brand is affected by the price movement of, for instance, a particular raw material. Such information can prove invaluable in brand pricing tactics.

Cost movements with various levels of volume are always difficult to estimate. But again the effort required to obtain a worthwhile indication of a competitor's position can often pay off handsomely. There is always a need to know just how much an additional amount of volume is worth in terms of unit cost reduction. For the maufacturer, if his brand is in an advantageous position it may be worthwhile to forego a price increase to gain extra volume, but such a move may be equally worthwhile for one of his competitors.

■ *At one time break-even charts were used frequently within business. Over recent years they appear to have lost some of their popularity. This is to be regretted for they have the effect of illustrating very clearly the importance of volume and the dramatic effect it can have on unit cost.*

As the capital equipment required for high-volume and high-speed production becomes more complex and more costly, and as the cost of advertising increases, so the importance of volume tends to grow. In many industries volume has become one of the most significant factors in the make-up of unit costs.

It is strongly recommended that a chart showing the movement of brand cost with varying levels of volume should be constructed for every brand as part of the operations plan formulation and review processes.

PRICE STRUCTURE AND THE MARKET

In an established market there is likely to be what is known as a price structure. Each brand competing within the market will have a price position and all of the positions will form the structure.

In a market where there is a dominant brand leader all the other brands will be spaced around the leader. The speciality brands and those providing a particularly high performance level will tend to be premium priced and above the leader. The brands offering lower quality than the leader will have unit prices below his level.

In this form of market the usual practice is for price increases and decreases to follow the leader. He sets the structure of the market, all the others watch him closely, but they tend to know their place. If the leader is following a low unit-margin approach then everybody else is likely to have low unit margins and relatively low unit profitability.

In a market where there is no clear leader but three or four brands are all of approximately the same standing, the position differs markedly. Each of the leading brands will have come to a balance between performance and price which enables it to hold its regular consumers. There may be speciality brands either at the top or bottom of the market price scale, their positions will tend to depend on the strength of their speciality.

The leading brands will all watch each other very closely; in particular they will study any product developments. But at this time most of the competition for the switchers in the market will tend to be in terms of advertising and promotions, each one making the best use of his skills in these areas. They are likely to try to avoid active price competition. They would prefer unit prices and margins to be relatively high so that all of them are able to make at least a reasonable level of profit.

Should one of the leading brands develop a product improvement of significance, an improvement which can rate as a competitive advantage, or a new brand with a competitive advantage enter the market, then the price structure is likely to go into disarray for a period as the new developments attempt to progress. Over the longer term the price structure will settle down again and its new form will depend very much on the degree of success enjoyed by the new developments.

For manufacturers competing in a mature market one of the most important questions must be: 'will competitors allow an established brand to change its position within the market price structure?' The follow-up question is: 'how can this be achieved without harming the brand or disturbing the market structure?' Again the strategy may plan for a change but it is in business operations that this very difficult manoeuvre has to be carried through. The questions receive attention in later paragraphs in this chapter, however, it is necessary that the subject of price dynamics receives consideration first. Also it is necessary to consider the two other *key* factors in this review – consumer response and competitive reaction.

PRICE DYNAMICS

Under this heading we are concerned with the movement of sales volume relative to the movement of price in a particular market, and very importantly, the price–sales volume relationship of the various brands competing in the market.

The price–sales volume relationship is often talked of in a manner which implies that it is a straight line. In the real life market-place it is much more likely to be a curve, whose actual depth and width varies from market to market, and from brand to brand.

■ *It is very important that the manufacturer should have a clear view of the price dynamics that apply within his markets and, even more important, that he should have a clear view of the price dynamics of his own brands.*

Some brands have a loyal group of consumers; they have to be wooed away from their chosen brand. Other brands have consumers who are much more willing to change, they are only loosely attached.

The manufacturer needs to know into which group his brand's consumers fit. He needs to be as sure as he can of the level of price elasticity that applies to his brands. If he has a sound knowledge as to how his brands fare in this respect he will be in a much stronger position in forming his pricing tactics.

Of course, it is also necessary that the manufacturer should have a sound knowledge as to how his competitors' brands measure in terms of price elasticity.

Research shows that one of the factors that is of consequence under this heading is brand personality. Where the *right* personality has been developed, so consumer loyalty is that much more firmly established.

How does the manufacturer find out how his brands stand? He can study in detail the effect of previous price adjustments. For his own brands he will have his actual sales and consumer research data, and for competitive brands he will have research data. He can study the effect of special price promotions for his own and competitive brands. He can also commission special research to provide him with guidance – in this respect, he should keep in mind one of the golden rules of price research: 'if you want to know what the consumer really feels, you must be sure he uses his own money.'

The manufacturer should also know, when he loses (or gains) volume following a brand price adjustment, just where the loss goes, or where the gain comes from. Does it come from competitive brands generally? Or does it come from one particular brand? Or from another brand in his own stable? These are important questions and while specific answers may be difficult to obtain, directional indications should certainly be possible.

There are a number of general guidelines that will help the manufacturer in his considerations. For instance, items that are purchased frequently are likely to be much more price-sensitive than infrequent purchase items. Necessities are more price-sensitive than luxury items. But the social or economic class of the consumer does not seem to be as significant a factor in price sensitivity as is popularly supposed.

■ *There is one elementary and basic rule which should always be kept well in mind when brand price comparisons and consumer reactions to price movements are considered: be sure your comparisons and other research data are in terms of their own money actually paid by traders and consumers for the brands concerned. This may not be the same as the prices that are quoted in the price-list or in other published data. Frequently price-list data will be later influenced by special discount arrangements and other forms of offer. These various trading agreements may have an important part to play in encouraging traders, and also possibly consumers, to enter into a special relationship with the manufacturer concerned. However, when considering consumer and trade reaction to price moves and competitive comparisons the actual money paid should form the basis of the studies.*

CONSUMER RESPONSE AND COMPETITIVE REACTION

When he moves his brand price the manufacturer has two specific areas where he can expect reaction. Both require his close attention and ideally he would like to be able to forecast accurately just what the reaction will be in each of them. One area concerns consumers

and the other his competitors. The interesting point is that the reactions are likely to move in opposite directions between favourable
and unfavourable for each of the groups depending upon whether
the price move is up or down.

Consumer response will be influenced by a number of factors, the
three most important are likely to be:

- The economic position within the country, in particular the
  buoyancy (or lack of buoyancy) of employment levels, and the
  general atmosphere with regard to price-levels. Where there is full
  employment, and a degree of inflation which means that prices
  move frequently, then a small increase in unit price may pass
  almost unnoticed. Where there is high unemployment and an
  almost static general price-level, then a small increase is likely to be
  noticed.
- Price movements within the particular market or market sector.
  Where there is frequent movement of price by the brands in the
  market, then another price move may be accepted without comment. Where the market has had a lengthy period without price
  movement, the first move is likely to get attention.
- The alternatives open to the consumer. The classic example often
  quoted concerns butter and margarine. If the price of butter rises,
  and margarine remains static, then a new competitive position has
  developed – some consumers will react to the new position and
  switch to margarine.

In general, when a brand price is raised the need is to minimize the
number of consumers who are likely to leave the brand and join a
competitor. When a brand moves its price down the requirement is
to maximize the number of new customers who can be tempted to try
the brand.

Normally, the manufacturer worries about the consumer response
to a price increase, but is more relaxed about a move down. He
should be concerned about moves in both directions, and take steps
to ensure that he does not lose on an increase and that he is getting
his money's worth from a reduction.

With competitive reaction the main concern is 'Will my competitors move with me, or will they leave me on my own?'

With a price increase, where the brand is the market leader competitors will frequently be pleased to follow, but they may take their

time. And if they do not follow it may be necessary to let them know this has been observed, and then to punish them.

If the market leader wishes to maintain a price discipline within his market, then the punishment may be very necessary.

If a brand is allowed to miss out on a price increase once, then it is possible that it will try the same move again. And if price is a material factor in changing brand market share and sales volume, the brand leader could find his dominant position slipping away from him.

Should the brand market leader move his price down, then he can expect the other brands in the market to follow. If they do not they will lose share and volume and their position will be further weakened.

Where a brand that is not a leader takes the initiative with either a price increase or decrease it should ensure it has *a line of retreat*. Without very firm data on the brand's price elasticity an increase could be very risky. The leader may decide to punish the brand, and other smaller brands are likely to extract as much extra business as possible out of their advantage. With a price increase, if a smaller brand leads then he may well be 'punished' by either the leader or the other small brands. There is much to be said for the smaller brands in a market 'following the leader' in price moves, unless exceptional conditions apply.

It is vitally important that the manufacturer keep the pressures and needs of his business with regard to brand price movements completely confidential. For instance, if the market leader ever lets it be known that a price increase for his brand is essential to him, then he could have given the smaller brands the opportunity to make him pay dearly. If they do not follow him he may be unable to punish them; once they know this, maintaining price discipline within the market could be impossible.

Similarly, smaller brands that let it be known that they are desperate for the revenue expected from a price increase may find themselves squeezed heavily.

■ *In chapter 5 the importance of knowing your competitors, knowing the people who manage competitive businesses, knowing their personalities, and how they might react in a given situation, was stressed. This applies most acutely to pricing – many of the shorter-term pricing decisions will hinge on the judgement of one individual within a competitive business. It could be very worthwhile to know his approach, his reasoning, and how he is likely to react in a particular circumstance.*

DIFFERENTIAL PRICING

A manufacturer may follow one of two broad approaches in the pricing of his brands to his trade customers. He may have a published price-list and have all of his customers purchase from it within the terms laid down. This does not mean they will necessarily all pay the same price, as the price-list may provide for volume discounts. But the discounts will be available to *all* customers who meet the volume requirements. This is often termed an 'open price-list approach'.

The second approach is known as 'differential pricing'. This means that the manufacturer will have a different price-level for each individual customer and the level will not necessarily be linked directly to volume.

The practical application of differential pricing frequently takes the form of the manufacturer having a price-list and from this he deducts an agreed level of discount for each customer, the level varying from customer to customer.

In some countries the law requires that manufacturers use a form of open price-list, but in many, including the UK, a differential approach may be used if it is considered advantageous.

■ *The decision as to which pricing approach to employ is of major consequence and should be regarded as a policy decision.*

To some considerable extent the decision will rest on the strength of the manufacturer's brands. If he has strong brands, including a number of market leaders, he is likely to opt for the open price-list approach. If his brands are weak he will almost certainly be forced toward differential pricing if he is to live.

We are concerned here with the operation of the two approaches, and how they might be used to gain an advantage.

Within the open list approach there is considerable skill required in structuring the list. The stages within the list are of consequence in that they can be set so that the retailer is encouraged to buy at a level at which the manufacturer prefers to sell and deliver. By manipulation of the stages he can encourage the smaller accounts to deal directly with him, or he can direct them toward area or regional distributors, as he chooses.

The open list is straightforward and protects the salesman from the continuous 'play-off' from big buyers looking for special concessions. Of course, there will be occasions where brands which are not leaders will be dropped by a retailer in favour of competitive brands where differential pricing has provided a much higher margin.

■ *Under the open-list approach the manufacturer can legitimately claim that he does not 'play favourites' among his customers. Providing his brands are secure, over time this approach should put him in a strong position and one that the traders will come to respect.*

For the manufacturer who opts for differential pricing the first, and vitally important, point is that he appreciates that he must keep all his dealings strictly confidential.

The reasoning behind the differential approach is that the manufacturer gives a better reward to those traders who co-operate with him than he does to those who are uncooperative. And this co-operation includes both stocking and featuring his brands. However, in practice, sheer buying power is often the key factor in deciding the extent of the differential negotiated with a particular trader.

The importance of confidentiality will be readily appreciated – without it the highest-level differential will soon become the going rate for all buyers.

Negotiating the level of differential is sure to be a difficult and problematical operation. The manufacturer will always be under pressure to give more. The requirement from him is to make as sure as he can that he is getting his money's worth from the discount payments he provides.

Frequently the discount (or 'over-rider', as it is sometimes known) is based on the achievement of a given level of sales volume. It is very much up to the manufacturer to ensure that the additional reward is earned and not something paid as the result of a buoyant market or a general development in business.

The differential approach is rarely completely satisfactory. Yet for ⁻he manufacturer with weak brands it may well become a necessity if he wants his brands to survive. As a limited number of retail chains get a firm grip on the bulk of the volume generated in a particular market, so it becomes essential that a brand should be stocked by a number of them if it is to have any prospect of surviving.

Unless a brand has a worthwhile consumer franchise, the odds in the manufacturer–retailer negotiations which consider it are heavily weighted in the retailer's favour.

■ *For the manufacturer who is highly skilled in negotiation, differential pricing can provide opportunities. It can be a means of obtaining vital volume, and it can be a way of building the strength of a brand which in itself can help cut the cost of the differential. But the negotiation needs to be highly skilled, completely confidential, and it should not be wasted on brands that are going to fail in any case.*

PRICE AND PROMOTIONS

In some markets there is very little promotional action. Prices are reasonably stable and theme advertising is the major field of activity. In other markets there is considerable promotional investment – every two or three months each major brand launches a new promotion. There are markets where the leading contestants reckon to sell say 80 per cent of their volume for the year in one major special offer in the first quarter, with others most of the sales volume is made in the autumn promotion period prior to Christmas.

In forming his brand-price tactics the manufacturer needs to be sure of the form of the market in which he competes, and also how he wants to compete within it.

If he wants to have his brand selling on promotion for a major part of the year then he needs to be sure his brand's price structure provides for this. Similarly, if he wants to sell the major part of his volume for the year at a discount in one month, he needs to provide for this in his pricing approach.

In effect, he needs to provide for what is often termed 'giving back'. His pricing must allow for a large proportion of his sales volume to be priced below his price-list level (in this respect a coupon, or a gift item for instance, will represent a form of price reduction).

Markets that are growing rapidly, and where there is a continuous movement into the market of new users, often respond to heavy promotional attack. Part of the value of the promotion is that it can command display and feature space in the retail stores. A price discount is often a key factor within a total promotional package.

A consideration of a rather different nature, but nevertheless one involving price and promotion, is that which recommends that a price adjustment (in particular a price increase) should be made at a time when the brand is carrying, or is about to carry, a major promotion.

In effect, this is an attempt to cushion the price increase. The reasoning is that with the promotional offer as the main feature, the consumer is less likely to notice, and to react against, the price increase.

In a market where there is very heavy promotional activity, it will be almost impossible for a price increase not to coincide with promotional pack on display in the stores.

There can be little doubt that the impact of the promotion will act to cushion the pricing move. But it will probably merely delay the consumer reaction – although, on occasions, the delay could be helpful to the manufacturer. Of course, it is also possible that the move may blunt the promotion.

PRICE BREAKS

The one pence difference between 99p and 100p is much greater than that between 95p and 96p! The fact is that in many of the consumer package goods markets, a brand priced at 99p would sell at a much faster rate than it would at 100p. And, very importantly, its sales level against its competitors would improve if it was priced at 99p against their 100p.

Similar remarks apply for prices such as £1.99 or 29p. There is considerable research evidence to show that these 'price breaks' can be dramatic in their effect on consumer buying behaviour. Frequently the real money difference is very small (the 1p between £1.99 and £2.00 is less than 1 per cent), but the change in sales volume the lower price generates can be substantial.

It follows that if a manufacturer can arrange for his brands to be priced by retailers at the right position for the break he may gain an advantage. Where the manufacturer owns the retail outlets through which his brands pass to the consumer then he can arrange for the prices to be pitched at the advantageous levels. This is, of course, one of the major advantages possessed by distributor brands. Where a system of retail price maintenance is enforced then the manufacturer can, if he wishes, set the retail price of his brands at levels which are well positioned for the price break. But the owning of retail shops by the manufacturer, and the enforcement of retail price maintenance, are the exception: most manufacturers sell through retail outlets which are owned by retailers and retail price maintenance is not enforced.

Where the majority of his retailers are known to take a certain level of margin on his brand, then the manufacturer can arrange his own pricing so that the final retail price is at the level he prefers. But in practice this will often be a most difficult operation to arrange. Any one retailer is unlikely to take the same margin on a brand all the time, and a series of retailers would be most unlikely to have the same margin for a brand over a lengthy period.

■ *It is with his periodic special discounts that the manufacturer can make his main effort to ensure that his brand's retail price is positioned at a desirable break level. Firstly, he can ensure that the level of discount he provides to his normal price gives a net level that allows a well-positioned retail price. Secondly, he can ensure that his salesmen in their trade negotiations use the discount in a positive manner to encourage traders to set retail prices at the right break level.*

PACK-SIZE PRICING

The manufacturer may like to get the same percentage level of contributory margin from each one of the brand pack-sizes he markets, and in this way he need not be unduly concerned which size pack the consumer decides to buy.

It can, of course, be questioned whether or not this is a desirable position for a manufacturer to aim for. The question is academic as the position is most unlikely to arise.

In considering his pack size pricing the manufacturer needs to be aware of two key considerations. The first of these is of a public relations nature, and the second is very much concerned with gaining additional market share and sales volume.

Consumers have come to expect that whenever they buy a bigger size of a pack they should pay a lower price per ounce or per pound or whatever measure applies. Thus, if the 8 oz pack sells for 10p then the 16 oz pack would be expected to sell for less than 20p. This may be annoying for the manufacturer as the larger pack is not necessarily cheaper per oz to produce. However, this practice is very firmly established with both traders and consumers and the manufacturer could be unwise to disregard it.

■ *Just as you should put your major effort behind your brand when its market is in its growth stage, so also should you put your major effort behind the brand pack-size which is experiencing the fastest growth.*

A typical pack-size development for a brand is for it to be introduced to the consumer through a relatively small pack, of say 8 oz. The consumer can quickly be persuaded to trade up to a 16 oz size, and then when he is an established user the move up to say a 32 oz size can take place.

During the early stage the need is to be aggressive with the small 8 oz size. The all-important consumer trial will probably come from this pack. During the early period the requirement is that it should be stocked and featured at a special trial price.

The major activity will quickly pass to the 16 oz size. It will offer the consumer sufficient stock of the product to cover his regular shopping visits, and encourage him to use the brand more frequently in his home.

At this time the 16 oz pack needs to be stocked and to carry the special offers. Now the small size is unlikely to be promoted, unless there is a steady stream of new users entering the market. At this time the small size contributory percentage margin per unit is likely to move well ahead of the 16 oz size.

The 32 oz size is for the large quantity users who are prepared to be loyal to the brand for a longer period. Its percentage contributory margin per unit will almost certainly be the lowest of the three packs. As the market develops so this pack will take a higher proportion of the special pack – the unit percentage contributory margins of both the 8 oz and 16 oz packs will rise moving well ahead of the 32 oz.

This is a very general description of how a brand's pack size activity is likely to move in a typical growth market. It would not necessarily apply in a country where consumers' purchasing power is very low and where the trade is concentrated in small shops. In such circumstances small sizes tend to be much more popular.

If the manufacturer wishes to obtain an advantage from the use of his pack sizes he should take care to ensure that he is strong and fully competitive in the *right* pack at the *right* time. He should be prepared, if necessary, to support the *right* size by taking a lower percentage level of contribution per unit, balancing this with higher levels on other sizes.

Apart from the part it can play in the market-place battle in attracting 'switchers' to the brand and providing them with an extended trial, the other great contribution of the larger size is binding the consumer to the brand for a longer period, lessening the likelihood that he will go out of stock, and encouraging a more frequent and greater consumption. It also acts to protect the brand from competitive attack. These are valuable brand advantages, but they may have to be paid for with a lower unit margin. The manufacturer should take care that his payment is at a reasonable level, and that he makes it work.

EVALUATING THE RISK

For what we are discussing in this section the term 'risk' is probably a misnomer. We are concerned here with putting a financial value on the probable effect on volume of a price movement, and providing for this to be expressed as a percentage level of current sales over a selected period.

Many executives are helped in their consideration of the proposal if the profit contribution return from a price increase is expressed in terms such as: 'If we increase price by 5 per cent we can lose up to 20 per cent of volume and still retain our profitability.' (The volume would normally be considered over a relatively short period such as six months.)

From such a statement the executive can get a *feel* for the downside risk. He can feel, for instance, that at worst he is unlikely to lose short-term profitability from the move.

The calculation is, of course, a rough one and would employ the shorter-term variable unit cost of the brand, as shown in the following example:

> Brand A's current sales price is 100p
> Price increase proposed is 5 per cent: new price 105p
> Variable cost per unit of brand is 80p
> Six-months sales volume is 10,000 units
> Break-even volume on price increase is
> $$\frac{10,000 \times 20}{25} = 8,000 \text{ units}$$

The effect of changes in volume and price increase on the profit contribution over the period for the brand in the example is shown below and in figure 13.1.

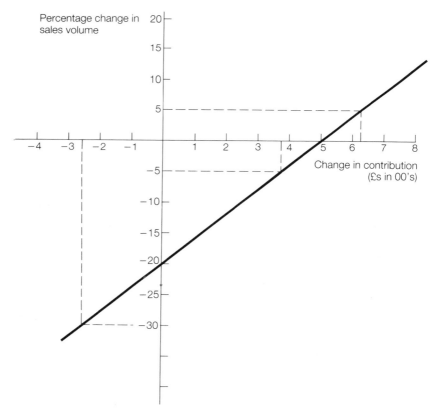

Figure 13.1   The effect of sales volume change on profit contribution

+ 5% volume means +£625
− 5% volume means +£375
−20% volume breaks even
−30% volume means −£250

Similar examples can be drawn up to show the level of volume increase that is necessary to maintain profitability for a price decrease.

It should be stressed that this statement is merely a *rough* guide. It can help provide perspective between proposals for various levels of increase with varying possible volume outcomes.

PROVIDING FOR A RETREAT

A medium-sized manufacturer with a brand placed near the middle of the market incurs a series of cost increases. He needs a price increase to restore his level of profitability. He feels his competitors in the market must also need a price increase, but he cannot be sure. If he leads with his own move, and others do not follow, he could suffer a fall in market share and volume, and have his profitability reduced to an uncomfortably low level.

In these circumstances, if the manufacturer instanced decides to move his brand price it is important that he leaves himself *an avenue for retreat* should he need it.

■ *The first and most important point to make is that in circumstances of this kind pride should not be allowed to enter into the manufacturer's action plan. He may have misjudged his competitors' need for an increase, they may be holding back to pick up his business, it really isn't necessarily important why they haven't moved. What is of consequence is that his brand's share and volume is at risk and he must act to rescue it. He must get his position right and swallow any pride that may be involved.*

Ideally, he needs to be able to withdraw his increase with a sensible dignity so that his trade relationships are maintained and his own staff morale is not unduly damaged.

One approach is for him to give a lengthy notice of increase, as this will allow him time to withdraw without causing confusion.

He can use trade bonuses extensively for a period – but he may have to give these at a rate higher than his increase. This approach can work over the shorter term but it could become confusing over a longer period and it may be expensive.

There are other shorter-term moves available to the manufacturer. The important consideration is that when he moves he does so decisively, with confidence, and with clarity – if he hesitates and is not clear he could cause trade confusion and this can be very costly. He may have a position where he fails to get his price increase and loses his volume.

For the very small operator the problem is in part alleviated as he is probably operating some form of differential pricing. This will allow him to apply his increase in different places at different times. Even so, the small operator is unlikely to enjoy the position of price leader.

For the market leader the position is very different. Providing his increase is within a reasonable limit he is unlikely to be thinking in terms of a retreat. However, if he wishes to maintain price discipline within the market he may have to teach a lesson to any of his competitors who do not follow him within a reasonable time period. This may be costly for him over the shorter term, but if he believes price discipline has a value then it could be a good investment.

PRICE WARS

When the brands competing in a market engage in widespread price cutting, and this continues for a lengthy period of time, it is often termed a 'price war.'

■ *Price wars can be started deliberately or by accident. To start a price war deliberately is a strategic move. It should follow a detailed research of the circumstances which apply within the market and of the competitors involved. The manufacturer concerned should have come to the conclusion that a price war is for him the most effective way to achieve a particular strategic objective. Before he makes his move he should be as sure as is possible that he will win.*

Operations are involved in putting this strategy into effect. A high level of skill and judgement will be paramount for a successful action. In particular, research into competitors, to show their financial strength, and just how much the particular market means to them, will be of vital importance.

If this homework has been carried out competently and the manufacturer has ensured that he has the necessary resources available himself, then an effective operator should be able to carry the move through and achieve his objective. However, he must be prepared for surprises. Under price-war pressures desperate moves are often made, and they can have surprising effects.

A price war that arises accidentally is a very different matter. A salesman reports that a buyer has informed him a competitor is reducing his price. Another salesman picks up the same story, and then a market researcher reports in similar vein. Action is taken on this information, and soon the whole market is involved with prices spiralling down. Later it transpires that the early reports from the salesmen were false rumours.

For any manufacturer who wants to compete actively in his markets a sensitive and efficient field reporting arrangement is essential. However to be of value the reporting must be accurate. Rumours should be reported, they can often be the prelude to an official announcement. But the rumours should be verified before they become the basis for action. An accidental price war can be an expensive and futile exercise for everyone involved.

How should a manufacturer whose brand is caught up in a price war, fight the battle? Of course, it depends very much on his circumstances. The general aim must be to fight in such a way that you hold your market share and limit your expenditures while your competitors are forced to spend heavily and make no gain.

The need is to ensure that you use your resources where you are likely to have an advantage. That you fight, as far as possible, on your home ground and that you retain the initiative through the course of the battle.

If you are the small man in the battle then you use those advantages that your size affords you. Flexibility is one such advantage that should be yours. You can use special packs prepared at short notice. If you employ differential pricing then you use this with *key* accounts and work to ensure you get all the help and assistance normally accorded to the small man.

If you are the big man then you employ the economy of scale which is yours and should provide you with lower unit costs for standard product. You avoid being thrown off your main line of attack, and you take care to be sensibly patient. You know that you are in a position to give the consumer *best value* over the medium term and so you play the game accordingly. You have greater resources and time should be on your side.

■ *Two basic points are of significance under this heading. If you are the small man and your business intelligence tells you that you are likely to be the subject of a price attack then you could be well advised to consider selling your business or merging it with a strong partner. You are likely to get a much better price and your brands have a better chance of survival, if you do this before the attack rather than after.*

Secondly, in price wars, as in all business battles of this kind, the business that is effective and efficient in its operations is much more likely to survive and prosper than is one that is ineffective.

PRICE ADJUSTMENT: EXTENT AND FREQUENCY

When a manufacturer makes a price adjustment there must always be a degree of risk. No matter how thorough his research and testing, when he makes his move in the market-place he can never be completely sure as to how his competitors will react or how the consumer will behave. All price adjustments create a certain degree of management apprehension, but it is with price increases that the greater level of unease usually occurs.

The purpose of a price increase is not to bring a high degree of risk to a brand; the purpose is to increase the revenue coming from the brand without damaging its sales volume or market standing. Indeed, in planning and forming a price increase proposal the aim should be to minimize the risk to the brand.

Major price increases tend to unsettle consumers, who start questioning whether or not the brand continues to be *best-value*. They provide a reason for trying an alternative brand.

If a brand is priced at 100p for five years and then makes a move up to 150p it is likely to be at considerable risk. To many of its customers the fact that its price has been unchanged for five years will be forgotten, the fact that it has increased in price by 50 per cent will get their attention.

■ *Major price increases attract attention, and put the brand at risk. They should be avoided. Smaller price increases are much more likely to pass without undue attention, they do not disturb the brand's performance–price balance to any great extent, and they put the brand at very much less risk. Smaller price increases are to be preferred. In the example quoted above it is suggested that the brand concerned would have been at much less risk if it had made an increase of 10p each year over the five-year period.*

Clearly there will be a need to balance extent with frequency. In the example, would it have been better to have moved by 5p every half year instead of 10p per year? It is very difficult to provide a specific answer, as so much will depend on the general movement of prices and the movement of prices in the specific market. In terms of avoiding unsettling customers a 5p increase is to be preferred to a 10p one – the question therefore centres on whether or not half-yearly is too high a frequency. Again a specific answer is difficult, so much will depend on the particular circumstances which apply at the time.

Key points

1 Price is a *key* factor in setting the level of a brand's unit margin. It is also a key factor in determining a brand's volume. It follows that price is of major significance in determining the brand's profit contribution.

2 Price is also a key factor within the brand's *best-value* equation. Beware of moving a brand's price against the reasoning of the *best-value* concept.

3 Price is an important *tool* of strategy. Used skilfully it can secure the longer-term position of a brand; used carelessly it can provide a competitor with a major opportunity. All operational price moves should have the brand's longer-term price objective in mind.

4 Know the price dynamics of your own and competitive brands. When you lose business on a price move find out where it has gone. And when you gain check where the gain comes from.

5 Beware of using price offensively unless you have a competitive advantage in unit costs, or you know that your competitors are unable, or unwilling, to respond to your price moves.

6 Where you have a strong, well-positioned brand with a significant competitive advantage in unit cost, and your market is growing, you should consider using price to help you secure market dominance. Such a move could pay off handsomely over the longer term.

7 If your brand is one of the smaller brands in the market then in all probability your best course of action in pricing will be to 'follow the leader'. But if you know he (the leader) badly needs the revenue from the price move then you may be able to make him worry, and improve your own position.

8 If you are the market leader and you want to maintain a price discipline in the market then you must ensure you punish those brands which do not follow your lead. If they get away once, then they will try again, and soon there will be no discipline.

9 Never start a price war unless you are very sure you are going to win it.

10 If, despite the fact that you have a small brand, you are forced to become a price leader in your market, be sure to provide an avenue for retreat. And if it is necessary for you to make use of the avenue don't let pride get in your way.

11 Large price increases carry a higher degree of risk than do small ones. Providing they do not necessitate an unduly high frequency, smaller increases should be used. The objective of a price increase is not to undertake major risk, but to increase the brand's revenue and to limit the risk to market share and volume.

12 A significant competitive advantage in price can be of great importance to a brand. Price is one of the most powerful of the marketing *tools*. Used positively and with skill it can be a major factor in a brand's growth, and in the development of its profit contribution. Used carelessly, it can greatly damage a brand and provide a competitor with a major opportunity.

14

◇

The Trade, the Sales
Force, and Distribution

◆

THE TRADE

Times and positions change. There was a period, not many years ago, when the manufacturer in the UK was king. He had a large, well-financed organization and he distributed his brands to his ultimate customers through many thousands of small retail outlets each of which would transact less than one per cent of his business. When the brands were strongly advertised the small retailers were almost bound to stock and display them. And if a few of them decided against stocking then it was not a matter that caused the manufacturer serious concern.

Through the forty-year period 1950–90 there has been a dramatic change in the positions of the retailer and the manufacturer in almost every developed country of the world.

Many thousands of small retail stores have been replaced by a limited number of large superstores. Each one of these new superstores is capable of a turnover equal to that of many hundreds of the old small outlets. Of the small stores that are left very few now trade directly with manufacturers, they buy either through cash-and-carry warehouses or wholesale groups.

The big stores have owners who are large companies, well financed, and professionally managed. Frequently they are much bigger organizations than are the manufacturers who supply them.

The indications are that the current trends will continue. The big stores will increase in number and they will take even more of the consumers' total spending. And the number of owners of big stores will tend to decrease, putting more and more of the total business into the hands of fewer and fewer major companies.

■ *Times and positions change. The manufacturer is no longer king, and he must be fully aware of this change if he is to operate successfully.*

THE TRADE AND OPERATIONS

By far the majority of manufacturers distribute their brands to their consumers through the trade. The term 'the trade' is normally used to describe the retailers and wholesalers who buy and sell the particular category of products in which the manufacturer is interested. There is a grocery trade, a jewellery trade, a sports trade, and so on.

With the development of the very large superstores the demarcation line between the various trades may have become blurred. But even the big stores are likely to arrange their buying under trade headings.

Here we are concerned with an analysis of the structure, the form, and the effectiveness of the trade. We are also concerned with the way trade is moving, and in particular how it is likely to move during the operating period. We are looking for ways of creating a competitive advantage out of a superior handling of the trade.

The trade is the same for all the manufacturers competing in a market. There are the same number of superstores, small stores, cash-and-carry warehouses, etc. available to all. The same buyers and store managers are involved with the brands of all the manufacturers.

The important requirement for the manufacturer is that he uses operating resources effectively and efficiently to get the best results from the trade for his brands. However, before he can do this he must make a study of the trade so that he can be sure just where, when, and how he should use his operating resources. If he carries out this analysis skilfully, plans wisely and then follows through effectively in his operations, he will greatly enhance his chance of obtaining a competitive advantage in his total trade operation.

■ *It is important to appreciate that the study must go beyond a detailed review of the numbers. The numbers are, of course, of consequence; but the need will be to go behind them and, in particular, to consider the managers in the trade who generate those numbers. Their aims and objectives, how they are likely to react to a particular form of business proposition, and how they are likely to behave in given circumstances, are all vitally important considerations.*

In any consideration of the trade, there are three basic questions that must be answered:

- Who does the business?
- Were is it done?
- How and when is it done?

In this context, the term 'business' is used to describe the sale to the consumer of the brands and products which make up the market or markets in which the manufacturer is interested.

Who does the business?

This requires an analysis of the total market, firstly into ownership type, e.g. multiple chain, wholesale group, cash-and-carry wholesaler, independent store.

The second requirement is an analysis of each class into in-dividual concerns. For instance, the multiple chains should each be named and their share and value of the business itemized. Most im-portantly, the trend of the business over recent years should be shown.

Beyond this there is a need to analysis each concern in detail. How many stores has it got? What kind of stores are they? Who manages the concern? Who takes the *key* decisions? How is the chain planning to develop? What are the main policies it follows in its business?

This leads through to a forecast of the business the particular concern is expected to do in the operating periods ahead, an examina-tion of the opportunities it presents, and how they should be best exploited.

The aim is to build up a detailed account of every concern doing, or likely to do, a worthwhile amount of business in the market.

Details of the special policies of concern are important for they may provide an opportunity for an exploitation. For instance: Do they allow merchandisers into their stores? Do they encourage coupon acceptance? and so on.

Beyond this it is important to know the *key* measures used by the concern. For instance, are they very conscious of profit per square foot of floor space? Is a straight percentage of *sales* their measure? Or is *volume* their main aim?

A further consideration of significance is the concern's attitude to own-label (distributor) brands. Do they rate as a major factor in the business? Are they sold aggressively, or in a passive manner? What is the performance–price relationship of their brands? What is their share of market in the stores?

Where is the business done?

Firstly, an analysis by volume and concern on a regional basis. Who is strong in the north? Who dominates the south west?, questions of this kind should be answered by the analysis.

The second requirement is to carry the analysis through to store type. How big a share of the market do the superstores hold? Are the small independents still of significance in the north west? This type of question should be answered.

With the superstores it should be possible to get a good idea of the extent of the business (within the market) transacted in each particular store and, from this, a guide as to the share of market held by, for instance, the top 100 stores. Similarly detailed data should be possible on wholesale groups and cash and carry operators.

How and when is the business done?

Is the business spread evenly over the year with sales made at standard prices? Or is it made spasmodically with big sales made at specific times on a special offer basis?

Do promotions play a major part in obtaining sales? Are individual brands promoted heavily? Or is the aim a good competitive position without major variation through the year?

For particular concerns – is advertising a feature of the concern's operation? Do they engage in co-operative advertising promotions? Are weekly sales concentrated over one or two days, or are they spread evenly through the week?

From a series of questions of this type it should be possible to build up a complete picture of the general position within the market, and then to go beyond this and to form a detailed analysis for each major concern operating in the retail wholesale market.

Research data providing answers to these questions can be obtained from a number of sources. Much of it appears in the form of information issued by the retail trade associations. Reports can be purchased from the professional marketing research companies. The company's own records should also provide a considerable amount of useful guideline data.

Data on the retail concern's financial position should be available from published accounts. Details on policy factors, development plans, and personnel can often be contributed by the manufacturer's own staff who have a frequent contact with the particular concern.

With the data which provides answers to these various questions, and the help of a suitable computer, it should be possible for the manufacturer to build up a form of data bank on the trade.

The purpose of collecting and analysing this trade data is that it should provide guidance to the opportunities that are available for the company's brands through the trade. A well-designed computer programme should provide for information to be withdrawn rapidly and for operational programmes which plan for an effective exploitation to be built up.

The aim is to ensure that the sales force, and other resources, are used in the place, in the manner, and at the time they can expect to bring optimum results for the company's brands.

Key points

1 The dramatic change in position between the manufacturer and the retailer over the last 40 years means that now the manufacturer should never take anything with the trade for granted.

2 At one time a high level of store distribution for a well advertised brand was considered automatic. Now, it certainly isn't automatic. But a satisfactory level of store distribution remains vitally important for a brand, as also is a reasonable frequency of brand feature. Now these, and other trade requirements, have to be planned and worked for.

3 There will be competitive market-place battles between the various retailers and wholesalers who compete in your markets. There will be winners and losers in these battles. You need to have good business relations with all the retailers and wholesalers, but in particular you need to be well acquainted with the winners. Be sure you know who the winners are likely to be as they will be important in the future.

4 Know your retail and wholesale customers well, in particular know the managers who design and control their operations. Work to ensure the business propositions offered to the trade provide for mutual benefit and progress, and are better than those of your competitors. In this way you can build a competitive advantage through the trade.

5 This certainly does not mean you give the trade everything they want — it does mean you never take them for granted.

THE SALES FORCE

When the grocery trade in the UK was made up of over 100,000 small independently owned and managed stores each one required an individual sales call, each one was able to decide whether or not a particular brand should be stocked, and each one took a personal decision on which brands should be featured and displayed. Similar positions applied in most other trades.

During this period a manufacturer who possessed a large, well trained and disciplined sales force, one that was able to call directly on a high proportion of the 100,000 stores, could often have a competitive advantage based on the sheer size and ability of his sales force.

There have been dramatic changes in the structure of the 'trade' and in the new circumstances the possession of a large sales force is unlikely to represent a competitive advantage, indeed it could well be a disadvantage for a large sales force is now a very costly resource to maintain.

However, competitive advantages can still be achieved in the selling area, but now they need to be created and developed in a different manner. Sheer numbers and a strong discipline are no longer enough.

THE BASIC JOB

The structure, the form, the size, and the method of operating for the sales force may have changed considerably over the years but the basic job required of it has changed very little:

1   To ensure store distribution of the brand;

2   To obtain brand feature, i.e. prominent display, in appropriate
    positions within the stores;
3   To obtain competitive brand pricing.

■ *Consumer penetration is vitally important for a brand. The most
effective way to increase sales volume is to increase brand penetration. Consumer brand penetration is invariably linked
directly with brand store distribution. This is understandable; if
the brand isn't available in his regular store the consumer is
unlikely to buy and try it. The brand advertising may be highly
persuasive, the promotions very attractive, but if the brand fails to
get an adequate distribution, they will be in part wasted.*

Two measures of brand distribution are usually employed. The first,
known as *actual* distribution, measures the number of stores stocking
the brand and expresses this as a percentage of the total number of
stores in the particular category. Thus, a brand may be stocked by
25,000 stores out of a total of 50,000, i.e. an *actual* distribution of 50
per cent.

The second measure, and usually the more important one, is
known as *sterling* or *turnover* distribution. This is concerned with the
percentage of the total turnover covered by the stores where the
brand is stocked. It appreciates that some stores are much bigger than
others, they have a larger turnover, and can be expected to sell a
greater volume of the various brands they stock. The brand quoted
above may have an actual distribution of 50 per cent, but if the stores
in which it is stocked are the larger ones then its *sterling* distribution
could be 75 per cent or possibly higher.

The first requirement is that the brand should be stocked, the next
is that it should be featured. This means that the brand will be
stocked in the right quantity, at the right price, and in the best position in the store. And when it isn't on feature display, then it should
have the best position on the store shelves.

A prominent in-store feature can make a dramatic difference to the
consumer off-take of a brand. It can act as a strong stimulant to brand
trial.

■ *In the majority of instances the price the consumer pays for a
brand is decided by the retailer; however, the salesmen can have
an influence on the retailer's decision. The way the salesman*

presents his brand will be important, the way he talks about its record, its advertising and promotions support, and its potential, these and other brand factors will be of consequence to the retailer in taking his price decision.

COMPETITIVE ADVANTAGE

How can the manufacturer get a competitive advantage in selling given the new circumstances which apply within the retail trade? For a very small number of manufacturers the large, well-organized, trained and disciplined sales force may still be the answer. Some markets continue to have a place for this form of sales organization. But they are very few, and the manufacturers who are able to follow the approach with any success are now a special minority. The majority of manufacturers will have to work for a competitive advantage in other directions.

The limited number of big stores, which are the *key* to a high level of brand *sterling* distribution, are controlled by a relatively small number of multiple chains. Entry to the large number of independently owned smaller stores, which go to make up a large proportion of *actual* store distribution, is controlled by a limited number of cash-and-carry wholesalers and wholesale buying organizations.

The executives within these organizations who have the authority to buy brands and to allocate brand feature opportunities in the various retail outlets which they control, are clearly vitally important people to the manufacturer.

■ *It is suggested that for the majority of manufacturers, if they are to gain a competitive advantage in sales force operation, it must come through their handling of the* key *group of executives who control access to the major and smaller stores throughout the country.*

A competitive advantage in selling must eventually show its worth in the performance of the brands concerned in the market-place. Whilst success in individual stores may be of significance they are unlikely to register in terms of brand market share movement. Success with the *key* executives will certainly register in terms of market-share movement.

From the selling viewpoint the performance with the *key* accounts is all about the performance of a relatively small number of salesmen. Of course, the results they obtain will be greatly influenced by the advertising, the promotion, the brand pricing and ultimately by the brand's total ability to win the customers *best-value* test.

■ *But the salesman's contribution is vitally important. He can take a good brand proposition and get complete distribution with strong feature through a particular chain, or he can fail to get acceptance. The manufacturer's aim should be to assemble a truly top class group of salesmen to handle the key accounts.*

BUSINESS PROPOSITIONS

The executives who control the group superstores, major supermarkets and cash-and-carry warehouses are unlikely to have received a formal training in the practices of the old-style grocery or other established trade. Essentially they are business men intent on using the resources available to them in an effective and efficient manner to achieve their particular objectives. Normally this will mean that they are concerned with making as much profit as possible, although in the shorter term they may have other objectives such as sales volume and market share.

In particular the retail executive will want to use his space effectively. To make profit he must get the consumers' custom, and before he can get this he must attract them into the store. It follows that certain parts of his space may concentrate on profit making while other parts will provide consumer attraction. Of course, if the executive is skilful he may be able to use much of his space to both make profit and attract customers.

■ *When a salesman makes a sales presentation to a retailer he is, in effect, making a claim for part of the retailer's space. In essence he is saying to the retailer 'My brands can work for you if you will give them your space. They can help you achieve your objectives.'*

This is a major part of the skill of the *key* account salesman, forming a presentation for his brands that will help the retailer achieve his (the retailer's) objectives.

Firstly, he must know what the objectives of his customer (the retailer) are. If he is a good salesman he will have an intimate knowledge of the account. He will know the objectives of the business and he will know how the buyer is working to achieve these objectives. When the buyer is looking for a feature to attract a particular kind of consumer the salesman will know of this, and when the buyer is looking for an opportunity to make a higher profit contribution the salesman will also know. And in addition he will know the buyer well, he will be aware of his timing needs, of how he tends to reason when he makes his decisions, and of the pressures he may be under.

The salesman will also know his own objectives for his brands. When a brand is looking for extensive in-store sampling he will know the form of feature it needs, and similarly when it requires a strong defensive promotion he will know.

Beyond this the *key* account salesman should have other relevant information available to him. He should know just how various forms of in-store feature have performed for his brands in other stores. He should know of the advertising backing his brands are to receive, of the consumer promotions they are mounting, and he should be aware of how this support can help brand sales. In particular he should know of the sales that feature support can bring for the retailer and the brand.

The salesman should be aware of the trends that are taking place within his markets and he should also know how his competitors are reacting to these developments. Most importantly he should be completely on top of the price terms he is able to offer the buyer in return for varying levels of co-operation.

Armed with this information the *key* account salesman must now put together a business proposition for his brand or brands for each individual account with which he is concerned.

His task is firstly to decide on the opportunity within the particular account that he intends to exploit, and then to formulate a proposition that meets the opportunity (i.e. it gives the buyer the benefits he is looking for), and meets the requirements of his (the salesman's) brands.

The cynic may argue that in the final analysis the success or failure of a business proposition will depend on the level of price discount the salesman is prepared to give.

Price discounts will certainly be of consequence. But it would be very wrong to suppose that they are the only factor of significance or even the most important consideration. There are many other issues that can be of at least equal importance, just which ones they are will vary from account to account and from time to time; part of the salesman's skill is contained in his ability to recognize which issues should apply for each individual account on the particular occasion.

Having formed his business proposition the second major skill of the *key* account salesman is his ability to present and negotiate it successfully.

■ *Successful negotiation is clearly both a science and an art. A superior knowledge of a whole series of relevant facts, together with an ability to use these facts in a positive and effective manner, are among the important assets the good negotiator must possess.*

There is an additional skill required of the salesman and this is the ability to ensure that he follows through the deal he has negotiated. This simply means that he ensures that his own company meets the terms of the agreement, and also that his customer meets the terms. When your customer holds, say, 25 per cent of your company's total business, ensuring that he follows through requires a very special form of tact and firmness, but it is essential for real success. If a customer fails to meet his responsibilities once, then he may fail again, and this could become a habit.

SPECIAL PACKS: STORE DISTRIBUTION

When a brand mounts a promotion a well-directed store distribution of the promoted pack will be essential if the promotion is to be competely successful.

Frequently the promotion will involve the issue of a special pack carrying an offer such as, 'Introductory offer – Save 50p', when the price of the pack is reduced by 50p. A promotion of this kind can be of strategic importance to the brand and involve a major investment. It will be vitally important that the resource involved be used effectively.

One of the key factors in deciding the level of effectiveness achieved by the promotion is sure to centre on the way the sales force manage the distribution of the special pack.

The prime objective of the promotion should be clearly defined and this must be the leading consideration for the sales force in planning their store distribution. If the objective is widespread sampling of not less than 30 per cent of homes in an area which contains some

10 million homes, then the promotion will need to issue a minimum of 3 million packs (in fact, more than this will be necessary to cover for unavoidable double sampling etc.) and these will need to be placed with stores throughout the area. To obtain widespread sampling the pack will need to be sold, in proportion to their customer throughput, to all the stores in the area, and not to any one type or class of ownership.

If the aim of the promotion is to gain distribution of the brand through the independant trade in a particular region, then the special pack should be sold in suitable quantities to the wholesalers in that region (and not to the multiple trade outlets).

Should the promotion be one that requires large-scale prominent display then it should be sold heavily into retail outlets (e.g. superstores) that are able to meet the requirement.

■ *It will be readily appreciated that the indiscriminate selling of special pack, particularly if it is of high offer value, can be a very wasteful and expensive activity. The salesman who sells all his allocation at his first and favourite account call may win a competition for the speed of selling his quota, but he is unlikely to help in the achievement of the promotions objective, and he could have wasted a valuable resource.*

Frequently the manufacturer will find that in his desire to issue what is considered to be a 'satisfactory' quantity of a special pack, and remain within his appropriation, he will be guilty of allowing the unit-offer value to drop to an unduly low level. A skilfully designed store distribution plan for the special pack can often show that a lower quantity of the pack will be fully adequate to meet the objective, and the unit offer value can be held at the optimum level to get the best results with the consumer.

Sales management has an important double responsibility under this heading of 'special pack distribution':

1 To play a constructive part in deciding just how much special pack should be issued in the promotion;
2 To formulate plans which ensure that the sales force has clear guidance as to where the special packs can work most effectively (i.e. store types, concerns, etc.) and how much should be placed in these outlets.

HOW MANY BRANDS CAN A SALESMAN SELL?

The operative word in this question is *sell* as distinct from merely taking an order.

Within the strategy formulation process, as the company plans to develop its existing brands and to introduce new ones, the question should be asked: 'will our sales force be carrying so many brands that it will fail to do a satisfactory job on any one of them?' If the unsatisfactory job applies only to a limited number of dying and relatively unimportant small brands then the problem is not acute. But if the failure goes beyond this then corrective action will be necessary.

If there is a problem under this heading, then it is really a strategic issue. In fact, a good strategist will not wait for the problem to arise; he will have seen it well in advance, and turned it into an opportunity to provide a superior sales force for his brands.

The terms 'simplify' and 'concentrate' have become linked with successful business and with successful operations. There can be little doubt that if you keep your operations simple, and concentrate your resources on a limited number, then your chances of success will be greatly increased.

Selling certainly is *not* an exception to this general rule. When a good salesman has a basically simple proposition to make, and he is able to concentrate on a limited number of brands, then his performance should be at a high level.

Over the last forty years or so the development of sales organizations in the UK has tended to move through three stages. In the early period there were many thousands of small stores to be called upon, and salesmen were relatively inexpensive to maintain. A successful call on a small store demanded a strong, well-directed, sales approach. There were many large sales forces within the country.

The second stage saw the beginning of the concentration of buying power, a great reduction in the number of small stores, and an increase in the cost of maintaining a sales force. There was a marked reduction in number of large sales organizations.

The third stage has seen an even greater concentration of buying power. If the grocery trade in the UK is used as an example, it will be seen that a very small number of *key* buyers now control over 80 per cent of the business. A small group of salesmen can cover this select band of *key* buyers and, when successful, provide access for their brands to by far the majority of UK customers.

This means that in a growing business with an expanding list of brands one of the approaches the strategist should consider for his sales force is that of divisionalization. Instead of one force carrying both household products and toiletries a two force approach could be used. And if the household products list becomes unduly long then this could be split into, say a household cleaning division and a clothes cleaning division.

The reasoning here is that the divisional salesman will be able to simplify and concentrate his efforts, and out of this will come extra business which will more than take care of any additional expenses.

While the strategist should list this topic as one to be covered, it is a consideration which is very close to the operator. He is in a good position to appreciate when the sales force is 'overloaded' and when this is having, or is likely to have, a material effect on results.

The development of the business may mean a growth in the number of brands marketed. The operators must learn to handle this increase. They must organize so that the necessary simplification and concentration can be applied; the business should not stop growing merely because some of its operators find growth difficult to cope with.

■ *Simplification in operations is a matter for which operators are, in the main, responsible. They should at all times guard against the cardinal error of* over complexity. *As the sales drive for each brand develops so additions are made to the promotions, extra trade incentives are added, small consumer offers are tacked on to the main offer, special packs are introduced for short periods, and so on. These moves may seem reasonable in themselves, but together they bring complications, each one small in its own right, but when totalled together they are of significance, and they can have a marked effect on the performance of the sales force.*

A second complication error to be avoided is that of trying to drive too hard a bargain with traders. It is the negotiation of this form of deal which takes up a large part of the salesman's time and effort. It is this form of bargain which turns the buyer off. It may only concern one brand, but it can affect the negotiation for the whole list. It can be for a small and relatively unimportant brand, but the problems can spill over onto major brands that are vying for leadership.

Clearly there is need for a sensible balance. The aim should be to give the trader a fair deal and one that rewards him for his contribution, it is certainly *not* necessarily wise to be over-generous – although with small brands it is probably better to be over-generous than unduly tight.

The whole area of evaluating the effectiveness of the sale force operation is one where good judgement will be at a premium. So many of the contentions will be difficult to prove by fact. For instance, is it correct to say that buyers put a limit on the number of features they will give to any one manufacturer during a given period? It is very difficult to justify this statement on a business basis – surely if the brand offers are good enough the buyer will feature all of them. But the argument is one with which many experienced and effective sales operators would agree and in practice it does seem to be of substance.

ACCOUNT PROFITABILITY

The old joke: 'We doubled the business through the account, then we doubled it again, and then we went bankrupt', is a valuable reminder to the manufacturer that volume is important, but *not* at any cost.

Some accounts are easy to handle. They do not look for an extensive service, and they pay on time. Others require a highly developed service, they place a number of restrictions on how business is conducted, and they are slow payers.

It is well worth the manufacturer checking, from time to time, how much it costs him to do business with each of his various accounts, and what sort of profit contribution each one is making.

However, great care is required in calculating the cost of servicing a particular account. It is also important to be clear as to whether the service is provided at the insistence of the account or voluntarily by the manufacturer. This is an area where arbitrary cost allocations can prove very misleading.

■ *In comparing account costs it is advisable to start with those items of cost which are directly incurred and essential to dealing with the account. Even with these items some allocations may be necessary. At this stage comparative-account absolute contributions, and contribution rates, can be calculated. Later when voluntarily-incurred costs are introduced it should be possible to get an indication of their worth in terms of the extra volume they generate and the profit contribution they make.*

The check on account contribution should show where service costs and selling prices have been allowed to deviate too far and where into the future correction is necessary. It should also help to highlight sales approaches which have been outstandingly successful and which could be used on a wider basis.

SALES FORCE: MANAGEMENT

Comments on the leadership and general management of the business are made in chapter 15. Here we are concerned with three special aspects of sales management, each one of which can be of material significance in ensuring that this important section of the business is working at its most effective level.

A high level of morale among personnel throughout the business invariably brings a better level of operational effectiveness. Nowhere is this more in evidence than in the sales force. The salesman is often working alone far from the company factory or offices. During his day he will probably have to listen to many complaints about the company and its brands, however unreasonable they may be. Even the most efficient operation will attract criticism – it is part of trading and negotiation. He will be told on many occasions of the good things his competitors are doing (rarely will he hear of their mistakes). All the delivery problems and the package breakages will be his fault. Through all of this it is important that he remains balanced and positive in his approach. If he has been carefully selected for his job and given sound training he will be able to handle the position successfully. He will know that every buyer has so many problems of his own that he just doesn't want to hear of any problems that he (the salesman) may have.

Given this position it is vitally important that the sales force receive strong backing from head office, including:

• Frequent and factual reports on the progress of the business and its brands. It is vitally important that the salesman should never be placed in a position where the buyer knows more than he does of his (the salesman's) business;

- An opportunity to meet with colleagues from time to time to discuss problems and opportunities;
- A periodic review of the company's development, and in particular the progress of the brands they sell (this can include a sensible level of technical information), and, where a competitive advantage has been developed, this should be fully explained and illustrated;
- An acknowledgement where a particularly good sale has been achieved, and where an account or accounts are proving difficult, an expression of encouragement.

Comments and reviews of this kind are all part of good sales-force management. They help to develop pride in the business and its brands, they help to keep the salesman's morale at a high level, and they can pay off handsomely in results.

The second of these special points concerns the use of the sales force as gleaners of information. The salesman is close to the consumer at the point of sale and he is also involved with the trader who controls access to the consumer through his stores. The good salesman uses his position to pick up valuable information. Frequently, for instance, he will be the first person to sense that a price increase is going wrong, that a particular promotion is going to be highly successful, or that a new pack design is causing confusion. Through discussion and careful listening he may get to know of a planned competitive move or an important policy change within the retail trade.

There is a need to be sure that the salesman is heard in the company policy and operational discussions. Often he is not as articulate as his marketing colleagues in the internal meetings, often he feels he is at a disadvantage; if this applies it should be corrected. The good salesman has much to offer, particularly in relation to the forming and execution of tactics, he should be given the opportunity to contribute.

The need to keep sales people, at all levels, selling is the third special point. As a business grows, as its brands get bigger, and its management layers increase, so more and more of its sales managers tend to become administrators. They can always find a good reason for being in the office; there are always important internal meetings which may benefit from their attendance, letters to dictate, and reports to prepare.

■ *The basic strength of a sales force is contained in its ability to prepare effective business propositions and then to get out and negotiate their acceptance for action. And this applies at all levels in the sales organizations. Administrators can take care of the administration; for this they should be rewarded as administrators and this is likely to be at a level well below that of a successful salesman.*

Key points

1 Decide where the *key* trade opportunities are for your brands. Decide on the form and style of selling approach that is *right* for your operation.

2 Your *key* account salesman will be vitally important. They will provide the best opportunity for the business to get a competitive advantage in selling.

3 Select them with great care, train them continuously, provide them with strong motivation, and ensure they are well rewarded for success. Be careful of the use of the typical job evaluation scheme in deciding on the remuneration of the *key* account salesman. Educational background, the number of years in training, and similar measures, are not necessarily appropriate factors in valuing this particular position.

4 Devote time, effort, and expertise, to the formulation of your business propositions. Ensure they meet the needs of both your customer (the buyer) and of your brands. Negotiate with skill, dexterity, and determination. Be sure, with tact and firmness, that both you and your customer meet all the terms of the agreement. If you fail to get business there is something wrong with either your business proposition or your salesman. Investigate carefully, and then put the problem right – fast.

5 The record shows that the maxim: 'Keep it simple and concentrate', has proved a good one to follow in general business management. It is certainly the right approach for an effective sales operation.

When you plan for your brand list to grow and your operations to expand don't accept a decline in your sales force performance – think positively and turn the position into an opportunity.

6 Never stop working to build the morale of your sales force. Encourage them to glean information, listen to their comments, and make sure they keep selling.

DISTRIBUTION

'Distribution' means the physical distribution of the manufacturer's brands to the warehouses and stores of his customers. It tends to be a somewhat unglamorous part of the business operation, and yet over recent years its cost has risen and in many instances it has become a major part of total company expenditure.

The aim of the manufacturer is to get his brands, in trays or cases, from the end of his production line to his customers' stores in an appropriate time period, in a satisfactory condition, and at as low a unit cost as possible.

Gaining a significant competitive advantage under this heading is extremely difficult; however an advantage is possible, and would normally come under one, or both, of the headings:

1   Effective and efficient operation;
2   Structure and planning.

Cases can be moved efficiently, or they can be moved in a slipshod and inefficient manner. Trucks can be maintained and driven in a good order, be free of breakdown, and have a low-level fuel consumption; or they can be driven hard and without satisfactory maintenance. Warehouses can be well controlled with correct stock rotation, or they can be badly managed with heavy stock damages. An effective and efficient operation can bring extensive benefits in physical distribution.

This is a field of operation where the manufacturer should question whether or not he needs outside specialist contractors for all or part of the job. Outside distribution contractors are frequently better positioned to get composite deliveries to warehouses and return loadings for their vehicles; this can help to provide for lower unit-operating costs.

'Structure and planning' refers to the way in which the manufacturer structures his price-list, and the way he plans the operation of his deliveries.

From a cost viewpoint, the manufacturer would like his brand to come straight off the production line into the waiting vehicle and then on to his customer's store. In this way he cuts his handling to a minimum, removes the need for finished product storage, and reduces the capital he has tied up in finished goods.

This requires the salesman to sell by the truck load, preferably for one brand in one size. If his brand is big enough, and he is prepared to give the trader an attractive enough incentive, then orders of this kind can be booked.

With the right kind of mechanization, it should be possible to arrange for a truck full of mixed brands to be loaded without extensive man-handling, again it may be necessary to provide the trader with the right level of incentive to buy the necessary quantity. There will, of course, be a need to arrange for the timing of a delivery to be reasonably flexible so that it can fit with the timing of the planned production of the brand.

It can be seen that the manufacturer has available in the structuring of his price-list, a powerful tool to encourage his buyers to order in quantities, and in timing, so that he can get the maximum cost savings in his physical delivery. He can go further by encouraging his customer to carry the stock in his (i.e. the customer's) warehouse rather than have it in his own storage.

To gain the full advantage from operations of this kind the manufacturer needs to link his sales force activity closely with his production planning, and beyond this with his own purchase and reception of raw materials and packaging.

There will be a need for cost and revenue estimates covering the various permutations of order size, production volumes, storage and handling costs, delivery costs, capital tie-up, and revenue receipts. It is a field where a suitably programmed computer should prove most helpful.

The discussion here has been primarily about the cost savings coming from volume operations. For some manufacturers the aim may be very different, for instance, the competitive advantage may be in product freshness; small deliveries, made frequently, can be all important. The need for an effective and efficient operation will be just the same, and the price-list can be used in a similar manner but with a different aim – the trader should be encouraged to buy frequently, possibly daily if this the best way to ensure a fresh product, and a fresh product is a form of competitive advantage.

Key points

1 The cost of physical distribution is likely to be a major part of your total expenditure. Distribution should not be treated as the 'Cinderella' section of the business. It is worthy of high calibre management.

2 Close liaison between the distribution, sales and production departments is essential. Picking up cases and putting them down again is a costly business – costly in terms of the personnel and handling charges, costly in terms of storage facilities, and costly in terms of the capital tied-up.

3 The price-list structure can be a powerful distribution cost reduction *tool*. Of course, it is important to remember that the aim is not merely to reduce distribution costs – the aim is to make the highest possible level of sales at an acceptable level of cost. If there were no sales then distribution costs could be reduced to nil – but without sales there would be no business!

PART V

15

◇

Leadership, People and Morale, and Culture

◆

In every chapter of this book, direct or indirect reference is made to the importance of a business managing its operations effectively and efficiently. No apology is made for this for it is very clearly one of the *key* factors in business success.

However, if we examine the truly successful businesses, and in particular those which are able to maintain their success over a lengthy period of time, we find they have something beyond effective and efficient operations. They have an *extra* ingredient which gives them the ability to produce a performance which is superior to that of their competitors at a time when it really matters. When they appear to be down and struggling they are able to somehow make a come-back and gain leadership, and when they are in a close fight for the lead they are able to pull out the *extra* which carries them through to the top.

A cynic may argue that the *extra* referred to is quite simply money, and of course, in the type of situations mentioned a liberal supply of money can be a very great help. But the *extra* referred to is not money. Indeed it is noticeable that many companies which are well supplied with money lack the *extra*.

The statement: 'The two most important assets a business should have are never included on its orthodox balance sheet' has already been made. It is a reference to the fact that the brands and the people of the business are never included as such among the listed assets.

The statement goes on to make the point that as the brands are created, developed, and maintained by people, then its people should be the company's No. 1 asset.

257

■ *Whether or not there is complete agreement with this statement is not really important. What is important is the fact that the people of a business can make or break it. They can give it great success or they can push it towards bankruptcy. The 'extra' mentioned in the preceding paragraphs is most certainly very directly linked to the people of the business, their attitude to its performance, and to the results it produces.*

When only one of the businesses competing in a market has the ability to produce this 'extra' then it has a competitive advantage, most probably a significant one. But even if more than one of the competitors is able to produce the extra *it is clearly an ability that is of great significance. If you haven't got it then you could be a loser at an important time.*

Just how a company creates within itself the conditions and an atmosphere which encourages its people to perform at an outstandingly high level, at important times and over lengthy periods, has been the subject of numerous research studies and academic treatise. There are many varying views but one point would appear to be clear; there is certainly no single simple approach which will produce the desired result in all conditions and at all times. Indeed, the record shows that an amazingly varied number of approaches have proved successful when practised by people with special abilities in particular circumstances.

Every business should be interested in developing a competitive advantage, and so every business should want to develop the *extra* ability within its people. In this chapter we are concerned with the development of this *extra*. It is clearly a factor of paramount importance.

The subject is, of course, a complex and involved one which we cannot expect to cover in great detail. Discussion here is centred under three headings, and it is accepted that these notes are limited in their scope. However, this is a vitally important consideration and one that must receive the full attention of any management which seeks to deliver a superior performance. The three headings are:

- leadership
- people and morale
- culture

Everyone agrees that outstanding leadership can be a great asset to a business. It can achieve exceptional performance in the most adverse circumstances. However, there is rarely the same level of agreement as to what constitutes outstanding leadership, how you develop it, or how you should put it into effect.

The level of morale within the business is clearly an important factor in operations. Happy people invariably contribute much better than do those who are downcast and aggrieved. How do you develop a high level of morale? Again there is no one simple answer, but there are a number of approaches which can be helpful.

Over recent years business researchers have become conscious of what is known as the company culture. Some of the researchers have gone as far as to comment that company culture can be a *key* factor in business success, and some enthusiasts have argued that culture *is* the *key* factor. There would probably be general agreement that a well-developed culture, of the right kind, can most certainly have a part to play in business success.

LEADERSHIP

Great national leaders come in all shapes and sizes – just check the great leaders of the last fifty years and this will be confirmed. They also come from varying backgrounds, have contrasting educational standards, and reach their prime as leaders at differing age-levels.

Leaders of business organizations are similar. They also have varying backgrounds and educational standards, and they also reach their prime at different age-levels.

Rather than try to examine in detail the training, career development and so forth, of those men who have become successful leaders in business, and then go on to form a view as to how such a leader might be developed, the approach used here is to turn the equation around and consider what the people who are to be led (i.e. the staff of the business) might expect of an outstanding leader.

Before moving into this consideration two points need further clarification. Firstly, the fact that within a business there are many leaders. Every person who is in any way supervising a number of others needs to be a leader.

Frequently, within a business there is a small group, for instance the board of directors, who are known as the leadership. In some companies a very limited number, say three or four senior board members, occupy what is known as the office of leadership. And then there is the one man who is the chief executive who is known and seen as the leader.

In these notes the reference is to the one man who is known and seen as the leader. Although it is accepted that many of the remarks would apply equally to the other groups.

Secondly, while the leadership tends to be referred to in terms of those people working in the business, it should be remembered that the chief executive (or chairman) is also the leader of the owners of the business, i.e. the stockholders. In many important respects the aims of the employees and the shareholders will be the same, but on occasions they will differ. It follows that on occasions the views of the two groups on the performance of the leadership is likely to differ.

In these notes, as we are primarily concerned with leadership and the development of competitive advantage, the remarks are made from the viewpoint of employees.

Leadership attributes

It is suggested that there are a number of attributes the employees would expect an outstanding leader to possess, and to give to the business.

A sense of direction

The people of the business will want to know where their business is going, what its objectives are, and how it expects to achieve them. A business without a sense of direction is like a ship without a rudder.

■ *An outstanding leader will ensure that this necessary sense of direction is provided. He will ensure that at all levels throughout the business there is an understanding of where the business is going and, in general terms, what it needs to do to reach its objectives.*

This does not mean that the objectives need necessarily be spelt out in great detail, very general terms will often suffice. There can be considerable advantages to the leader if he is able to avoid detail and remain with more general objectives.

The leader may choose to vary the level of detail he uses depending upon the understanding of the people concerned. Similarly, the way the objectives are to be achieved does not have to be spelt out in great detail. But the approach must be practical and expressed in a manner which can be understood.

It is important that the business objectives, and their achievement, be seen as realistic. With the objectives it is better to build in steps to a final objective level rather than to set out with an unduly high level which appears unrealistic. This can be of particular significance where there is a need to build confidence.

The advantage in expressing the objectives, and the means of achieving them, in general terms is that it helps to avoid the unnecessary debate which invariably follows detail. It also avoids problems when objectives have to be changed as they do from time to time. The good leader wants his people engaged in productive pursuits rather than in unproductive debates on objectives.

Confidence

The leader gives the people of the business confidence in a number of ways, two of which are of particular significance. Firstly, by the results he achieves in his management of the business. As the business makes progress under his leadership so the confidence of the people in him and in the company will grow.

Secondly, the leader gives the people of the business confidence by his own behaviour and self-conduct.

■ *If, by his actions, he demonstrates his confidence in the future of the business this will be noticed and reported. Equally, any move by the leader which appears to show a lack of confidence, will quickly be reported through the organization.*

The leader needs to exercise considerable care in his personal reactions, and in his public (and private) comments on business progress. It is very difficult to keep all the discussions held within a tightly knit business community completely confidential and rumours of the wrong kind can be particularly damaging to confidence. The leader needs to have a positive approach, and to ensure that this is conveyed to the people of the business.

Integrity

■ *Complete integrity in all his dealings will be of great importance to the outstanding leader. His word really must be his bond. The respect of the people he leads will be vital to him, real respect can only come with complete integrity.*

Success

■ *The outstanding leader is successful. He has the skill, ability, and the shrewdness, to ensure that the resources available to him are used to achieve the objectives of the business. His people expect him to bring success – this is one of the reasons why he is an outstanding leader.*

Intelligent employees realize that only a successful business can provide them with security, good working conditions, and satisfactory rewards. They need a successful business and they appreciate that their leader is of paramount importance in achieving this.

How is the success measured? From the employee's viewpoint, primarily in terms of profitability and performance in the marketplace. These are in turn reflected in job security, promotion prospects, and reward levels.

This is not to say that the company must become market leader or have a higher level of profitability than any competitor. But it does require that the business should make progress in terms of profit and market share.

There may be shorter-term periods when the business is defending its position against competitive attack, or building its resources ready for an advance – these periods can and should be explained. But if the leader is to become an outstanding leader he must, within a reasonable time period, bring the business through to success.

The argument that as a business gets bigger the leader cannot be held responsible for its success or failure as others take many of the *key* decisions, is not accepted. The leader should be involved actively with the *key* decisions, and he should also be involved in the selection of his immediate associates to whom he delegates certain of the vital performance requirements.

The chief executive should be given the credit for any success the business achieves, equally he must take responsibility for any failure.

It has been explained above that success is important to employees in that it can bring material benefits. It is also important to their pride. They want to be proud of their business in just the same way as the leader and his fellow senior managers want to be proud of it. As we shall see later, this pride factor is of great significance to company morale.

It is very difficult to have a fully developed pride in a business that is unsuccessful.

Strength, justice and sincerity

Employees appreciate that to be outstanding their leader must be a strong man. Strong in terms of will, but also in terms of reasonable physical strength. He must not weaken under pressure, his nerve must be good, and he must have a reserve of energy to carry him through particularly difficult periods.

Employees may not always appreciate his strength when he is involved in negotiations with them. Although even here they will accept his strength if they have also come to see him as a basically just man.

A weak man cannot become an outstanding leader. He will be unable to deliver business success or to warrant the respect which is so important.

Shrewdness, especially in business tactics, should not be confused with weakness. Shrewdness is part of a good business man, and therefore part of a good business leader. For instance, there may be occasions when it is good tactics to withdraw from an impossible market position with a view to fighting again another day – this is certainly not weakness and it should not be allowed to appear as such.

There will be differences between people within his organization from time to time, and the leader must not allow these differences to impair the progress of the business. If necessary he must settle the differences himself, and this is where it is of consequence that he is a just man and is seen as one.

■ *All outstanding leaders are sincere men. They believe in their business, they believe in its place within society and they believe in the benefits it brings to the community. Their sincerity is of the deep and genuine kind. One of the reasons that outstanding business leaders are often good at talking about their business, but not about other subjects, is that they believe very deeply in their business. They speak from a sincere base, but when they speak on other subjects they are not so sure of themselves and are less convincing.*

Decisiveness

Throughout the business, from time to time, decisions will have to be taken if the business is to function and progress is to be made. Some of these decisions, usually the most important ones, will be the responsibility of the leader.

■ *The manner in which the leader faces his decision-making responsibility will be of importance to the whole business. That he should get the decisions right is, of course, of paramount importance. Beyond this it is necessary that the decisions should be taken at the right time, and in the right manner.*

One of the most harmful experiences a business can have is a leader who finds it unduly difficult to make up his mind. His hesitation and indecision will quickly be interpreted as a lack of confidence and ability.

The requirement is that decisions be taken without unnecessary delay. Sometimes delay will be appropriate; there may be new information to come, changes in circumstances, and so on. In such conditions the clever move could be to delay the decision. The important qualification is 'without unnecessary delay'.

Decisions should be clear and straightforward. Decisions which avoid facing the main issue clearly, decisions which aim for compromise merely to keep the peace and avoid offence, are never satisfactory.

Decisions taken without regard to the facts which apply, decisions taken out of bias, and decisions taken out of personal interest can have a material and damaging effect on the attitude of the people towards the leader. The cynic may argue that as long as the decision is *right* what does it matter? How the decisions are taken and conveyed does matter in that it can have an adverse effect on the attitude of the people toward the leadership. How the leader takes his decision will be noticed, and he will be cited as an example – the example needs to be a good one.

Enthusiasm

In some circles enthusiasm appears to be looked down on. It is considered to be unsophisticated and naïve. The reasoning seems to be that enthusiasm and profound thinking do not mix, and are not to be found together in one person.

This is, of course, completely unsound reasoning. The record shows very clearly that all great leaders are enthusiasts. And this most certainly applies to business leaders. They are enthusiastic about their business, about its brands, its new developments, its potential, its people, in fact they bring enthusiasm to everything they do and are involved with. Their enthusiasm is infectious, and gets to all their associates.

■ *The outstanding leader has the ability to know when he must take a hard, cold, calculating look at the appropriate data, seek sound unemotional views, and come to a decision. He also knows there is a time when he needs to get his colleagues enthusiastically involved in a project, he knows their enthusiasm can bring about a difference in performance which will ensure success.*

You don't have to stand on a box and shout to be an enthusiast. Enthusiasm is very much an attitude of mind. All the great inventors have invariably been enthusiasts. They keep going despite difficulties. They have an ardent zeal for their idea, and they stay with it until it is successful. People of this kind are good to have with you in a business battle.

Discernment

The leader cannot do everything. He can't take every decision or be involved in every action. As the business grows so he will need to delegate more and more. It is important that the people to whom he delegates are of a sufficiently high calibre to take the *right* decisions in their turn, and ensure they are carried through in a manner which provides a superior performance.

■ *The leader should be involved in the selection of his more senior associates. This task is too important to the business for him to delegate it, although he could well seek suitable advice and assistance. It is one of his most consequential responsibilities. It is vitally important that he gets it* right.

In some instances the need will be for a person who balances his own contribution, a person who has skills that he (the leader) does not possess, a person who, when appropriate, will argue with him and challenge his view. An ability, and a will, to deliver in terms of performance should be the *key* criterion in selection. If the business and the leader, is to record the success which is so vital for its future, a superior performance from his associates will be very necessary.

The attributes have not been listed in order of priority, and it is accepted that other important ones can be added. Nevertheless, any company which has a leader who possesses all the attributes listed is most fortunate.

There is an argument which reasons that the attributes of an outstanding leader will need to vary depending upon the circumstances of the company with which he is concerned. The qualities required when the company is in deep trouble will differ from those necessary when the need is to continue a successful run. There is some evidence from the practical business scene which supports this argument. And from the wider world the fact that a number of outstanding war time leaders have been less successful during times of peace would seem to support the basic proposition.

As a counter to this, it can be claimed that the leadership attributes required for success do not change with the circumstances; there is merely a change in emphasis and use. The outstanding leader will appreciate this and conduct himself accordingly.

Putting attributes to work

How does an outstanding leader bring his skills to work within the business? He needs a formal organization, preferably one which is as simple and straightforward as possible. This will include board meetings and the other more official means of communication. However, if he is to be truly successful he needs more, he needs an unofficial means of *giving and receiving* communications with members of the business. How he does this will depend very much on his personality, the approach he prefers, the approach which works for him. There is no one correct way. Some successful leaders use short, sharp, memos, others hold frequent small conferences at breakfast, while some just walk about and talk. The important point is that the leader must both give and receive. He can decide on the approach he prefers but the small and very important point is that it must work.

From the record it would seem that the most important requirement is that the leader should be himself. He should not try to imitate the approach of others, as he is most unlikely to have their characteristics and specific abilities. However, he is likely to have certain characteristics and skills of his own and these he should use. Of course, he may work to improve, for instance, his communicating skills. But if he tries to change himself to any great extent in his presentation he is likely to fail. Better that he concentrate on the development of his own approach and be sure to make it work.

It has been claimed that outstanding leaders are born, and not made, trained or developed. Of course, this claim has been challenged on many occasions.

It would seem to be generally agreed that outstanding leaders frequently have a strong will, and a strong desire to be leaders. They also have a deep and sincere belief in the specific cause, or project they are leading. However, there does not appear to be any particular reason to accept that they were born with these attributes and feelings.

In many cases the outstanding leader also has an exceptional personality, but again this personality frequently passes through a number of phases as it develops and it may differ significantly from beginning to end.

■ *The record shows that many outstanding leaders have possessed the basic requirements such as a strong will, integrity, and sincerity from an early age. To this they have added a sound training and good experience. As they have achieved a degree of success so they have gained maturity, confidence, a feel for people, and an astuteness in their particular area of activity. They also develop an ability to appreciate rapidly which are the key issues and over time they come to possess an innate shrewdness to recognize the big opportunity.*

The company that has an outstanding leader is most fortunate. It should ensure that he continues to be satisfactorily motivated and rewarded. He could, in himself, represent a significant competitive advantage.

Beyond this they should make certain that the leader is taking appropriate steps to ensure that when it is time for him to vacate the leadership there are others available with the appropriate attributes and experience to continue the business progress.

What of the company that has an unsuccessful leader? The first requirement is to recognize that the leader is unsuccessful. The most elaborate checks before appointment cannot guarantee that the man given the job will be successful. Only when he is in position and actually operating can a true judgement of his performance be made. Even at this stage a worthwhile judgement at a specific time may be extremely difficult. Frequently leaders take time to bring their ideas into operation. A successful business strategy may require a number of years to work through to real profit growth. There may well need to be a period of rough going before the success begins to show. There may be a need for personnel moves within the senior management and for a difficult morale period as the business needs to settle.

The assessment of the business leader will always require great care and sensitivity. It cannot be a simple operation for there are so many complex considerations to be taken into account.

If it is decided that a change in leader is necessary then once the decision is taken the move should be made with a sensible degree of urgency. A long period of impasse in the leadership of the business can be most harmful, and a significant competitive disadvantage.

PEOPLE AND MORALE

When we talk of the morale of the business we are in fact talking of the attitude toward, and feeling about, the business held by its people. People and morale are at one.

Here the plan is firstly to consider people under the headings of selection, training, and motivation, and then to discuss a number of other factors which concern the people of the business and have a marked effect on their morale.

It will be appreciated that this whole subject is a most complex one, and one that has been at the centre of many long and detailed research studies. In these notes the aim has been to consider the more basic influences.

■ *Successful companies tend to have a high morale, unsuccessful companies tend to have low morale. Is it cause, or effect? Probably something of both. The important consideration is that high morale can be competitive advantage, and so management should be concerned to develop it.*

'The business gets the people it deserves' is a statement often heard in personnel discussions. In that the business has the privilege of selecting those people it employs the statement must be correct.

Selection

It is customary to ensure that an applicant for a position with a business is suitably qualified in terms of training and professional ability. For instance, that fitters have carried out an approved training period and have followed this with appropriate experience. That accountants have gained an appropriate qualification and have followed this with a desirable form of experience. This is understandable and is clearly a very reasonable procedure.

Companies of course differ in their make-up and in their personality. They also differ in their approach to business and in the way they operate. The company that manufactures and markets consumer products normally has a very different atmosphere to the one that is engaged in making heavy-duty metal forgings.

Both atmospheres may be perfectly right in their place. But they do differ, and they differ primarily because the tempo of the business, its atmosphere, the methods employed, and the approach to the customer are of a very different nature. If you make and sell battleships you can be very successful with just a single sale every three years; if you make washing powder you may need to sell at least one million packets each week to enjoy a modest success.

■ *The suggestion here is that companies should be prepared to spend more time and effort in ensuring that their new recruits are well suited for their business. That they have the approach and attitude that will fit well in their particular atmosphere. In effect they should ask the question; 'will this person really enjoy working in our business?'*

It is important that a satisfactory number of the new recruits stay with the business over time. Some movement in and out of personnel may be necessary, and indeed should be welcomed, as new thinking, and a new approach, can often be very effective. But excessive personnel movement can be most wasteful and unsettling for a business. Where the movement is widespread and frequent, company morale is likely to be low and company culture non-existent.

Training

■ *Every job in the business can be done at a higher level of performance than at present. And this applies irrespective of the level of the job, or the level of current performance. Acceptance of this statement – and the record shows most clearly that it is a correct statement – automatically makes the case for an effective training programme within the business.*

Progressive businesses accept this approach. They realize that a programme of continuous training is necessary for everyone in the business.

It does not follow from this that members of staff should be frequently withdrawn from their workplace to attend a series of lectures. In some instances a period away from business in a lecture room may be appropriate, but often the best kind of training is actually on the job.

In many cases there will be a good case for taking the training outside the actual professional field of the individual. The business is part of the free enterprise system, it is a part of capitalism. Many employees may not fully appreciate this or, for instance, such factors as the importance of profit performance in attracting new capital, and the fact that new capital will be essential if employment levels are to be maintained. There would seem to be good reason to include, at an appropriate level, items of this kind within the training programme. Good performers are rarely satisfied with merely doing the job. They want to know how it fits into the wider company activity, and they need to understand how that activity is justified within the community.

Motivation

Here we are concerned with the motivation of personnel as individuals, and as members of the total company team, to produce a superior performance.

Basically two forms of incentive may be offered to staff as a form of motivation; financial and non-financial incentives.

Financial incentives range from the straightforward commission on sales for the salesmen, through the output bonus for production staff, to a stock-option scheme for senior executives.

In some companies incentive schemes work remarkably well at all levels, in others they are considered more trouble than they are worth. They can differ in structure from individual, to group, to total-company reward. They can be based on profits, sales volume, production output, and so on.

The successful incentive schemes would seem to:

- Be designed specifically for the particular unit or operation concerned;
- Relate specifically to a unit of measure that the individual concerned materially influences and understands;
- Enable the individual or individuals concerned to be aware of their benefits at frequent intervals;
- Be relatively simple to understand and to administrate;
- Be seen and recognized as *fair*.

Companies that run successful incentive schemes have invariably taken great care in their design and implementation. And they insist that the schemes are reviewed and adjusted as appropriate on a regular basis.

Profit-sharing schemes have many advocates, but they can encounter difficulties when profits drop for reasons beyond the control or influence of the workforce.

Schemes that provide employees with a share in ownership of the business can be most helpful in removing the 'them and us' attitude between employees and owners. They can give employees a deeper, longer-term association with the business and they can also help to provide an understanding of the free enterprise system of which the business is a part.

In many instances the success or failure of schemes of this kind hinge on how they are used. If you set a scheme in motion and then refer to it once each year the chances are it will be forgotten for some eleven months of the year. To have an effect on the output of the people concerned the progress of the scheme needs to be publicized at frequent intervals – the scheme is after all a form of investment and should be used in such a manner that the return coming from it is maximized.

Non-financial incentive (or motivation) schemes can take many forms. One of the most prominent and effective centres on the careers and promotions of employees.

■ *Management has full control of the employee selection and promotion process within the business. Used effectively it can be a great motivating* tool *and bring substantial benefit to the business. Used ineffectively it can even become a form of de-motivation.*

Successful applications ensure that the process and its workings, in particular how it affects individuals, is continually brought to the notice of the staff. Many factors may be included but successful applications invariably major on performance. Every effort is made to ensure the application is fair, and seen to be fair.

One of the most potent motivating approaches centres on the pride of the people in the business. The pride of the individual in his own performance, the performance of his group, and the performance of his company. Given the right atmosphere within a business, good management can use pride to get exceptional results without high-level expenditure. To be acknowledged as the outstanding performer in a group, or acknowledged as the outstanding group, is sought after by all 'professionals' whether they be production staff, salesmen, managers, or clerks. The rewards do not necessarily have to be extensive, it is the acknowledgement that is all-important.

Non-financial incentives can provide management with the opportunity to bring home the point that business is fun. A 'race for a Christmas turkey' between production units, or a 'Christmas party contest' between sales groups, are the sort of incentives that can, in the right circumstances and with good timing, prove great motivating events.

Morale

We have considered very briefly the selection, training and motivation of the people of the business. Even when these factors have been handled skilfully and effectively it is still possible to have a low level of morale within a business.

Company morale is difficult to define satisfactorily and it is difficult to be completely clear as to how it can be developed, indeed it has been argued that if you try too hard to develop it you will fail. When you visit a business with a high morale you can feel its presence; equally where morale is low this can also be sensed. A high level of morale among employees is certainly a most valuable asset for any business to have. Among the more prominent factors that can help to develop morale are:

Information and consultation

It is very difficult to have a pride in the performance of your company if you do not know how it is performing. It is very difficult to appreciate your own performance if you are not given any indication as to how it compares with your competitors.

Good people want to have pride in their company, and they should be given appropriate information on the business and its progress at regular intervals. The information needs to be presented in a manner which is positive and which they can understand without difficulty.

Good people also have a pride in their section or unit of the business. They want to know how it performs and how it can be developed. And they like to contribute to the development.

There are two particularly good reasons for encouraging consultation on the progress of the unit and the company. Firstly, it can help develop morale, and secondly it can bring forth suggestions which can enhance performance.

Conditions

The conditions within a business do not necessarily have to be de luxe to help in the development of morale, but they do have to be satisfactory. It may not be impossible, but it is certainly extremely difficult to develop a high level of morale if the people concerned are expected to work in unsatisfactory conditions.

Rewards

It is often claimed that the level of the reward paid in a business has no effect on morale – 'The small business on the corner has much better morale than the big business up the road, and they pay much lower wages.' This may be so, but nevertheless the rewards paid do have an effect on morale.

If employees do not believe they are receiving a reasonable reward in the circumstances then it will be difficult to build high morale. The wages in the small business quoted may be lower, but if they are seen as reasonable in the circumstances they will not affect the morale.

It should be possible to make sure that high level rewards contribute to a high level morale. But if the high levels are administered and managed ineffectively then they can actually cause morale problems.

■ *The level of the rewards paid are always of consequence. From the viewpoint of morale development, it can be equally important that they are seen to be paid in an equitable manner as between members of a particular group, and members of the company.*

Success

It can, on certain exceptional occasions, be excusable to lose, but it is always better to win. There can be little doubt that success, handled adroitly, can be a major factor in building morale. People like to win, and the stronger the competition, the more valuable the win becomes.

Effective and efficient operation

The more efficient the unit the higher the morale of the personnel concerned is likely to be. One of the most frustrating experiences is to work in a production unit, or any other kind of unit, where supplies are continually held up, where repair parts can never be obtained, and so on. Frustration of this kind is rarely ever partnered by high morale.

Appreciation and encouragement

Good people like to feel their efforts are appreciated. They give of their best, and they like to know this has been noticed and acknowledged. And they like to receive encouragement, particularly in difficult periods. Appreciation and encouragement are not costly considerations – except when they are missing.

To these factors others may be added. In the development of morale what is said will always be of significance; when and how it is said will also be of major importance.

CULTURE

A lengthy dictionary definition of the word 'culture' would be 'The pattern of human behaviour in speech, thought and action that is concerned with man's capacity for learning and passing knowledge to others.' A more practical definition and one that fits much more closely to the use of the term in current business circles, is to say that company culture is: 'What we believe in, and how we do things in this company.'

The case for the development of a company culture hinges on the fact that a number of researchers working mainly in the USA have highlighted the fact that many of the more successful companies have a well-developed company culture. The culture isn't the same for all the companies, each one has been individually developed. The researchers would probably accept that the successful companies have also had well-planned strategies and were effective and efficient in their operation.

It would seem that if the values within the culture have been well chosen and developed, then the existence of the culture helps ensure these values are followed at all levels of the business. At times of stress the culture provides a set of values which company members can refer back to for support if they are ever in doubt.

For the company, the culture is a form of philosophy. It is always there as a reminder to management. They may on a particular occasion and for some very special reason, choose to ignore it, but this would be after careful and detailed consideration.

Some companies have a culture which has just happened to develop. They haven't designed it, it has come out of the way their management has behaved. In these cases the company may need to ask the question; 'Do we have the right culture?' If the answer is 'Yes' then they can continue its development.

If the answer should be 'No' then the question which follows is 'What do we want our culture to be?' In forming their answer they must remember that it is not enough merely to want a particular culture; if it is to mean anything they must make it a reality. For instance, if part of the culture is a 'fair deal for every employee' then care must be taken to ensure that every employee gets, and is seen to get, a fair deal.

With a new company there is an opportunity to decide what sort of culture the company wishes to develop. Of course, the need to *make it happen* applies in exactly the same way.

■ *Company culture concerns everyone in the business. When well developed it permeates every part of the business. Operations also concern everyone in the business, and so the wise selection and development of a sound company culture can be of significance for operating effectiveness.*

A well-developed company culture does not remove the need for a winning strategy or for effectiveness and efficiency in operations. It is a valuable addition to these basics and should help to sustain company progress.

Key points

1 The truly successful companies have the ability to produce an *extra* performance to meet a special requirement. It is a perform-ance which places them ahead of their competitors.

2 The *extra* can be, in part, an additional supply of money, or the in-troduction of special plant or some other resource; but, in the main, the *extra* will be associated with the people of the business, with their skill, their ability, their effort, and their attitude. In particular, the willingness of the people of the business to make, as both indi-viduals and as members of a team an outstanding contribution when it is especially required.

3 Any business which has the ability to produce this *extra* has a competitive advantage, possibly a significant one.

4 All the people of the business are concerned in this process – all have a part to play. However, the responsibility for creating the conditions and atmosphere within the business which are conducive to the development of the *extra*, rests with a limited number of people – the management, and in particular those who have the privilege to lead the business. The business leader has the major responsibility.

5 Outstanding business leaders come in all shapes and sizes, and from varying educational and social backgrounds. Invariably, they are sincere men of high integrity. They are enthusiasts and their enthusiasm is infectious, spreading to all sections of the business. Beyond this they are shrewd in their business dealings, and they are able to use the resources of the business to achieve its objectives. They bring the business through to success.

6 Successful businesses select their people with great care, train them continuously, reward them satisfactorily, and ensure they receive the right form of motivation.

7 In general, winning businesses have high morale, losing businesses have low morale. It is in part cause, and in part effect. High morale can represent a competitive advantage, it is an important part of the *extra* possessed by the truly successful companies.

8 The desire to have pride in the company and its achievements is not limited to the management. Good people throughout the business will have the same desire. They will also want to understand the part the business plays in the community, to be part of the business success, and to contribute to its progress. And understandably they will also want to share in the rewards of the success.

9 An effective management is very much aware of the importance of meeting, in a prudent manner, the desires of the people of the business. They realize that a sensible pride, properly developed, can have a major part to play in ensuring a high level of company morale. In particular, they appreciate the vital importance of giving and receiving good communications with the people of the business.

10 People should be the company's most valuable asset. The people of the business should represent a competitive advantage. But this will not come about by accident. It will require outstanding leadership, effective management, and a willingness to work at it.

PART VI

16

◇

Commercial Management

◆

In some businesses the term 'commercial' is applied to the sales management. Here the term is used to cover that section of the business which is primarily concerned in the provision of information (mainly cost, revenue, and output data) to management to help them use the resources of the business effectively, and to achieve the business objectives.

In many cases the function described would be the responsibility of the finance director. Within business generally the term 'finance' has tended to be closely associated with accounting and account presentation. The concern here is with a function which is more broadly based than account presentation. In effect, the main interest here is with a form of business economics, and 'commercial' is thought to be a more suitable description.

■ *A highly proficient commercial staff will provide line management with the* right *information at the* right *time. There is, of course, a considerable skill in deciding what is the* right *information. The shrewd operator who demands the figures that are* right *for the particular occasion is fully justified in his requirement.*

The field of commercial management is an extensive one affecting every part of the business. Here discussion is limited to three topics.

- operations: commercial support;
- periodic reporting;
- finance.

Under the first heading we are concerned with the commercial influence on decision taking within business operations. All proposals for action need to be evaluated. The figures produced will clearly have a material influence on the decisions taken. The figures had better be *right*.

In some companies periodic reporting appears to have become a purpose in itself. It most certainly has a part to play in successful business management. But in some instances the emphasis appears to be misplaced — the important control input is surely before the money is spent and not afterwards!

Businesses go bankrupt through lack of cash. A shortage of profit may have prompted the lack of cash, but it is the cash shortage that actually sparks off the big problem. Effective management of finance is important, and it could bring a competitive advantage.

OPERATIONS: COMMERCIAL SUPPORT

All operations incur a cost and have an objective. The achievement, or failure to achieve, the objective can ultimately have an effect on profitability. But this effect is usually indirect, delayed, and often difficult to isolate. It is frequently more helpful to consider the cost of operations in terms of the cost of achieving the objective rather than in terms of profitability.

This reasoning is acceptable for individual projects such as a specific promotion, or a particular production output project, but when, for instance, the operation is a brand's total performance over a period of time then it is necessary to reason in terms of profit contribution.

The company operations plan itself is, in fact, a business proposal. It will contain investment proposals for all the brands marketed by the business, and will need to reason in terms of profit.

For individual projects the usual problem is centred on the calculation of the cost. The output (i.e. the objective) is normally more easily arrived at, although there can be occasions when there are difficulties. Where it is necessary to reason in terms of a profit objective the problems are twofold; the cost may be difficult to calculate and the profit most certainly will be.

Costs

There is, of course, a whole series of cost concepts and it is not intended to attempt a review of them here. Economists have dwelt on this topic at length and, in the main, their views have been accepted in business. This is why the shrewd operator is right to insist on 'the figures for the occasion'. He agrees with the economist, he appreciates that there is no such thing as actual cost or a cost that should be used at all times. For practical use the term 'cost' always requires further definition, e.g. marginal cost, opportunity cost, or replacement cost.

The most important cost concept in business is undoubtedly that of *opportunity cost*. If it is accepted that opportunity cost takes the form of the price a particular item, or combination of items, would command in the best alternative use that has been sacrificed, it follows that the concept should be applied continuously.

There should always be competition between the company's brands, both existing and proposed new brands, for the resources of the business. Acceptance of the opportunity cost concept automatically ensures that alternative proposals will be examined. Rather than restricting its thoughts to what it is doing, management also considers what it is *not* doing.

The practising business man will rightly protest that opportunity costs are often extremely difficult, if not impossible, to calculate with any confidence. There is truth in this point, and it means that while the concept is often accepted in theory, it is used less frequently in practice.

Replacement costs are often at a level very similar to opportunity costs, and normally much nearer than are either current or historic costs. There is certainly a strong case for the use of replacement costs in brand and other project cost statements.

A factor that is invariably of great significance in the calculation of unit costs is *volume*. With the development of more advanced plant, computers, and other forms of electronic equipment, so the potential for lower unit-production costs has grown. But if this plant and equipment is to perform effectively and produce at the lower unit cost levels it needs volume. For many manufacturers, an examination of their brand cost statements will show that volume has become a (and possibly the) major influence on their brand units costs.

To ensure that this volume factor is fully appreciated it is common to present costs, within statements covering shorter-term periods, under the headings 'fixed' or 'variable'. An often-quoted example of a fixed cost is depreciation. An example of a variable cost would be the raw material ingredients used in the brand products.

The period of time covered by the particular statement is clearly a key consideration in deciding whether or not a cost should be included as fixed or variable. It is true to say that over a long enough period all costs are variable. But over the shorter operating period some costs move almost entirely with volume and others hardly move at all.

Over shorter periods strong movements in volume can have a marked effect on brand unit costs, on brand profit contributions, and ultimately on the reported profit for the period.

The skilled operator will know how much it is likely to cost in advertising and promotion to obtain these strong volume movements over the shorter term. It follows that if he has available information which shows the effect of volume on unit cost and total cost, he should be well positioned to decide whether or not a move for the volume would be a feasible business proposition.

There is need for caution. Some 'fixed' costs do not remain fixed even through a shorter-term period. And some 'variable' costs do not remain completely variable; as volume falls they tend to become more fixed.

There are a number of costs which come under the heading of semi-variable. They vary with volume but the relationship is not a direct one. The good commercial man will know of this from his records and experience, and he will allow for it in his estimates.

Of course, it is always possible for a particular cost item to be either fixed or variable depending upon the circumstances which apply. Personnel engaged in a packing operation and paid on an output basis provide an example. The manufacturer may be able to provide a steady production flow for the personnel for, say, eleven months of the year. During the twelfth month he may have no packing work for them, but as their training requires a heavy investment he will not wish to lose them, and so he retains them on the payroll for the month. In these circumstances a cost that is normally variable has become fixed for the single month.

Plant capacity, in particular new plant capacity can have an important influence on costs. Frequently when capacity needs to be increased it requires the introduction of an additional unit, but the volume may not be sufficient during the earlier periods to keep the new plant occupied for more than say 50 per cent of its capacity. At this time the total unit cost of the product produced may rise with the increased cost of the new plant, but the variable costs per unit could fall as the higher volume provides economies such as lower raw material prices.

Always beware of cost figures which include *allocated costs*. Frequently the allocation is based on some arbitrary percentage. Very often so-termed 'total' costs contain a number of allocations. They should be examined closely especially when they are used in comparisons such as in the cost of performing a service. A specialist unit without allocations will usually beat a unit burdened with them, but examination of the costs involved may show that the case is not necessarily quite so clear.

Full costing: the contribution approach

Under what is termed the *full costing* approach a trading profit is calculated for each brand. This means that each brand is expected to carry its various direct costs such as packaging and raw materials and in addition an allocation of the total indirect costs which would include such items as the sales force, general administration, and the marketing department.

Under the *contribution* approach the various indirect costs are not allocated to brands. The brands make a contribution, and the indirect costs are deducted from the total contribution (i.e. from the contributions of all the brands) to arrive at a trading profit for the business.

■ *This subject is often featured as a presentation issue. In fact there really is no presentation problem for it is quite simple to have both approaches set out, with clarity, on the same sheet of paper. What is much more important is the reasoning behind the two approaches and the effect on decisions for the future that this reasoning can have.*

The full-costing approach has many followers and included among them are some very successful companies. It is possible they would have been equally successful without the approach, but their success implies the approach must merit some attention.

Advocates of the full-cost approach make such statements as: 'We do not want lame horses in our stable', and 'We want all of our brands to stand on their own feet'. There also seems to be a feeling that there is 'safety' in the full-cost approach. This applies particularly in pricing where a proposal for a brand price below full cost is agreed to only with great reluctance.

It is very difficult to accept that the full-cost approach has any real substance for shorter-term considerations involving any particular brand. Where the indirect allocations are of consequence so much will depend on the movement of other brands within the business. Without any change in its own position, or in the resources placed behind it, a brand could find its trading profit showing a substantial change merely because another brand has experienced a great success or a marked failure which has caused a major change in the overhead allocation.

Over the longer term the full-cost approach can have a greater value. If the business is to show a trading profit the general costs of administration, etc. have to be more than covered by the profit contributions of the brands. It is possible that, in a very rough way and over the long term, the allocation system applied within the business does make a reasonable charge against each brand for the services it receives.

The attraction of the contribution approach is that it is concerned with the *additional* costs and revenues that a proposal is expected to bring about. Additional revenues less additional costs equal additional contributions.

Advocates of the contribution approach would argue that the manufacturer in his application of the approach should ask himself three questions:

1 Can the contribution from this brand, or brand line, be increased?
2 Can the resources that are at present used on this brand, or brand line, be put to another use which will bring a higher contribution?
3 Can a higher total contribution be obtained if the resources used on this particular brand, or brand line, are sold and the cash realized re-invested?

If he can answer a firm 'No' to each of the three questions, then the manufacturer is proposing to put the resources concerned to their most profitable use.

Under the contribution approach there will, of course, be the difficulty of estimating accurately the costs that the project concerned is expected to incur; the semi-variable costs are likely to be at the centre of any problem.

There are two particular dangers often associated with the contribution approach. The first one is that management, seeking to increase sales volume, may be encouraged to drop price to a level which is dangerously low. Secondly, that management will be tempted to accept business that delivers a marginal profit contribution, but which fails to deliver a worthwhile net profit.

These are real dangers and they are always present. They are essentially problems of management judgement. Business can be lost through over-pricing and this can be equally costly. Often the need is to ensure that the shorter term is not allowed to obscure the longer-term aims and objectives. When it is proposed that brand margins should show marked variations from planned levels management should take care.

Activity-based costing

While it may be accepted that the arbitrary allocation of overhead as followed in product full costing is unsatisfactory, it can also be argued that the contribution approach has weaknesses. There will be occasions when management needs valid guidance as to the cost of a particular product through a given period and the contributory approach does not meet this requirement.

Activity-based costing, a technique which gained a degree of acceptance in the second half of the 1980s, attempts to provide a better level of guidance on product costs.

The approach subjects every cost item, and in particular the overhead items, to a rigorous analysis. The focus is on where costs originate and the activity which generates them. From the analysis the costs are traced back to the underlying causes and then to the products. The aim is to minimize arbitrary cost allocations.

The advocates of activity-based costing claim it has much to offer management, and that it is well worthy of the additional time and expense incurred in the very detailed analysis it requires.

Cost per objective

It is suggested that for many of the operational investment proposals the return should be measured in terms of the cost per objective to be achieved. Thus, in a sampling operation the objective could be 'number of homes sampled' and for a production proposal 'unit output per hour or per minute'. While proposals of this kind ultimately have an effect on profit it is an indirect effect. For wider proposals, e.g. a brand plan for a year, the measure would be in terms of contributory profit.

It follows that in judging a proposal it will be important to know what the main objective is. It will also be of significance to know over what time period the investment is to be judged. These factors should be clear so that comparisons between proposals are possible.

Small differences between objectives can make a big difference in the judgement. For instance, is the objective to 'sample homes' or to 'sample homes that will become regular users'? It could be that repeat buyers (i.e. the regulars) come primarily from rural homes. It is known that rural homes are more expensive to sample than those in the towns but a sample promotion directed to rural homes would possibly get a much higher proportion of regular buyers than would one directed to the population in general. Samples to the rural homes would be more expensive on a 'homes basis' but much less expensive on a basis of 'homes to become regular buyers'.

What if there is more than one objective? For many of the major operational investment proposals it is advisable to have one main objective. The danger of having a number of objectives is that the effort will be dispersed and no one aim will be achieved. Nevertheless, it is accepted that it can be possible for a proposal to have more than one objective. When this applies the manufacturer must decide the value of the various objectives so that he may get some measure of probable effectiveness between the proposals.

The time factor can, on occasions, be of major significance. Possibly a competitor is also racing to market a new brand, and in these circumstances it may be more important to be first with 70 per cent of the population rather than second with 90 per cent. Again this will be a judgement issue with the manufacturer having to decide the value of the time lead.

Where profit is the objective

How you define and measure profit has been debated at length over the years. There is no one simple and accepted approach and it is not intended to attempt to provide a definition here.

The various operational proposals prepared within the business must eventually come together to form brand proposals, and then on to form the operational investment plan for the period (this is the company operations plan expressed in financial terms). The measure of this plan is profit. There may be periods when the business is concentrating on market share, sales volume and other objectives, but even so, there will still be a profit objective.

While the various investment proposals will have been formulated and evaluated in terms of the appropriate cost concepts as discussed in the paragraphs above, the financial operations plan will be drawn up in more orthodox terms. The management of the business will eventually have to report to the owners in orthodox terms, and it is understandable that they (the management) would like to have the operations plan prepared in a manner which links directly with the report to the owners.

At one time financial plans where profit is the objective were measured in terms of their return on sales. This still continues in some companies, in particular it is often used in businesses where the investment in fixed capital is relatively low, and expenditure on sales promotion and advertising high. Over recent years the measure which has enjoyed widespread acceptance is that of 'Percentage Return on Capital Employed'. It is assumed that capital is a scarce resource that has a cost, and should be used in the most effective manner possible.

If a representative sample of business men were asked to name one index which they believed would provide an indication as to how effectively a business is managed, there is a high probability that they would select the percentage return on capital employed.

There are, of course, many problems involved in arriving at this figure in a manner which is considered equitable to both the management and the owners. The major problem invariably revolves around the question as to how the capital should be valued. An historic cost evaluation is unlikely to be satisfactory; replacement cost is probably the best approach although this also has weaknesses as, for instance, some of the plant may not be replaced.

Recent years have seen the introduction of a number of techniques for actually calculating the rate of return. A consideration of significance is that these techniques have the ability to provide for the importance of time – they allow for the fact that £1 received today is worth more than one to be received in the future, say in twelve months time.

■ *It is right that management should make every reasonable effort to obtain an accurate measure as to the rate of return the proposed investment plan is likely to produce. It is also right that they keep in mind that the calculations are based on a series of estimates that will almost certainly be subject to error. The resulting measure is a guide to management – it is not the answer. In the final analysis, management will need to use its judgement as to which investment plan it accepts for action – after all, getting judgement decisions of this kind* right *is one of the traits of successful management.*

PERIODIC REPORTS

Periodic reports on the financial progress of the business are now well established as part of the management control approach in a very large number of operating companies.

The reports are usually prepared every four weeks, or every month, or in some instances, every quarter. Where it is considered appropriate they can, of course, be issued on a more frequent basis.

Normally the reports take the form of a comparison of actual expenditures against a budget or an operating standard. They are often designed to show comparisons for the current period, and also for the cumulative period, from the commencement of the operating year.

A well managed system of budgetary control and periodic reporting, provided it is not unduly complex and is produced in good time, can become a very helpful tool to management. Frequently, the introduction of a well managed control system into a loosely managed business will be enough in itself to turn a loss position into profit.

It should be remembered that the purpose of the 'control' approach is to help management to improve its performance. The term 'control' is somewhat misleading for the expenditures reported have already been spent – they are not going to be 'controlled'.

A good management will not have to wait for a monthly report to know that a particular machine is creating a large amount of waste, or to know that the engineering workshop is booking excessive overtime. Daily and weekly data will have already made facts such as these known to the appropriate managers. Indeed, if a major variation comes as a surprise to the manager concerned there is something badly wrong with his personal control.

However the financial report will act to express all the activity of the whole unit, section, or department covered. In this way the variation will be seen in better perspective.

It is suggested that the reports should always attempt to present information in such a way as to show the trend over time of the particular expenditure. And also, wherever possible, show the outstanding commitment for the period ahead.

The daily or weekly reports can show current variances that require immediate attention. The monthly reports when viewed over time, are better for showing trends.

'Control' presentations are said to facilitate management by exception. The manager can concentrate his efforts on correcting deviations from budget or standard. This will often prove to be a very sound approach. However, the objective is to improve total performance, and an item that is already below budget should not escape attention for it may well produce yet an even lower level if it is suitably pushed.

The presentation of the data should always attempt to provide management with guidance as to what action it should take to produce better results in the future. In this respect it is important that management know clearly where the major expenditures are made in terms of money, and the variations expressed in total money terms and not merely in percentages. A 5 per cent variance on small expenditure items will not be a big sum; a 5 per cent variance on a major expenditure item will be of consequence and should receive attention accordingly.

The design of, and the particular information contained in, the control system forms will vary from business to business. The system must fit the business. Senior executives may have certain preferences as to how they want the information presented; some prefer graphical layout while others prefer straight figures. If this can be arranged at a reasonable cost it should be provided – if charts provide the chief executive with a much greater stimulus than do figures, then he should have charts.

The importance of timing in presentation has already been mentioned. It is a factor of great significance for two prime reasons. Firstly, if the figures are to prompt corrective action, the sooner they

do this the better. Secondly, if the figures are always late then soon
the whole system will lose credibility and be regarded as just a piece
of interesting history. To be of value the data must meet a satisfactory
standard of accuracy, but this does not mean accuracy to the last
penny in every instance. Better a reasonably accurate set of reports
within 24 hours than a completely accurate set in a week.

Periodic control reports should be directed to those individuals
who have authority, and responsibility, for the expenditures (inputs)
and revenues (outputs) contained in them. Allocated charges over
which the individual has no control should be avoided if possible.

What should be the content of the periodic control reports
received by the chief executive of a medium-sized operating
company? The content should vary depending upon the type and
form of business, the markets in which the business competes, the
frequency of the reports, and the preferences of the particular chief
executive.

Set out in figure 16.1 is a suggested set of ten schedules that the
chief executive of an operating company might find appropriate to
receive on a monthly basis. The list is certainly not intended to be
exhaustive and it can be argued that other schedules should be added.
It is envisaged that the schedules would compare actuals against the
budget or standard for both the current period and for the cumulative periods, and would also include an estimate of actual compared
with budget for the year. In some instances the monthly performances could be set out in detail so that any trend becomes ap-
parent, and where appropriate a graphical presentation could be used.

The schedules are not set out in an order which would necessarily
apply in practice, although they do follow a form of logical approach
through to the profit statement. It is accepted that schedule 10 (the
profit statement) would often appear as schedule 1 in real life.

A statement showing the balance sheet position as at the close of
each period could be added to this list, although it would probably
be acceptable to prepare this on a quarterly basis.

The period reports should be most helpful to management, but it
is important to stress that the figures contained within them are not
necessarily the same as those which would appear in the proposals
which come through on a continuous basis from operating managers. In the operating proposals the need is for 'the cost for the
occasion'. If the commercial manager ever forgets this he is likely to
be in error in his evaluations, and this could prove to be very costly.

SCHEDULE	CONTENT
1 Markets	• The market/s in which the business competes – its size, its movement, and the movement of the brands competing within it. • Show market size etc. in terms of value, and any other appropriate measure, e.g. weight. • Arrange details so that the movement etc. of the various sectors of the market is clear.
2 Sales	• Brand sales by value and volume. • Detail to include brand market shares. • Show sales by regions and also sales to *key* customers.
3 Brand margins	• Brand contributions/margins by unit and in total value. • Show sales value, raw material, packaging, and other direct costs. • Include estimates for periods ahead.
4 Promotion expenses	• Advertising and sales promotional expenditures. • Detail to include analysis by brand, also various types of media, and major promotions. • Where possible include estimates for major competitors. • Detail expenditure already committed for following periods.
5 Product costs	• Product raw material and packaging costs. • Detail to include prices, volumes etc. of major consumption items. • List outstanding commitments
6 Process costs	• Processing and production costs. • Analysis by production centres, by product type, etc. as appropriate.
7 Overhead	• Indirect (overhead) expenses. • All the general costs of running the business, analysed under appropriate headings.
8 Working capital	• Working capital movement including cash. • Analysis of the holding and movement of all the *key* items, and in particular a statement of the cash position with estimates for approaching periods.
9 Capital expenditure	• Capital expenditure analysed by *key* projects with commitments for future periods.
10 Profit and loss	• Profit and loss statement. • Bring together data from other statements which go to make up the business position. • Include forecasts period by period for the reporting year.

Figure 16.1 Ten schedules that may be required monthly

There are, of course, a number of successful businesses with good operational management which are run with very limited periodic reporting – the 'back of the envelope' is frequently quoted as their control system. On more detailed examination it will often be seen that the chief executive, through experience and sound judgement, has come to recognize the limited number of *key* factors which determine the success of his business. In some cases it may be possible to report these factors on the back of an envelope. This does not mean that a sensible degree of additional data might not make the envelope even more effective.

■ *It is worth adding the very basic and important point that a well designed periodic reporting system does not actually bring about a performance improvement. This requires management action taken following a study of the relevant data.*

FINANCE

Any business that is intent on making progress will need new capital. Machinery will need replacement, new buildings may be needed and old ones require additions. There may be a need to increase stocks and work-in-progress. Even in a period when the business is not progressing in all probability there will still be a need for new capital.

New funding can come from the raising of capital from either existing shareholders or from the market generally. It can come from internal re-investment, which means that existing shareholders will be required to forego immediate returns. There are, of course, many other ways in which new capital can be raised.

Within the business strategy there should be a plan which covers the financing of the business development. Financing a business is very much a strategic issue, and it is also very much a competitive issue.

Finance raised at the wrong time, at high rates, can be crippling for a business. The issue of new shares, which have an entitlement to a share in ownership, can be very costly for existing shareholders. Raising new finance can be both a complex and time consuming operation.

Unless the chief executive and/or his finance officer is exceptionally knowledgeable and skilled in this particular part of business, it is normal to use specialist consultants such as a merchant banker, to administer the raising of new capital from the market. If the capital is to be raised by a simpler approach such as a bank loan then it would probably be handled within the company.

With the major strategic financing arrangements operations will be concerned if, for some special reasons, it is necessary to delay, or bring forward, the actual task of raising the capital. This often happens; the capital markets change at relatively short notice, and the needs of the business can also change rapidly.

Delay may mean that extensive adjustments are necessary to the operations plan. Without the appropriate financial backing the brand launch may have to be cancelled, or a new plant extension postponed. At times the chief executive may have to make a trade off between raising his capital at the most opportune time, paying extra for shorter-term capital, or postponing certain operations. The commercial men should ensure that he is fully aware of the various costs and benefits involved.

Probably the major contribution of the operator in financing is made not in the detailed raising of the new finance, but in the way he uses the capital already invested in the business. The more effectively existing capital is used the less new capital will be required. If the business can be run efficiently on a one-month level of finished stock clearly this will be much better than a level of two or three months. If raw and package materials can be effectively fed into the production process on a 'just-in-time' basis rather than after a month of warehousing, the capital tie-up in stocks will be greatly reduced.

Cash control is always an important area in capital utilization. Suppliers should be paid in the manner and at the time agreed in the supply contract, but not before. And customers should be expected to pay in line with the terms of their contract and, as appropriate, they can be given a suitable incentive to pay earlier.

■ *The requirement is that at all levels throughout the business everyone should be aware that capital, in all its forms, has to be financed. In simple terms capital costs money, and it should be used and controlled accordingly. Management communication will be all-important on this topic. To many people within the business 'capital' is likely to convey investment in buildings and plant and not in consumable resources such as packaging material. The*

*fact that three weeks' supplies are sitting in a nearby warehouse
may be a comforting thought for a production manager eager to
avoid any shortage whatsoever that might spoil his production
output figures. But the stock may be costly to hold and possibly
require expensive double handling.*

The good commercial manager will ensure that his operating colleagues are kept fully aware of the capital they are tying-up in their
operations, and he will be sure they have a clear indication of the cost
of the capital they are using.

If the production manager quoted in the previous paragraph is
held responsible for production output performance, but not for
capital tie-up, it is understandable where his priorities are likely to be.
Only if he knows the cost of his stocks, and has a responsibility for
them is he likely to exercise the necessary control.

Key points

1 The commercial manager should play his full part, at all levels in the business, in the formulation of plans for action. With his knowledge and experience of cost (input) and revenue (output) movements in particular conditions his contribution can be of vital importance.

2 He should take the lead in the evaluation of the proposed plans. He needs to be sure to use the *right* costs for the occasion, and also to be sure that any index he applies is well suited to the particular project.

3 The 'control' process has an important part to play in the management of successful operations. The commercial manager should ensure that it presents the *right* information at the *right* time — 90 per cent accuracy in one day may be more valuable than 100 per cent accuracy in ten days.

4 Wherever possible the control data should provide information on future commitments — it is into the future that the real control action can apply.

5 Capital costs money. Everyone in the business should be aware of this and should receive information on the extent and movement of the capital they employ.

6 The good commercial man needs to be skilled in the 'use of figures' in particular in the formulation of cost and revenue estimates for business propositions. Of even greater importance, he should have a positive and constructive approach. The operator wants a commercial man who will help him to make his projects successful; and the business needs successful projects.

7 The really good commercial man is more than just a scorer; he is an active and valuable player.

PART VII

17

$\diamond$

Forming the Company Operations Plan

$\blacklozenge$

In this chapter the formulation of the plan is considered slightly more formally than elsewhere in this book. The aim is to suggest a simple and logical step by step process of formulation.

It must be emphasized that the approach is merely a guide. There is no one correct approach to operations plan formulation. The method employed will tend to vary with the size of the business concerned, with the particular industry and markets in which the business competes, and with the style of management and leadership employed within the business.

Some form of plan is essential. At one extreme, it may be on the back of an envelope, with the detail carried in the head of the leading operator. In a small one man business this form of operating plan can be very successful.

In a large business the chief executive is likely to delegate responsibilities for much of the plan formulation to his marketing director who in turn may have a senior manager with full-time responsibility for the task and for the continuous review and control of the plan.

■ *It is worth repeating that the plan is the means whereby the chief executive directs the shorter-term activity of the business. Following the strategic plan, the operations plan is the most important action plan for the business. It allocates priorities, it marshals resources, and it co-ordinates the activities of all sections of the business.*

From the company operations plan flow a series of other action

301

plans which will affect every section of the business. The plan is also the source of the company financial plan (or budget) for the period.

It follows that the formulation of the plan should be an important process within the business, one that is worthy of the concentrated and active attention of the managers concerned.

In this short summary, the formulation of the operations plan is considered as a simple seven-stage process. The approach is probably too formal for the very small business, and unduly simple for the bigger operator. The notes are more concerned with the reasoning behind the approach, than with the actual procedures.

Within the approach suggested three considerations are of basic importance. Firstly, it is essential that the approach should be a simple one and avoid any form of undue complexity. Simplicity should provide for a better understanding in all sections of the business; it should also act to help concentrate attention on the really important factors.

Secondly, the approach should provide for consultation with those people within the business who are going to have to make the plan work. At least they must be consulted on those sections of the plan with which they are closely concerned. There may be occasions when a decision for action will be taken which goes against the view of a manager who is actively involved in the particular move – he should be informed of the reasons why the decision has been taken, how it fits into the total plan, and the advantage it brings. Most importantly, he should be assured that his views have been given consideration. At times this may appear to be an unduly lengthy process, but it need not be so, and it is likely to pay very worthwhile dividends in getting a full commitment to the selected approach.

The third point is that the formulation process is a 'rolling' one; that is, it is repeated two or more times each year. This means that in many instances within the process the need will be to up-date previous estimates or reports.

The time-period a plan covers will vary with the particular business concerned and the markets in which it competes. In some instances a period as short as three months may be considered most suitable, while in others a period of say eighteen months may be appropriate.

For the purpose of these notes we shall reason in terms of an operating plan covering a period of twelve months with a half-yearly formal review which also plans twelve months ahead. The seven-stage approach is shown in figure 17.1.

Stage 1: The Forecasts

- *General*
  Population movements, consumer expenditure, unemployment levels, income movements etc.

- *Specific*
  Market developments, research and development activities, capacity movements, trade activity etc.

Stage 2: Competitive Activity

- Ownership and finance, management developments etc.

- Brands: strengths/weaknesses and probable activities.

Stage 3: The Opportunities Review

- Selecting *key* opportunities for action.

- Identification, assessment, classification, and evaluation of the available opportunities.

- Brands: major priorities to be agreed.

Stage 4: Brand Proposals

- Consider and agree (as appropriate) proposals for the development and exploitation of major, minor, and proposed new brands through the period of the plan.

- Form the first draft operations plan from the agreed brand proposals.

Stage 5: Review of the Support Facilities

- Each support facility (ie. sections such as sales, marketing, administration, commercial etc.) to be reviewed.

- The effectiveness and efficiency of each facility to be examined and appropriate developments agreed.

- Agreement to be reached on a financial budget for each facility for the period of the plan.

Stage 6: Forming the Operations Plan

- The following plans, with financial budgets, have to be agreed: brand plans, support facilities, profit and cash.

- The plans need to be brought together, any necessary adjustments made, and the operations plan formed.

- *Key* objectives for sales volume, market share, and profitability within the plan to be agreed and responsibilities assigned.

- The company operations plan to be issued to the management for action.

Stage 7: Deviations from Plan

- A series of contingency plans to be formulated to cover for any major deviations from the agreed plan.

Figure 17.1   Formulating the company operations plan: a seven-stage approach

STAGE 1: THE FORECASTS

We are concerned here with firstly the general forecasts. That is the movement of those factors which can have an influence, possibly a major influence, on the development of business through the period; but they are factors which are in the main, outside the direct influence of the business.

Secondly, we are concerned with the specific forecasts. These are specific to the industry and the markets in which the business competes. It is always possible for the business to have a direct influence on these items, but in most cases the influence will be of a limited nature.

General forecasts

The best example of the general forecasts required are those which cover the economic scene. They could include:

- population movements
- gross natural product growth
- consumer expenditure
- unemployment levels
- income estimates
- wage and salary developments
- housing construction
- interest rates, credit controls
- taxation and special grant charges

There is a need to provide guidance as to the level of movement under these and other headings. Also required is guidance on timing, possibly in quarters or in terms of months. Where appropriate, forecasts covering items that are of particular significance in specific industries and markets should be included.

Other items that can be included under this heading include:

Media trends and costs

The cost of advertising via the various types of media will be of importance in forming brand support plans.

Legal considerations

Any changes in the law which are likely to affect business operations should be listed and outlined.

Environmental issues

These can include for instance, such items as changes in manufacturing processes under safety regulations, or the barring of certain chemical ingredients that have previously been used on a widespread basis.

Household durables and electrical appliances

Items such as this, as they apply to the particular industry and markets, should be covered. For instance, many markets are affected by the movement in the production of motor vehicles, for others the production of radios and television sets may be a key factor. Whatever is of consequence should be covered.

Many of these general forecasts can be purchased from specialist consultants. It is important that there should be confidence that they are at least reasonably accurate as the specific forecasts which follow are, to some considerable extent, built on them.

Specific forecasts

These forecasts are specific to the industry or markets concerned. They are in effect, within the general forecasts and will be influenced by them.

As a general rule the specific forecasts should start with a factual statement of the current position and should show how this has been developed over recent periods.

Among the more important specific forecasts are:

Market development

A forecast of the development expected over the period for each of the markets in which the company competes or intends to compete. The forecasts should show the market movement over time through the period – this may be monthly, or whatever period is appropriate.

Within the total market it is important that each market sector should be covered in details.

Accompanying each market development forecast should be the latest available consumer research study of the market. This study should include all the existing brands in the market, their performance levels, their price positions, and their strengths and weaknesses. Wherever possible the study should include a statement of the consumers' feelings about existing brands (their personalities), their criticisms of them, and their requirements for the future.

The aim is to build up a factual view of each market, its size, its make-up, and its movement through the period.

Research and development

Here the requirement is a statement detailing the various research and development projects expected to move into the market through the period. There will be a need to forecast the extent of the projects, their likely effect on the market, and their timing.

This is a difficult area to forecast with accuracy. Information coming from the market-place of consumer and market tests, details gleaned by buyers from suppliers, and field reports by the sales force, can all have a part to play in helping to build a complete picture.

For the periods immediately ahead it should be possible to provide a list of 'definite' market-place moves; for the periods beyond, a list of 'probable' moves should be possible.

Capacity

In industries and markets where capacity is of importance it is necessary to know who has it, and equally important to know who is likely to be short of capacity. It is also important to know what is the condition (e.g. new and modern, or old and in poor shape) of the available capacity. Again firm information under this heading can be difficult to obtain. A careful logging of information gleaned from plant and machinery suppliers can be helpful.

The trade

On their way to the consumer the manufacturer's brands and products must pass through the trade – the retailers and wholesalers who buy and sell the particular categories concerned.

The trade and its developments can play an important part in helping to stimulate a market or a particular sector of a market. The trade can, for instance, play a major role in speeding the acceptance of a brand pack size, or it can be helpful in stimulating particular kinds of promotions; probably most important of all, the trade can greatly affect the availability of a brand.

The ownership, the type of store that is growing in significance, the type that is in decline, the pricing policies likely to be followed, these are among the considerations which can be significant in the development of the trade; they can have a marked effect on the size of a market and on the growth or decline of particular sectors within the market.

Within the trade there will be some growth sectors, e.g. the superstores; and some sectors in decline, e.g. the small stores. There will be changes in the share of business held by the various owners – the multiples, the independents, the variety chains, etc. – which will be a factor in the competitive development of the market-place.

These trade factors can apply at differing levels of intensity in the various regions of the country, and so a regional analysis will also be necessary.

Many of the developments are publicized through the retail associations' own publications and in trade journals. Details of brands' movements through the various trade sectors, nationally and by regions, are recorded and are sold by commercial marketing research companies.

STAGE 2: COMPETITIVE ACTIVITY

It can be argued that this competitive activity forecast should be included in Stage 1. It is a particularly important area, requiring an analysis which extends beyond the current strength of competitive brands, and therefore warrants separate consideration.

What is required is analysis of each competitor, including its management and their effectiveness, its brands, its financial standing and production capacity.

When this analysis is complete the need is to consider the probable activity of the competitor in each of the markets in which he competes over the period of the operating plan.

■ *The study of the competitive management is especially important. Their abilities, the pressures on them, their ambitions, the requirements of their owners, considerations of this kind do not appear in orthodox marketing research reports and yet they can be of great significance in determining competitive market-place activity, and how it is conducted.*

The financial standing of each competitor should be examined carefully. For instance, the ability of a competitor to finance a new brand in a strong growth market may be questioned – his present and probable future financial standing can provide the answer to this form of question.

A detailed competitive analysis is a very important *tool* in the formulation of an operations plan. The aim must be to forecast the major competitive brand actions through the period. The strength of the actions in terms of investment will be significant as also will be their timing.

Knowing the competitive disciplines in terms of consumer and market testing can be of importance. Checking on the actions of the competitor in the markets of other countries, picking up odd pieces of information from suppliers, gleaning details from advertising sales people. These and other similar avenues can provide small items of information which, when brought together, can help to pin-point probable competitive actions.

■ *Know your competitors, know them well, and remember they are the enemy. There is no such thing as a friendly competitor. The operations plan must be competitive. It is about you winning and your competitors losing.*

STAGE 3: OPPORTUNITIES REVIEW

It is at this stage that the opportunities for action are selected, and the basis of the operations plan is formed.

Each one of the existing brands, and the proposed new brands, should have identified opportunities they wish to exploit during the period of the operations plan.

Some will be major opportunities of vital importance to the brand and to the company. Others will be of lesser significance.

Of course, it is not only important that the brand should have identified the opportunity; it must also have developed a means of exploiting it. With a major opportunity the proposed exploitation approach should be supported by appropriate research backing.

During this stage it is necessary to arrange the opportunities in order of priority to the company, and then to position them as appropriate through the operating period.

It is probable that all the brands will claim the peak selling period, e.g. the spring or the autumn. None will be keen on the period immediately prior to Christmas (unless this period is a good one for the type of product), some may want the holiday months, and so on.

The requirement is that the necessary priorities should be allocated on a sound business basis, with the major opportunities taking the lead position at selected periods, and the lesser opportunities acting to balance the programme.

There will be much pushing and shoving between the various brands as each one attempts to get the best positions for its activities and also attempts to build a strong, well-balanced, brand programme through the period.

■ *This is the stage where the foundations for the operating plan are laid. The* key *requirement is that the really important opportunities should be identified and given an appropriate priority in the plan. Beyond this the plan needs to be sensibly balanced – there is, for instance, no point in over-loading during say, March/April and having nothing at all during May/June.*

There will be a need to balance the requirements of the established brands, some of which may be valuable cash contributors, with the demands of the new brands fighting to win in the growth markets.

At this stage the priorities are awarded to brands on what could be termed a 'draft' plan. Later, as each brand proposal for the period (including its financial plan) is considered, and a total plan begins to take shape, adjustments may be necessary.

STAGE 4: BRAND PROPOSALS

This stage must be followed through for *existing* and *new* brands.

Each brand is now required to prepare a detailed proposal covering its activities for the period of the plan. It is, in fact, an investment proposal in which the brand sets out the objectives it proposes to attain and the support in terms of such factors as advertising, promotions, and sales force activity, it considers necessary to achieve them.

The proposal should set out, in detail month by month through the period, the brand's proposed sales volume and sales revenue, its direct costs, and the proposed level of profit contribution it expects to make. Both the revenue and the costs should be based on the best estimates for the period.

The proposal should show these details for each week or month within the operating period. The brand proposals should be the subject of a rigorous examination, Where a major opportunity has been highlighted, and a competitive advantage developed to exploit it, then it should be pursued vigorously. Failure to develop a brand to its full potential can prove very costly. However, it is important to be sure the opportunity is a major one, and that the proposed exploitation makes good business sense.

Every effort should be made to ensure the brand proposals are realistic, with undue pessimism or optimism removed. All the various marketing *tools* discussed in earlier chapters have a part to play; considerable skill will be required to ensure that they are used effectively and in a manner which moves the brand towards its objectives in sales volume, market share, and profit contribution.

Drawing up worthwhile proposals for new brands can often prove difficult. The brand plans may not be firm, there may be production problems, the formula not agreed, the packaging may be unsatisfactory, and so on. However, a proposal is necessary and priorities must be arranged. They may well need extensive alteration at a later review, but the proposals should be the best possible at the time of the operations plan formulation.

■ *Consideration of the brand proposals should rank as one of the most important sessions within the business management. It is here that the individual brand's programme towards its strategic objectives is plotted, the action plan for the whole business aligned, and the base for the company's trading profit for the period constructed.*

The session is one where the good brand manager proves his worth. He is in a strong position for he is the brand specialist, he should know more of its strength, weaknesses, and potential, than anyone else at the session. His skill, and his attitude will be vitally important.

STAGE 5: REVIEW OF THE SUPPORT FACILITIES

The term 'support facilities' is used here to describe all those services which provide support for the brands. Thus they would include:

- research and development
- production
- distribution
- the sales force
- administration ,
  to include accounting,
  general administration,
  marketing, and general
  management

If the total cost of maintaining the support facilities is deducted from the total profit contribution coming from the brands, the balance remaining is the company's trading profit.

The review of the support facilities has three main aims:

1   To ensure that each one of the various services has the ability to meet the demands that will be made on it by the brands through the period of the operations plan;
2   To act as a review of the effectiveness and efficiency of each one of the services;
3   To agree a financial budget for the service through the period of the operating plan.

A review of particular significance is that of the plant capacity. There will be a need to ensure that the plant has the ability to meet the volume demand of the brands at the time periods specified, at a satisfactory level of cost, and at the specified quality.

It may be necessary to think in terms of extra shift working at particular periods, or to use weekend working for an extended time, with a view to ensuring sufficient volume. Alternatively, the possibility of building and holding stock may be considered.

This form of reasoning may also be necessary in other sections. The distribution fleet may need to be augmented for a period, the sales force may need the assistance of a team of merchandisers during the new brand launch, and so on.

With all of the various administrative services it is important to keep a strict control on the costs involved.

If the services are allowed to increase in size and then later have to be reduced, the reduction process can be both painful and troublesome.

■ *In effect, the review of the support facilities is a continuation of the opportunities review. 'There is always a better way.' This applies to the whole business and most certainly includes the service departments. They should be encouraged during the course of the review to come forward with proposals showing how they can provide a more satisfactory service to the brands with a reduction in costs.*

An important part of the support facilities review is the consideration of capital expenditure. This will include such items as plant and machinery, new office buildings and equipment, motor vehicles, and distribution warehouses.

It is usual to have an approach to capital expenditure which requires that proposals are examined in terms of the savings they generate and the percentage level of return on capital invested which they produce. These measures can provide a very useful guide, but it is only a guide, and it should be viewed accordingly. Sound judgement is always at a premium in the consideration of capital expenditure proposals.

Many of these proposals will have arisen from the strategic plan. In reviewing them it is necessary to be sure that they are still required in the form and size, and at the time, as originally planned.

■ *Probably the most important review under this stage is the review of personnel. Its aim should be to ensure that the people who are currently managing the business are of a satisfactory calibre and ability, and also that the business is developing an adequate flow of younger managers who will be available to take it forward into the future.*

The personnel review should extend beyond the management level, to encompass the personnel needs of the whole business. In particular it should cover the many highly skilled positions that are invariably present in modern marketing and manufacturing organizations.

STAGE 6: FORMING THE COMPANY OPERATIONS PLAN

With his brand proposals agreed, and the review of the support facilities completed, the chief executive can move forward to the formulation of the first draft company operations plan.

This first draft is unlikely to be satisfactory. However, after more detailed considerations and probably a number of adjustments, including deletions and additions, the plan should begin to take shape. It should emerge as a plan that is set to achieve the shorter-term objectives of the chief executive in terms of sales volume, brand strength, and profitability.

There is now a need to ensure that the company can finance the plan. Will it have available the necessary cash to provide for the development of its sales volume, carry the additional raw materials and packaging necessary, meet the capital expenditures, and pay the dividends? And if the cash isn't readily available can it be obtained on terms, and at a time, that are acceptable?

If the answer to this question is 'No' then the draft operations plan will need further revision. The company will need to adjust its operations so that the liquidity problem is overcome. There is no point in having a great market success and going broke, or becoming the easy victim of an unwelcome take-over bid.

If the answer to the question is 'Yes', then the operations plan is no longer a draft: it is now a firm plan for action. It will need to be communicated clearly to the appropriate management throughout the business, and a whole series of supplementary action plans will need to be formed and aligned with it.

■ *The company operations plan is the* key *plan within the business over the shorter–medium term. It sets the priorities, allocates resources, outlines responsibilities, and links directly with the financial plan.*

A skilful formulation of the operations plan will be a key *factor in ensuring the business uses its limited resources in a manner,*

*and at a time, which should enable it to move forward and achieve
its shorter term objectives, and ultimately its longer-term strategic
aims.*

STAGE 7: DEVIATION FROM THE PLAN

The company operations plan may have been formulated with great
skill, and the people actually operating it may be of high quality and
very resourceful, yet the actual results in the market-place are almost
certainly going to be out of line with the plan.

The wise executive knows there will be deviations from the plan,
and he ensures that the business has contingency plans available to
provide a reasonable cover.

Deviations in the minor activities within the plan are unlikely to
cause undue problems; they can usually be covered in operations
without any difficulty. Problems are likely to arise if there are deviations from plan, particularly large deviations, with the major
activities. Contingency plans should be made to cover both an outstanding success and a failure for each of the major activities – an
allowance for plus or minus 10 per cent from target would normally
be a reasonable cover (although this will vary from business to
business).

Contingency plans for successful operations are just as important
as are those for possible failures – the cost of not being able to con-
solidate an outstanding success can be very high.

The chief executive may well decide to give these contingency
plans a very restricted circulation within the business. He may limit
them to the three or four managers who have been involved with him
in their formulation. They could possibly have an adverse affect on
the morale of some of his people. But he would be wise to ensure that
the contingency plans are drawn up and available for action, even if
he keeps them from view in a bottom drawer.

REVISION OF THE OPERATIONS PLAN

Operations are about winning in the market-place. They are shorter
term, and at times require rapid action. They are concerned to outmanoeuvre competitors and this can on occasions necessitate a swift

change of direction. Operating opportunities have to be taken when they appear; there is unlikely to be a second chance.

It follows that the company operations plan must always be kept reasonably flexible. It must provide for frequent review and change, if change is really necessary. Of course, a change in plan will invariably have a cost attached to it, and so the operative words are 'really necessary'.

Within the business it is important that a correct balance should be maintained. Brand managers, and others concerned should not be encouraged to request a change in plan for any minor problem that arises. If they use their initiative they can usually overcome minor problems without causing any extensive upset. However, it is important that managers appreciate that when there is good cause the plan can, and will, be adjusted.

In an approach where the company operations plan is drawn up to cover a year ahead, and is formally reviewed on a rolling basis every six months, major changes should be limited in number.

Key points

1 The company operations plan is a vitally important action plan within the business, ranking second only to the strategic plan. It has a significant part to play in directing, co-ordinating, and concentrating the resources of the business through the shorter term.

2 For real success the business needs a winning strategy backed by effective and efficient operations. A well-designed and skilfully formulated operations plan will be essential for fully effective operations.

3 It is important to appreciate that the very highest level of skill in plan design and formulation cannot guarantee success.
Real success in business operations requires skill, effort, enthusiasm, commitment, in effect the *right* total attitude from the people of the business. They turn the plan into actual effect. Only they can add the *extra* so essential if the business operations are to be superior to all competitors.

4 Formulating a winning business strategy can be a great challenge and most stimulating. 'Making it all happen' in the market-place through successful business operations can, in many respects, be even more rewarding. It can also be most enjoyable.

Index

◆

316